World Economic and Financial Surveys

Global Financial Stability Report

Market Developments and Issues

September 2003

International Monetary Fund
Washington DC

Production: IMF Multimedia Services Division
Cover: Phil Torsani
Photo: Padraic Hughes
Figures: Theodore F. Peters, Jr.
Typesetting: Choon Lee

ISBN 1-58906-236-1
ISSN 0258-7440

Price: US$49.00
(US$46.00 to full-time faculty members and
students at universities and colleges)

Please send orders to:
International Monetary Fund, Publication Services
700 19th Street, N.W., Washington, D.C. 20431, U.S.A.
Tel.: (202) 623-7430   Telefax: (202) 623-7201
E-mail: publications@imf.org
Internet:http://www.imf.org

recycled paper

CONTENTS

Tables

Figures

The following symbols have been used throughout this volume:

. . . to indicate that data are not available;

— to indicate that the figure is zero or less than half the final digit shown, or that the item does not exist;

– between years or months (for example, 1997–99 or January–June) to indicate the years or months covered, including the beginning and ending years or months;

/ between years (for example, 1998/99) to indicate a fiscal or financial year.

"Billion" means a thousand million; "trillion" means a thousand billion.

"Basis points" refer to hundredths of 1 percentage point (for example, 25 basis points are equivalent to ¼ of 1 percentage point).

"n.a." means not applicable.

Minor discrepancies between constituent figures and totals are due to rounding.

As used in this volume the term "country" does not in all cases refer to a territorial entity that is a state as understood by international law and practice. As used here, the term also covers some territorial entities that are not states but for which statistical data are maintained on a separate and independent basis.

PREFACE

First launched in March 2002, the *Global Financial Stability Report* (GFSR) provides a regular assessment of global financial markets and identifies potential systemic weaknesses that could lead to crises. By calling attention to potential fault lines in the global financial system, the report seeks to play a role in preventing crises before they erupt, thereby contributing to global financial stability and the sustained economic growth of the IMF's member countries.

The report was prepared by the International Capital Markets Department, under the direction of the Counsellor and Director, Gerd Häusler. It is managed by an Editorial Committee comprising Hung Q. Tran (Chairman), Donald J. Mathieson, David J. Ordoobadi, and Rupert Thorne, and benefits from comments and suggestions from William E. Alexander, Axel Bertuch-Samuels, Charles R. Blitzer, and David Cheney. Other contributors to this issue are Francesc Balcells, Burkhard Drees, Martin Edmonds, Toni Gravelle, Janet Kong, Markus Krygier, Gabrielle Lipworth, Chris Morris, Jürgen Odenius, Kazunari Ohashi, Lars Pedersen, Jorge Roldos, Calvin Schnure, Alexander Tieman, and a staff team from the Monetary and Financial Systems Department (MFD) led by Anne-Marie Gulde, S. Kal Wajid, Udaibir Das, and including Gianni De Nicoló, Greta Mitchell, and others. Silvia Iorgova, Anne Jansen, Yoon Sook Kim, Ned Rumpeltin, Kalin Tintchev (MFD), and Peter Tran provided research assistance. Caroline Bagworth, Jane Harris, Vera Jasenovec, Ramanjeet Singh, and Joan Wise provided expert word processing assistance. Jeff Hayden of the External Relations Department edited the manuscript and coordinated production of the publication.

This particular issue draws, in part, on a series of informal discussions with commercial and investment banks, securities firms, asset management companies, insurance companies, pension funds, stock and futures exchanges, and credit rating agencies in Brazil, Chile, China, Hong Kong SAR, Hungary, Poland, Russia, Singapore, South Africa, and Thailand, as well as the major financial centers. The report reflects mostly information available up to August 4.

The report has benefited from comments and suggestions from staff in other IMF departments, as well as from Executive Directors following their discussions of the *Global Financial Stability Report* on August 22, 2003. However, the analysis and policy considerations are those of the contributing staff and should not be attributed to the Executive Directors, their national authorities, or the IMF.

The bursting of the equity bubble, geopolitical developments, and corporate governance scandals have severely tested the global financial system in recent years. In the fall of last year, these developments contributed to high levels of risk aversion, increased market volatility, widening credit spreads, and limited access to external financing for many emerging market countries. Even in the face of these strong headwinds, however, financial markets have remained remarkably resilient. Indeed, markets strengthened in the first half of 2003, notwithstanding continued lackluster economic growth.

Since the March 2003 issue of the *Global Financial Stability Report* (GFSR), further progress has been made in addressing the lingering effects of the bursting of the equity price bubble. Household and corporate balance sheets have continued to improve gradually and corporate default levels have declined. Companies in mature markets have cut costs, enhancing their ability to cope with slower growth and other potential difficulties. While unambiguous signs of stronger growth are still lacking, corporations—particularly in the United States—have made good progress in their financial consolidation efforts and are in a better financial position to increase investment spending.

The reduction of policy interest rates to postwar lows in the major financial centers has facilitated progress in restoring financial soundness. The prospect of a protracted period of low short-term interest rates and ample liquidity sparked investors' quest for yield that proceeded progressively out along the risk spectrum. After a period in which risk-averse investors sought the safety of mature market government bonds, driving down their yields, risk aversion began to dissi-

pate rather quickly starting in the fall of 2002. Since then, the pendulum has been swinging toward increased risk appetite. Investors moved into corporate and emerging market bonds, leading to a swift compression of credit spreads in these sectors. Flows were also attracted to higher-yielding local emerging markets, contributing to the appreciation of their currencies. Finally, mature equity markets—shunned by investors after three successive years of steep price declines—have rebounded since mid-March 2003. Monetary stimulus, an easing of geopolitical concerns, more attractive valuations relative to alternative asset classes, and indications of stronger growth in corporate earnings all underpinned the equity market rally.

Benchmark yield curves in the major financial centers had been pushed to quite low levels, setting the stage for a snapback in mature government bond yields when signs of stronger economic growth emerged (Table 1.1). The March 2003 GFSR highlighted the risk that such an increase in yields would trigger an unwinding of carry trades; indeed, the rebound in yields evident in all major markets since mid-June appears to have been accentuated by an unwinding of such trades. Also, credit spreads on corporate and emerging market bonds and credit default swaps may have been overly compressed, making them vulnerable to a rebound in government bond yields, although spreads have to date remained little changed. In addition, given the high level of portfolio managers' exposure to emerging market bonds, the rotation of funds away from fixed-income instruments in favor of equities could hurt emerging markets.

Ultimately, however, a further steepening of government bond yield curves in the major financial centers, driven by prospects for

Table 1.1. Financial Market Data
(Percentage change; unless otherwise noted)

		Change to August 4, 2003 from			
	Peak (March 24, 2000)	2001		2002 December 31	2003 March 31
		September 11	December 31		
Equity Market					
Major stock indexes[1]					
S&P 500	−35.7	−10.0	−14.4	11.7	15.9
Nasdaq	−65.5	1.1	−12.1	28.3	27.8
FTSE Eurotop 300	−47.7	−21.7	−31.4	1.0	16.4
Topix	−43.0	−11.7	−9.5	10.8	18.6
Bank indexes					
S&P 500 bank index	19.3	11.5	8.7	13.1	19.9
FTSE Eurotop 300 bank index	−19.1	−9.6	−21.7	9.3	24.9
Topix bank index	−60.6	−44.1	−23.2	2.3	19.4
Bond Market					
U.S. corporate bonds					
Yields (level change; basis points)					
AAA	−176	−107	−74	−22	10
BAA	−132	−78	−91	−30	14
High-yield bonds	−223	−286	−300	−245	−140
Spreads (level change; basis points)[2]					
AAA	15	−59	3	−69	−39
BAA	59	−30	−14	−77	−35
High-yield bonds	−32	−237	−223	−292	−188
U.S. corporate bond price indexes[3]					
AAA	. . .	3.6	4.3	−1.7	−2.3
A	. . .	3.6	4.6	−1.0	−1.7
BBB	. . .	−0.6	1.3	1.6	0.3
European corporate bond spreads[4]					
AA	−12	−16	−15	−19	−14
A	−13	−43	−25	−20	−24
BBB	25	−81	−44	−64	−48
Japanese corporate bond spreads[4]					
AA	−10	−2	−5	0	0
A	0	−4	−27	−10	−5
BBB	−24	2	−35	−24	−9
Government bond yields (level change; basis points)[5]					
United States	−191	−48	−77	47	49
Germany	−111	−66	−86	−6	10
Japan	−89	−44	−39	7	27
Government bond price indexes[6]					
United States	9.6	0.8	4.0	−5.4	−5.3
Germany	10.1	8.9	7.6	−0.1	−0.4
Japan	11.8	8.1	7.0	0.1	−4.1
Exchange rates					
Euro/U.S. dollar	−13.9	−19.6	−21.7	−7.6	−3.9
Yen/U.S. dollar	12.6	0.8	−8.6	1.3	1.9
Trade-weighted nominal U.S.dollar	−3.8	−11.7	−15.1	−6.0	−3.8

Sources: Bloomberg L.P.; and Datastream.
[1]In local currency terms.
[2]Spread over a 10-year U.S. treasury bond.
[3]Merrill Lynch corporate bond indexes.
[4]Merrill Lynch corporate bond spreads; level change, in basis points.
[5]Ten-year government bonds.
[6]Merrill Lynch government bond indexes, 10+ years.

stronger growth, would be a positive development. A return to strong growth will improve the financial conditions of firms and households, while a steeper yield curve will allow banks and other institutions to generate income through well-managed maturity mismatches. The risk lies in the transition to a higher level of bond yields, as market participants must manage the inevitable losses on bond portfolios and increased market volatility. So far, the transition process appears to be orderly, notwithstanding the widening in credit spreads and rising market volatility.

A related risk lies in rising bond yields driven by a further weakening of the dollar in a disorderly fashion. However, since the dollar has recently recovered somewhat in line with the rebound in bond yields—both reflecting expectations of strong U.S. growth—this scenario is less likely.

A more serious risk would emerge if corporate earnings fail to validate the recent strong rebound in mature equity markets. Equity markets would fall again, undermining corporate and household balance sheets and undoing some of the progress achieved in the first half of this year. Unless economic growth decelerates substantially, however, weak earnings growth is unlikely to pose a serious threat to the resilience of the international financial system. Having strengthened their balance sheets, most corporations and financial institutions are now better prepared to cope with slower growth than they were last fall.

In addition to assessing recent financial market developments and current vulnerabilities (Chapter II), this GFSR considers financial market stability issues in a more medium-term context. Chapter III analyzes past episodes of extreme asset price volatility in mature markets. It highlights the role of amplifiers that can transform volatility into market instability and identifies measures to limit their impact. The lessons learned from those episodes remain relevant. Chapter IV assesses the changing pattern and volatility of capital flows to emerging markets, identifies the factors

that have contributed to changing patterns of flows, and suggests ways to mitigate the impact of abrupt changes in flows. These two chapters represent the first installment of work to examine the interrelationship between market volatility and financial stability. Such work aims to draw policy lessons to help strengthen the resilience of financial systems in both mature and emerging market countries.

Balance of Risk and Vulnerabilities

The two major risks going forward—namely, *a continued rise in bond yields* and *disappointing corporate earnings*—have a number of potential consequences.

Bond Yields

Bond yields could rise further in the face of convincing signs of a strong economic recovery and an increased supply of government securities. Since the U.S. Federal Reserve has indicated that the Fed funds rate will be kept low for a sustained period, the U.S. treasury yield curve would likely steepen further. Given the historically high correlation among government bond markets, yield curves in other major financial centers can be expected to do likewise. Ultimately, the combination of a steep yield curve and stronger growth would contribute to more robust global financial conditions. The transition period, however, would entail risks that need to be carefully managed to ensure an orderly adjustment:

- The sharp increase in bond yields in the major financial markets has apparently weakened the wave of mortgage refinancings in the United States, which may unsettle the support extended throughout the downturn by consumers. Rising interest rates could also undercut property prices, undermining the net worth of the household sector, whose exposure to real estate has increased with the refinancing and house price boom.

- Bond investors, or their hedging counter-parties, would incur losses on their portfolios. Those attempting to benefit from the carry trade and other bond investors with short-term liabilities would suffer.
- U.S. mortgage agencies would need to engage in continuous hedging, as rising rates would rapidly increase the expected duration of their portfolios of mortgage-backed securities from relatively low levels. Hedging by shorting cash or derivative instruments could amplify the rise in bond yields—highlighting the role of amplifiers in accentuating market price movements. The liquidity of the markets for fixed-income cash and derivative instruments has come under pressure given the hedging need for the unprecedented size of holdings of mortgages and mortgage-backed securities.
- Emerging bond markets are vulnerable to a correction, given the rapid spread compression and the apparently reduced investor discrimination over issuer credit quality during the recent search for yield.

Corporate Profitability

The alternative risk—that of continued lackluster corporate profitability and weak economic growth—could be more serious. Corporate earnings reports—especially for the second quarter of 2003—suggest that the probability of this happening, while not negligible, does not appear to be very high. Lower-than-expected earnings growth in the second half of 2003 could lead to an equity market sell-off, as the recent rally was built on the inflow of funds being pushed away from low-yielding alternatives and encouraged by expectations of better earnings. If a renewed equity decline were substantial, it could undo some of the financial improvements to date and thereby weaken the global financial sector. This would be a particular risk for insurers and pension funds, which would be hurt both by a further equity

market sell-off and by the continued low interest rates such a weak growth scenario would entail.

Policies to Promote Financial Stability

Policy Implications of Recent Market Developments

The favorable performance of financial markets has anticipated, and improved the prospects for, a stronger recovery in the real economy. Policies must continue to boost consumer and business confidence. Confidence is important to help spark renewed investment spending—so far the missing key ingredient in the recovery—as corporations have improved their balance sheets. It is appropriate that monetary policies in the major financial centers remain accommodative for the present. Low short-term rates and ample liquidity would contribute to further balance sheet repair and underpin investor risk appetite, even though this could cause problems for some financial institutions.

As for the major financial centers, many of the measures discussed in previous issues of the GFSR remain salient. In a range of areas, the authorities must persist in implementing reforms to strengthen market foundations:

- Corporate governance must be strengthened further to restore investor confidence, including through the full implementation of recent measures to enhance the independence of corporate boards. At the same time, corporate executives must not feel constrained from undertaking profitable investments.
- Most investment managers, mutual funds, and pension funds should play a more active role in enhancing corporate governance. They have typically viewed proxy voting as a back office function, often voting with management by default rather than conviction. More active exercise of ownership rights would increase transparency and board independence.

- By virtue of their size, rapid growth, high leverage, and complex hedging of interest rate risk, the U.S. mortgage agencies warrant careful monitoring. Such monitoring should include an assessment of whether these agencies are sufficiently capitalized against the shocks arising from fast-moving markets. Thin capital coverage can increase the pressure on these agencies to conduct continuous hedging strategies that have the potential to amplify interest rate movements.
- The regulation and supervision of the financial activities of insurance and re-insurance companies must improve further (see Appendix I of Chapter II).
- Pension fund accounting and regulation are in need of reform. Such reform should aim at increasing transparency and improving risk controls. Possible measures that need to be studied include putting pension fund assets and liabilities on the balance sheet or as a separate trust fund, valuing pension fund assets at market prices rather than actuarial assumed rates of return, and speeding the recognition of pension fund shortfalls and surpluses. But given the magnitude of corporate pension funds, and of the potential cost of implementing such reforms, the appropriate pace and degree of reform will need to be carefully calibrated.
- More generally, given the sizable buildup in liquidity searching for investment outlets, there is a risk of excessive accumulations of positions or exposures in certain instruments or credits. While low interest rates are needed to spur activity and investment, investors need to remain discriminating. Supervisors, as well as private sector risk managers, should be on the lookout for signs of concentration or mispricing of risk.

Policy Lessons from Past Episodes of High Volatility

Price volatility is an inevitable and, to a large extent, desirable feature of markets as it represents the price discovery mechanism at work. Nevertheless, it is important to ensure that volatility is not amplified to a point where it triggers instability. Chapter III studies price volatility in, and correlations between, the equity, bond, and foreign exchange markets since the 1970s. It notes that only the equity market has experienced persistently high volatility in recent years and identifies four episodes of extreme volatility in equity and other markets. Case studies of these four episodes show that the lessons learned about the need to limit the impact of amplifiers continue to be relevant. At present, they are particularly relevant for the potential risk that the continuous hedging of mortgage-backed securities portfolios could amplify interest rate movements.

A number of these lessons relate to the need to avoid mechanisms that amplify volatility in a crisis by forcing, or creating incentives for, asset sales into falling markets:

- The injection of liquidity by the authorities or emergency netting and settlement agreements between market participants can help break the cycle of increasing volatility in a crisis by allowing counterparties to meet margin requirements or otherwise settle transactions without having to sell assets.
- Excessive leverage often turns volatility into instability. Supervisors must continually improve the sophistication of their leverage measurement—both on- and off-balance sheet—to keep up with market innovations.
- Dynamic hedging strategies—while useful during periods of moderate price fluctuation—can have severe limitations in coping with a rapid price fall and they have, in a number of crises, sharply accentuated selling pressure. Currently, hedging strategies for prepayment risk in mortgage markets are similar to the strategies of those past crises in that they could lead to price-insensitive sales.
- Rigid risk limits, similar to automatic hedging rules, can lead to forced sales in a crisis.

Developments such as value-at-risk models and the ratings-based approach in Basel II greatly improve risk management. They also, however, carry the risk of pro-cyclicality and amplifying volatility by requiring asset sales as volatility increases.

- Incentive structures that promote herding and "short-termism" among institutional investors, or the companies they invest in, have also contributed to boom-bust cycles. While conflicts of interest can be mitigated by regulation or better enforcement, the pro-cyclical effects of excessive focus on short-term returns or index tracking are more difficult to address.

- Adequate transparency both from financial intermediaries and the corporate sector is needed to permit risk assessment and management. But the information disclosed must be meaningful and put within an appropriate long-term context. Measures such as fair-value accounting illustrate the difficulty of achieving this for institutions with long-term investment goals. There may be scope for a middle ground to smooth the more extreme effects of using mark-to-market snapshots of balance sheets.

Policy Implications for Emerging Market Countries

Past issues of the GFSR have highlighted—in a less favorable external financing environment—the need for emerging market countries to consistently implement sound macroeconomic policies and reforms to improve their investment climate. In the current, slightly improved external financing environment, complacency must be avoided. Emerging market countries must take advantage of the recent improvement in access to capital markets to pursue structural reform and to make progress on putting public finances on a sound footing. They also need

to improve the structure of liabilities. Indeed, a number of countries—including Brazil, Mexico, and Poland—have undertaken successful liability management operations that have extended the maturity of their obligations and conducted debt swaps out of existing Brady bonds. Brazil has also taken advantage of improved investor sentiment to reduce the share of dollar-linked liabilities in its domestic debt, thus reducing a major past source of vulnerability. South Africa has used some of the proceeds of its recent 10-year bond issue to pay down maturing short-term debt and to eliminate the Reserve Bank's net open forward position.

More, however, can and is being done by emerging market countries. As Chapter IV and previous GFSRs emphasize, emerging markets have taken measures to self-insure against the potential volatility of external flows, particularly private debt flows. These measures have included:

- changes in external asset and liability management practices. In part, this has involved large-scale accumulation of foreign exchange reserves, particularly in Asia;
- adapting exchange rate arrangements to the degree of capital account openness;
- strengthening domestic financial institutions;
- enhancing prudential supervision and regulation in order to increase resilience to volatility; and
- developing more efficient and liquid local and regional securities and derivatives markets.

Finally, the relationship between emerging markets and international capital markets has changed fundamentally in recent years. Indeed, although some emerging markets remain dependent on borrowing from international markets, emerging markets, as a group, have become net exporters of capital since 1999, including through the accumulation of international reserves.

CHAPTER II

GLOBAL FINANCIAL MARKET DEVELOPMENTS

Low interest rate policies in the major financial centers were a key driver of financial market developments in the first half of 2003. Low rates induced investors to move out along the risk spectrum in search of better returns, investing in corporate and emerging market bonds and then in equities. They also allowed corporate and household sectors to lock in longer-dated borrowing and enabled many emerging market sovereigns to complete early their 2003 borrowing program. However, low rates presented problems to some financial institutions, such as life insurers and defined-benefit pension funds.

Since mid-June, mature market government bond yields have rebounded and yield curves have steepened, raising the possibility that a transition to a higher interest rate environment has begun. The rises in yields have at times been sharp, and the total increase has already been significant. At the same time, the U.S. dollar has shown signs of stabilizing, most notably against the euro, as a result of market expectations that growth in the United States would outpace that in the euro zone.

This chapter examines the impact of low interest rates across a wide range of mature and emerging markets. It notes that, on balance, financial stability concerns have eased. Household and corporate balance sheets have improved, the equity market rally has strengthened insurers and pension funds, and emerging market countries have increased their international bond issuance. However, significant concerns remain. Insurers' and pension funds' balance sheets remain weakened by the low long-term yields, and the equity market recovery remains highly dependent on corporate earnings meeting expectations. Meanwhile, there could be risks to stability if a sudden rise in long-term interest rates is amplified by factors such as herd behavior by market participants, hedging practices in the mortgage market, or the unwinding of carry trades. The signs of reduced investor discrimination in the emerging markets (and other credit markets) also heighten the risks of a more pronounced reversal in that market.

- The first section reviews recent developments in mature markets.
- The second section analyzes key vulnerabilities in the major financial centers.
- The third section assesses developments in secondary markets for emerging market debt.
- The fourth section describes the rebound in emerging market access to financing.
- The fifth section examines financial soundness indicators in emerging market banking sectors.
- Appendix I considers regulatory challenges and responses in the insurance and other sectors.
- Appendix II looks at the market implications of convergence by European Union applicants.

Ample Liquidity Dominates Developments in Major Financial Markets

Mature Bond Market Yields Rise from Near Historic Lows

Through most of the first half of 2003, mature government bond markets discounted sluggish growth and low inflation and

Figure 2.1. Inflation-Linked 10-Year Bond Yields
(In percent)

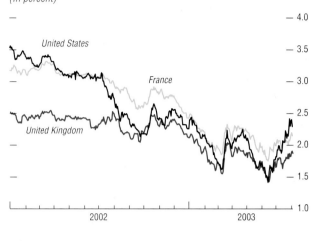

Source: Bloomberg L.P.

Figure 2.2. Inflation Expectations
(In percent)

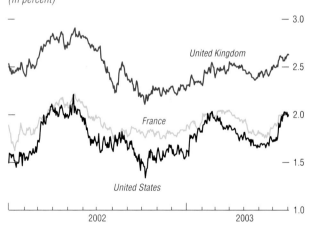

Sources: Bloomberg L.P.; and IMF staff estimates.

reflected expectations that short-term rates would remain low for an extended period. Government bond yields in the major financial centers approached postwar lows, reflecting in large part a decline in real yields. Inflation expectations—as proxied by the spread between the nominal yield on conventional government bonds and the real yield on their inflation-indexed counterparts—remained low (Figures 2.1 and 2.2).

Beginning in mid-June, however, markets began to anticipate improved prospects for economic growth and a greater supply of government securities, while reducing their assessment of the likelihood that the U.S. Federal Reserve might purchase longer-dated treasury securities to avert deflation. Nominal government bond yields in the United States, Europe, and Japan rose significantly and yield curves steepened. The sell-offs in these markets were closely correlated with each other. The increase in nominal bond yields largely reflected an increase in real yields, as market-based indicators of inflation expectations rose only modestly. In the United States, longer-term nominal rates are around 40 basis points above levels prevailing at the beginning of the year, but in Japan they have returned to around end-year levels and in Europe they remain around 20 basis points lower. Nevertheless, the speed with which yields have risen since mid-June highlights the risk of further rapid rises in yields from still historically low levels should further signs of a return to robust economic growth materialize.

In Japan, tenacious deflationary pressures, continued low expectations for economic growth, and the Bank of Japan's monetary policies kept government bond yields at virtually zero for maturities of three years or less. Yields on 10-year Japanese government bonds reached a low of about 45 basis points before almost tripling after mid-June to over one percent, as investors began to switch back into equities. The persistence of deflationary pressures has led to an increased direct and indirect ownership role of the government in

Table 2.1. United States: Changes in Government Securities Yields[1]

(In percent)

	October 15, 1993– November 7, 1994	October 5, 1998– January 20, 2000	November 7, 2001– April 1, 2002	June 13, 2003– August 4, 2003
3-month	2.28	1.35	−0.01	0.11
2-year	3.27	2.47	1.41	0.60
10-year	2.87	2.63	1.25	1.17

Source: Bloomberg L.P.

[1]Dates chosen for changes are from the trough to the peak of the respective periods of rising 10-year treasury bond yields (apart from the present period, for which data ends on August 4, 2003).

financial intermediaries and the wider economy.

Yield curves steepened as markets continued to expect policy rates to remain unchanged for an extended period. The steepening of the U.S. yield curve in particular during the recent rebound in yield was much more pronounced than during other periods of sharp treasury market sell-offs and further suggests that technical factors affecting long-term securities, such as mortgage market hedging activity, have played a contributory role (Table 2.1).

Rising U.S. treasury yields resulted in an increase in mortgage rates and a fall in mortgage refinancing activity. A reduction in mortgage refinancing, including in particular cash-out refinancing, could potentially undercut household consumption. Moreover, rising interest rates and falling refinancing levels have extended the expected duration of outstanding mortgages and mortgage-backed securities (MBSs). This in turn necessitated widespread hedging by U.S. mortgage agencies and other holders of MBSs, which has tended to amplify the trend toward higher interest rates and resulted briefly in the largest jump in spreads between the swap rate and government yields since the Long-Term Capital Management crisis in 1998.[1] (The hedging process is described in detail later in this chapter.)

Investment Flows Shift into Corporate Bonds and, Eventually, Equities

Corporate bond spreads narrowed substantially as investors were increasingly prepared to assume credit risk and interest rate risk in the search for yield (Table 2.2). There were signs of reduced investor discrimination, as shown by the lower coefficient of variation in the spreads of individual U.S. corporate issuers over treasury securities compared with the peak in credit spreads last October. This could leave corporate bonds vulnerable to a sell-off in the treasury market. However, to date, corporate bond spreads both for high-grade and below-investment-grade issuers remain below their levels at the mid-June low point for the treasury market, which may be another indication that the recent rebound in yields is partly accounted for by technical factors in the treasury and swap markets.

Continued low short-term interest rates triggered an exodus from money market mutual funds up to May, as investors appeared to be moving out along the risk spectrum (Figure 2.3). In addition to low interest rates on government bond yields across the maturity spectrum and the compression of credit spreads, the rekindled investor interest in equities was sparked by an easing of geopolitical tensions and signs of a revival of corporate earnings. Since May, although money market fund out-

---

[1]The swap rate is the fixed interest rate that a market participant can pay in exchange for receiving floating-rate LIBOR interest payments. The swap market is frequently used as a method of hedging fixed-rate exposures, including exposures arising from the mortgage market. A rise in the spread between the swap rate and treasury bond yields can indicate an increase in demand to hedge fixed-rate assets by making fixed-rate payments.

Table 2.2. U.S. Corporate Bond Spread: Coefficients of Variation

	Oct. 31, 2002	Jul. 31, 2003
Mean of spreads (basis points)	219	108
Standard deviation of spreads	195	73
Coefficient of variation	0.89	0.68

Source: Lehman Brothers; largest 100 U.S. corporations measured by market value of issuance.

flows have come to an end, equity inflows have continued.

As a result, mature equity markets rebounded from their March lows and implied equity volatility moderated (Figure 2.4). Moreover, expectations that earnings volatility would decline helped raise equity valuations. Low interest rates on government bonds also made equity valuations appear relatively attractive, pushing bond-to-earnings yield ratios to long-term lows, which have been only modestly offset by the recent rise in bond yields (Figure 2.5). More recently, U.S. corporate earnings in the second quarter have outstripped analyst projections, further boosting sentiment.

The Dollar Stabilizes Amid a Recovery of Equities and Foreign Exchange Intervention

In tandem with the equity market recovery and rising bond yields, expectations that growth in the United States would outpace that in Europe contributed to a rebound in the dollar from mid-June, following its steep decline (Figure 2.6). Portfolio flows into the United States remained strong, reflecting in part efforts by Asian central banks to stem the appreciation of their currencies against the dollar. Nevertheless, concerns over the size of the external financing need of the United States and the large share of U.S. financial assets held by foreigners remain strong. Moreover, markets have been increasingly concerned that the euro will continue to bear the brunt of any adjustment in the U.S. external accounts, further undermining sluggish growth in the euro area.

Figure 2.3. Cumulative Net Flows to U.S. Mutual Funds
(In billions of U.S. dollars)

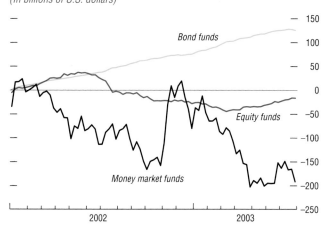

Source: AMG Data Services.

Mature Market Vulnerabilities Have Eased

The March 2003 GFSR, and earlier issues, highlighted a number of vulnerabilities stemming from the continuing adjustment to the bursting of the equity price bubble in 2000. Since then, on balance, vulnerabilities have eased in the global financial system:

- *The rally in equity markets since March has reduced stability risks.* It has improved the balance sheets of insurers (particularly in Europe) and of pension funds. It will have increased household wealth and strengthened corporate balance sheets (not least through its effect on defined-benefit corporate pension funds).
- *Both corporate and household sectors continued to build up liquidity in early 2003.* More recently, they have begun to be less risk averse, as investors have acquired corporate bonds and equities and the pace of corporate balance sheet restructuring appeared to slow down, which could help to increase private sector investment.
- *The recent increase in long-term interest rates appears to have led to the unwinding of some carry trade positions.* It will also have eased pressure on insurance companies and pension funds by reversing part of the rise in the discounted value of their liabilities.

However, some risks remain:

- *Higher long-term interest rates could still cause problems if not accompanied by stronger economic growth.* A further rise in interest rates is likely to be accompanied by stronger economic growth and to strengthen many financial balance sheets. However, in the unlikely event that interest rates were to rise while growth stayed weak, then equity as well as bond prices could fall.
- *Risks arising from the mortgage market should receive particular attention.* The sheer size alone of the U.S. mortgage market makes it of systemic importance. As the U.S. mortgage market has grown, some of the common strategies used to hedge the prepayment risk in MBSs (described below) could amplify any upward trend in overall interest rates.

Figure 2.4. Equity Market Performance

Source: Bloomberg L.P.

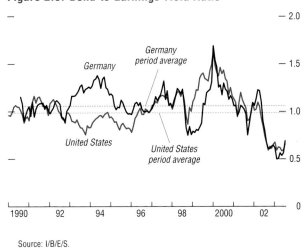

Figure 2.5. Bond-to-Earnings Yield Ratio

Source: I/B/E/S.

- *The equity market rally could be reversed if corporate earnings disappoint.* There are encouraging signs that earnings are matching expectations despite slow economic activity, but uncertainty remains high, particularly in Europe.
- *Although insurers' and pensions funds' balance sheets have improved, they remain vulnerable.* Life insurers in many countries still suffer from negative spreads between their assets and guaranteed liability returns, and many pension funds still face funding gaps.

This section discusses these vulnerabilities in more detail.

Balance Sheets of Household and Corporate Sectors Are Gradually Strengthening

Previous GFSRs noted a withdrawal from risk-taking and buildup of cash positions in the household and corporate sectors in the United States, Europe, and Japan since early 2000. The liquidity buildup continued in the first half of 2003, as households in particular increased their bank deposits further. But there were some signs of less risk aversion, with U.S. households beginning to acquire equities as the share market recovered and European companies acquiring short-term finance. Meanwhile banks' balance sheets generally improved as corporate earnings began to recover.

Household Sector

Despite the equity losses in recent years, household balance sheets in the major countries show few signs of strain. Debt levels are historically high, but low interest rates have kept debt service manageable and the high deposit balances provide a cushion. Rising real estate prices in the United States and Europe combined with low interest rates have stimulated increased mortgage debt, including for home equity withdrawals. Much of the interest rate risk in the housing market at this point would seem to have been passed to the investors in fixed-rate mortgage products (see

Figure 2.6. U.S. Dollar Performance

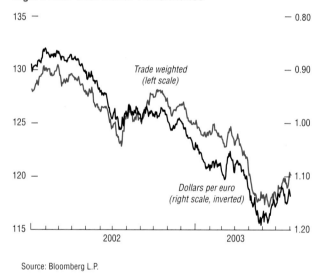

Source: Bloomberg L.P.

Table 2.3. United States: Balance Sheet of Households and Nonprofit Organizations
(End of period; in trillions of U.S. dollars)

	2000 Q1	2002 Q4	2003 Q1
Total assets	**50.25**	**48.1**	**48.24**
of which:			
deposits	4.18	5.08	5.23
corporate equities	9.22	4.33	4.17
pension fund reserves	9.26	8.01	7.94
real estate	11.79	14.92	15.11
Total liabilities	**7.01**	**8.77**	**8.93**
of which:			
home mortgages	4.6	6.05	6.22
consumer credit	1.44	1.76	1.74
Net worth	**43.24**	**39.33**	**39.31**

Source: Board of Governors of the Federal Reserve System, *Flow of Funds.*

the discussion of the mortgage market below).

In the United States, household net worth was flat in the first quarter of 2003, as a decline in equity values offset gains in the value of real estate (Table 2.3). Subsequent increases in both stock and housing prices have perhaps led to a recovery in net worth of about 4 percent, leaving it still 5 percent below the peak in early 2000. In the first quarter households made direct net purchases of equities for the first time since 1993, though this partly reflects the cyclical absence of cash-financed takeovers that had returned funds to investors during the boom (Figure 2.7). Household wealth has become more sensitive to the real estate market. Over the past three years, real estate has risen from 23 percent of total household assets to 31 percent. Mortgage debt (including cash-out refinancing) has also continued to grow rapidly. Owners' equity in their homes in the first quarter continued to decline as a share of home value. As a result, based on end-March 2003 figures, a 10 percent fall in house prices would reduce household net worth by 3.8 percent, compared with 2.7 percent three years earlier.

The growth of euro-area household debt rose slightly in the first quarter of 2003, but remains below the U.S. pace. Favorable mort-

Figure 2.7. United States: Household Net Acquisitions of Financial Assets, Selected Items
(In billions of U.S. dollars)

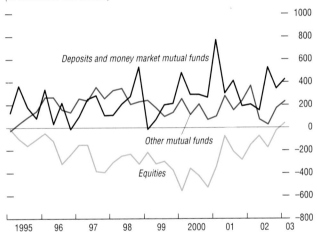

Source: Board of Governors of the Federal Reserve System, *Flow of Funds.*

Table 2.4. Euro Area: Nonfinancial Sector Net Asset Purchases[1]
(In billions of euros)

	2000	2001	2002
Currency, deposits, and money market mutual funds	126.4	420.8	307.4
Securities other than equities	141.6	132.9	89.8
Mutual fund shares[2]	113.1	61.3	55.5
Equities	223.0	38.9	−6.6

Source: European Central Bank, *Monthly Bulletin*.
[1]All nonfinancial sectors other than central government.
[2]Other than money market mutual funds.

gage interest rates have encouraged borrowing, but at a much slower rate than in the United States. Euro-area consumer credit grew slower still, in line with weak spending and as low long-term rates tended to channel credit demand into the mortgage market. Nevertheless, the consumer borrowing market remains less concentrated on mortgages than in the United States. Around two-thirds of bank lending to households in the euro area is for house purchase (31 percent of GDP), whereas almost three-quarters of U.S. household debt is through mortgages (58 percent of GDP). Although most euro-area mortgages, as in the United States, are fixed-rate and demand has therefore been boosted by historically low interest rates, there is much less tendency to use them for equity withdrawal and thus as a substitute for consumer credit.

Data showing separate breakdowns of euro-area asset portfolio allocation in 2002 for the household and corporate sectors are not yet available, but figures for the nonfinancial sector as a whole show that the strong preference for liquidity that began in 2001 continued in 2002 (Table 2.4). Bank deposits and other low-risk assets continued to receive the bulk of portfolio allocations. Monetary data for the first six months of 2003 indicate that this trend has persisted, and in particular the rapid growth of money market mutual funds has continued.

Portfolio allocations by Japanese households continue to be overwhelmingly into bank deposits, with continued outflows from uninsured bank debentures and trusts. Portfolio allocations into foreign securities, although small, have picked up in recent years.

Corporate Sector

Corporate balance sheets in the major countries continue to strengthen, and the main question at this point is whether expectations for earnings will be validated by results (see the discussion of corporate earnings below). But even though companies have lengthened the maturity of their debt, leverage remains high. Another risk would be a rise in interest rates, which would rapidly widen corporate credit spreads from their current compressed levels and would restrict access to new funds.

U.S. corporate profitability and liquidity continued to improve in the first quarter. Capital spending remained weak, contributing to a slow pace of debt growth. Nevertheless leverage remained high, with the debt-to-net-worth ratio rising to 53.2 percent, a little short of the 55 percent peak shortly after the end of the previous recession in the early 1990s. Firms continued to restructure their balance sheets, albeit at a slower pace than in previous quarters, as they lengthened the maturity of debt and locked in low interest rates, while maintaining a high level of liquidity (Figure 2.8). Outstanding commercial paper and bank lending to corporates declined to 26 percent below its end-2000 level, while corporate bonds outstanding rose to 23 percent above its end-2000 level. High corporate bond issuance levels in the second quarter suggest that this trend is continuing.

In contrast to the United States, euro-area nonfinancial corporations increased their short-term financing in the first quarter (based on preliminary data) after lengthening the maturity of their financing during the previous two years (Figure 2.9). This may partly reflect a seasonal rebound from typically slimmed down year-end balance sheets but also may reflect a more underlying increase in demand for working capital.

The Japanese corporate sector significantly reduced its debt in FY2002, while also narrowing the financing gap in its pension fund reserves. This was financed through improved profits and a reduction in deposits, while investments in stocks increased.

Banking Sector

Banks' balance sheets in the major financial centers generally improved in the first half of 2003. U.S. banks continue to be well capitalized, with strong earnings benefiting from wide net interest margins and slightly declining problem loan books. Mortgage and consumer lending grew strongly, while business lending has continued to decline as borrowing demand remained weak. The recent volatility in the mortgage market may present hedging problems for some banks, although ultimately higher long-term rates should help to keep their interest margins robust.

European banks are recovering from a difficult business environment in 2001 and 2002. Capitalization levels have remained well above regulatory minimums, although some banks sold business assets to ensure this. Cost-cutting programs, involving reductions in staff and branches, have continued at many banks. Profits began to improve in early 2003, despite continuing provisioning needs. As in the United States, lending growth has focused more on households than companies, although corporate lending has begun to rebound. Assuming the real economy continues to recover, banks' performance should improve further, although conditions remain challenging for German banks, and there could be some vulnerability to the real estate sector in some countries.

Japanese banks reduced nonperforming loans by 18 percent during the year ending March 31, 2003, but the resolution of loan quality problems remains a major source of uncertainty. Banks have started to take steps to meet the supervisory requirements to halve

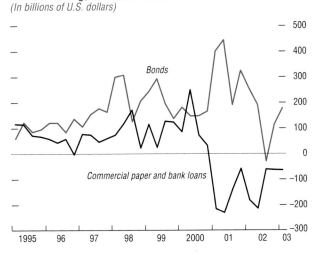

Figure 2.8. United States: Nonfinancial Corporations' Net Borrowing, Selected Items
(In billions of U.S. dollars)

Source: Board of Governors of the Federal Reserve System, *Flow of Funds.*

Figure 2.9. Euro Area: Nonfinancial Corporations' Net Borrowing
(In billions of euros)

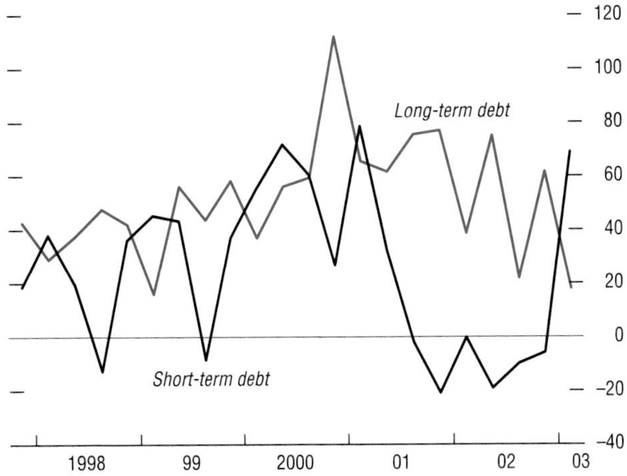

Source: European Central Bank, *Monthly Bulletin.*

their share of nonperforming loans by March 2005 and to reduce the amounts of equity holdings within Tier 1 capital by the end of September 2006. Several banks have announced the setting up of special purpose vehicles (SPVs), in cooperation with foreign banks, into which nonperforming loans would be transferred, and one bank transferred equity holdings into a similar SPV. The fifth largest bank, Resona Bank, received a capital injection from the government after a stricter accounting treatment of deferred tax assets revealed it to be undercapitalized. These developments, together with improved corporate earnings, have helped to create a tentative market view that the worst of Japan's nonperforming loan problem may be behind it, and by the end of July bank shares had generally more than recovered their losses earlier in 2003.

The U.S. Mortgage Market, Fannie Mae, and Freddie Mac

Fannie Mae and Freddie Mac, the U.S. government-sponsored housing enterprises, have come under increasing scrutiny because of their rapid growth and the possible risks they pose to financial stability. Recent developments have highlighted the extremely large, highly leveraged, nature of these enterprises and the risks they are managing. The ability of homeowners to fix their mortgage rates while preserving prepayment rights has transferred complex and increasingly large risks to these enterprises and other investors. While it is prudent for Fannie Mae and Freddie Mac to hedge their exposures, the very large size of their balance sheets implies that their hedging operations can accentuate sharp market moves. Although other countries also have seen booms in mortgage activity as a result of low long-term interest rates, the size of these two enterprises and the volume of mortgage

prepayments and hedging are much larger than activities in other countries and thus raise particular financial stability concerns.

Fannie Mae and Freddie Mac were chartered as agencies by Congress to provide liquidity to the home mortgage market. They are owned by private shareholders and have no explicit government guarantee, but are believed by many market participants to enjoy an implicit one. This perception, which helps lower their borrowing costs, has been reinforced by a number of factors, including a line of credit from the U.S. Treasury; exemption of their debt from banks' large-exposure limits; exemption of their income from state and local taxes; exemption from SEC registration requirements; and, perhaps most important, the belief that they are "too big to fail." They have an AAA rating but the rating agencies have stated that, absent the implicit government guarantee, the rating would be AA instead.

The size of the U.S. mortgage and agency debt market has grown rapidly in recent years to surpass that of U.S. treasury securities (Figure 2.10). At the end of March 2003, securities directly issued by U.S. government-sponsored agencies (including, but not limited to, Fannie Mae and Freddie Mac) totaled $2.4 trillion and mortgage-backed securities issued by the agencies totaled $3.2 trillion.[2] The total of these two amounts was 161 percent of the size of outstanding U.S. treasury securities, compared with 73 percent as recently as 1996.

Fannie Mae and Freddie Mac manage large exposures to interest rate, prepayment, and credit risks. They provide credit guarantees for the mortgages they have securitized. In addition, they hold on their balance sheets nearly $300 billion of home mortgages, plus an additional $1.2 trillion of MBSs, compared with a total $6.6 trillion of home mortgages outstanding in the United States. Some observers have warned of the systemic risks

---

[2]Subsequent references to "agencies" in this chapter refer only to Fannie Mae and Freddie Mac.

inherent in the agencies' large mortgage portfolios and their hedging operations, and have criticized the agencies for lack of transparency.

The Office of Federal Housing Enterprise Oversight (OFHEO), which supervises the two agencies, oversees quarterly stress tests to ensure that they can withstand severe market conditions for interest rates and house prices. Based on these stress tests, OFHEO found that the capital of Fannie Mae and Freddie Mac has consistently exceeded the minimum required. However, regulators need to look closely at whether agencies' capital adequacy is sufficient, especially bearing in mind the questions about internal controls that have emerged in Freddie Mac. Their core capital-to-asset ratio at the end of 2002 was only 3.2 percent, and it is unclear whether they have taken sufficient account of the risk that the markets may not be deep enough to allow them to continuously hedge their growing portfolios in times of stress. More comprehensive stress tests and a greater safety margin for operational risks within the capital requirement are two possibilities that could be considered, which would increase the robustness of the agencies, allow them to take a longer-term investment horizon, and reduce the pressure on them to conduct precise, continuous hedging.

The expected volume of prepayments is strongly influenced by the level of interest rates, and this changes the duration of mortgages and MBSs. (When interest rates go down, borrowers can refinance at lower cost, but when rates go up they can continue paying at the originally fixed rates.) Dynamic hedging requires continuously adjusting the duration of agencies' liabilities to offset changes in the duration of mortgage-related assets. In August 2002, the duration gap between Fannie Mae's assets and liabilities widened to minus 14 months, as falling interest rates increased likely prepayment rates and thus shortened the expected duration of its mortgages. This gap prompted OFHEO to

Figure 2.10. United States: Debt Outstanding
(In billions of U.S. dollars)

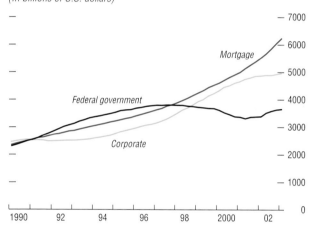

Source: Board of Governors of the Federal Reserve System, *Flow of Funds.*

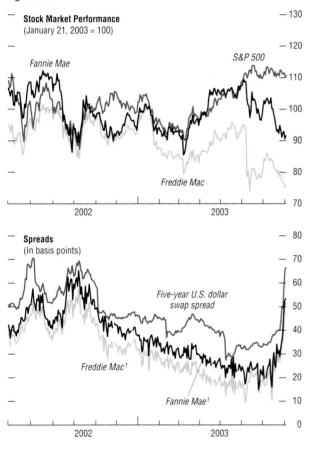

Figure 2.11. United States: Government-Sponsored Agencies

Stock Market Performance
(January 21, 2003 = 100)

Spreads
(In basis points)

Source: Bloomberg L.P.
[1]Spread over five-year U.S. treasury note.

require an action plan to correct this imbalance and to monitor Fannie Mae's maintenance of its duration gap for the following six months before it declared itself satisfied in April 2003.

In January 2003, Freddie Mac announced it would restate its earnings and capital for prior years due to incorrect accounting for derivatives transactions, and in June 2003 three top executives left the firm over a corporate governance scandal. The firm's former auditor had mistakenly allowed various transactions to be used to smooth financial results and thus defer profits from marking to market hedges as required under the "fair value" accounting rules introduced in 2001. Its new auditor, appointed in 2002, insisted that the accounts be restated to remove this smoothing. Freddie Mac has stated that it expects retained net earnings at end-2002 to be increased by between $1.5 billion and $4.5 billion as a result of the restatement, and that future earnings would accordingly be lower than under the previous treatment. In addition, the new accounting practices will likely result in greater future variability of earnings.

The news of accounting and corporate governance problems at Freddie Mac unsettled the market. The biggest effect was on the equity price of Freddie Mac (in both January and June 2003) and to a lesser extent Fannie Mae (Figure 2.11). Interest rate spreads of agency over U.S. treasury debt widened. The market's initial reaction seemed to suggest more concern about the agencies' future profitability than about their creditworthiness.

Hedging in the Mortgage Market Can Amplify Interest Rate Movements

If U.S. bond yields rise further, one source of additional market volatility may be the dynamic hedging practices in the mortgage and MBS market, by both the agencies and other investors (Box 2.1). The size of mortgage indebtedness and recent historically low interest rates greatly increased the volume of prepayments to be hedged in the last three

Box 2.1. Mortgage Hedging Mechanics

The hedging of mortgages and mortgage-backed securities (MBSs) is complicated by the need to predict, and constantly adjust to, the future tendency of borrowers to prepay their mortgages. A portfolio of fixed-rate prepayable mortgages will, ex post, have an actual duration much shorter than the average contractual length of the mortgages because of prepayments. Prepayment rates will depend partly on future interest rates, as borrowers prepay when there are cost savings from refinancing, but will also depend on other factors, such as the frequency with which borrowers move house or the promptness with which they seize opportunities to refinance more cheaply. Past experience enables investors and analysts to estimate expected prepayment rates, depending on the interest rates and terms of the mortgages in the portfolio and the current level of interest rates.

The complicated nature of the prepayment risks means that the interest rate risk on mortgages or MBSs cannot be fully hedged away by other instruments, such as conventional bonds or derivatives. At any given instant, the exposure of an investment in MBSs to small interest rate changes can be hedged by a short position in conventional fixed-rate instruments, once the average duration of the MBSs has been estimated. But the hedge would need to be constantly adjusted, as the expected durations of the MBSs would change much more than the durations of the conventional instruments in response to interest rate changes. For instance, as interest rates rise, expected prepayment rates for MBSs fall, and their durations rise, leading hedgers to need to sell extra conventional instruments to remain fully hedged. The required hedging ratios would change over time even if interest rates remained the same, as the expected prepayment rate would continue to evolve.

Several hedging strategies can be used by investors. One common one is to sell treasury securities. This provides a very liquid market for hedging, but its accuracy depends on a stable spread being maintained between treasuries and MBSs, which is not always the case. The swap market similarly provides an avenue for hedging. Both types of hedge require continual readjusting of hedge positions. Because of a poor experience with government bond hedges in 1998–2000, including during the Long-Term Capital Management (LTCM) crisis, many participants turned to the swap market to hedge investment portfolios of MBSs and other securities. One visible consequence was the strong correlation of swap *rates* and swap *spreads over U.S. treasury yields* as U.S. mortgage rates fell in 2000–01. As rates fell, mortgage prepayment suddenly became more likely and hedged investors needed to receive fixed-rate interest payments in the swap market. This demand to receive fixed-rate payments was revealed by the decline in swap spreads at the same time as the overall level of rates fell.

An approximate attempt to hedge against larger interest rate movements can be made by using option-related products such as buying swaptions (the option to enter into a swap at a certain fixed rate) or selling callable bonds (which give the issuer the right to prepay the bond). Both these instruments can allow investors to match some of the prepayment features of MBSs, but will not exactly duplicate the likely behavior of the pool of mortgage borrowers. The growing size of the mortgage debt market appears to have encouraged the use of a wider range of hedges, such as these to absorb more easily the shifts in mortgage duration. While these sorts of hedges can be more exact than conventional bonds or swaps, they can be more expensive to implement and more illiquid.

A more fundamental way for mortgage lenders to reduce their hedging needs would be to price adjustable-rate mortgages more aggressively to limit the creation of new fixed-rate mortgages with prepayment rights, although persuading borrowers to accept adjustable-rate mortgages when fixed rates are still at historically low levels would undoubtedly be difficult.

Figure 2.12. United States: Mortgage Market and Hedging

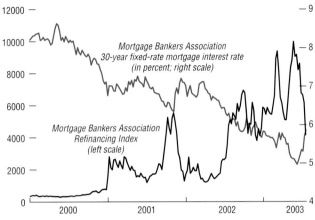

Source: Bloomberg L.P.

Figure 2.13. United States: Mortgage-Backed Securities
(Over one year maturity)

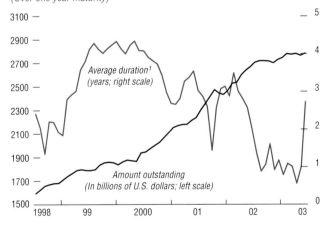

Source: Lehman Brothers Inc.
[1]Modified adjusted duration.

years (Figure 2.12). Therefore the effect of these prepayments, and the consequent need for hedging transactions, has become a more important issue for financial stability. As dynamic hedgers see the expected duration of their assets increase when interest rates rise and the likelihood of prepayments falls, they will reduce duration elsewhere on their balance sheet by, for example, selling treasury securities, thus potentially accelerating the upward movement in yields in the overall market.

As mortgage interest rates have risen from their historic lows in June, the volume of mortgage prepayments has already fallen rapidly. Those borrowers with new mortgages or who have recently refinanced have locked in rates well below what are now current market levels. Meanwhile there are relatively few mortgages still outstanding that were taken out in the period before 2001 when rates were well above current rates and that have not already been refinanced.

As the volume of actual and prospective prepayments has fallen, durations of MBSs, which had declined dramatically, have increased rapidly again. In May during the peak of the refinancing boom, for example, the pace of refinancing was such that the average expected duration of MBSs fell to 0.5 years, compared to over four years in early 2000, and it has widened again to over three years in early August (Figure 2.13).

The speed and magnitude of this change in duration has generated the need for large amounts of extra hedging. The exact proportion of MBSs whose hedges are adjusted on a continuous basis is not known, but around 40 percent of MBSs are held by the agencies, which have a policy of hedging. If we assume that around half the total outstanding are held in continuously hedged portfolios, the rise in duration since the low point in May has already created the need for hedgers to sell the equivalent of $500 billion of 10-year conventional securities, which is more than double the amount of total U.S. government debt issuance with maturity two years and over in the year ending June 30, 2003.

The strains of accommodating this hedging activity have been clearly evident and were illustrated dramatically in the swap market at the end of July. After swap spreads had remained stable during the first phase of interest rate rises from mid-June to late July, the five-year spread between the swap rate and treasury yield rose from 41 basis points on July 25 to a peak of 66 basis points on August 1 before falling back again below 40 basis points on August 7 (Figure 2.11). Swaption volatility also jumped sharply. Many analysts attributed these developments to the strong demand from investors to pay fixed rates under swaps to hedge their increased fixed-rate asset exposure.

The likely continuous hedging needs from the mortgage market remain very high. One market analyst has estimated that, if long-term interest rates were to rise by a further 50 basis points, the expected duration of the MBS market would increase by almost one year, leading to additional hedging sales equivalent to around $200 billion of 10-year securities, while a 50 basis point fall would create the need to reduce short positions by a similar amount (Modukuri, 2003). Given the amounts involved, a sudden rise or fall in interest rates could be further amplified by this hedging, particularly at longer maturities, as hedgers sell into markets where prices are already falling, or buy into rising markets.

Institutions affected by these hedging needs include the agencies, banks and other investors in mortgage-related instruments, and counterparties that have taken on some of the positions hedged by these investors. The agencies have the largest and most concentrated positions, and so the impact on them is perhaps the most important for financial stability.

The close regulatory and public attention to Fannie Mae and Freddie Mac may have caused them to hedge more exactly on a continuous basis, presumably amplifying the effect of interest rate moves still further. This hedging also has likely costs for the agencies arising from the bid-offer spread of transactions. For every $100 billion of MBSs dynamically hedged on a continuous basis, the total hedging cost of adjusting to an additional one-year change in average duration would be $10 million per basis point of bid-offer spread paid. The speed of market movements and illiquidity during periods of rapid rate movements, illustrated by discontinuities (so-called "gapping") in prices, also mean that the agencies face increased interest rate exposure during these market moves.

Meanwhile, the funding costs have gone up for the agencies as spreads have widened further. Continued stories of accounting uncertainties and investigations appear to have led to sales of agency debt by some investors. Foreign central banks, for instance, which increased holdings of agency securities rapidly in the early part of the year as part of the search for yield, appear to now be making net sales, despite their continued buildup of dollar reserves. Ten-year agency spreads against U.S. treasury bonds have widened to over 50 basis points from 37 basis points at the end of May, for instance. Spreads are currently highly volatile, but if this increased funding cost is sustained, it will reduce the agencies' profitability, although it should be noted that they reported comfortable net interest margins of over 100 basis points at the end of 2002.

It may be that other investors—such as banks, securities firms, or hedge funds—have sustained considerable losses during the recent market turbulence, especially if they have been attempting to benefit from the interest rate carry that can be earned on MBSs or longer-term instruments or otherwise felt less need than the agencies to hedge their full interest rate risk. However, no specific information of such losses has emerged, nor any additional market disruption that would arise from feared failures of significant counterparties. It is also possible that some of these institutions will have moved recently to hedge

Figure 2.14. Germany and Switzerland: Insurance Companies' Credit Default Swap Spreads (CDS) and Stock Prices[1]

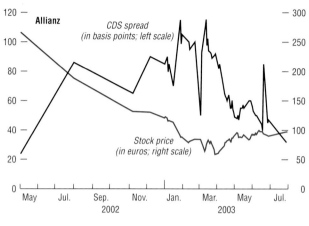

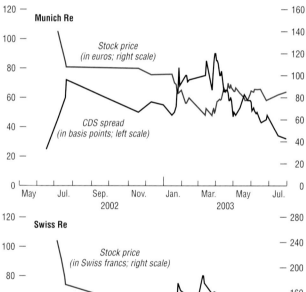

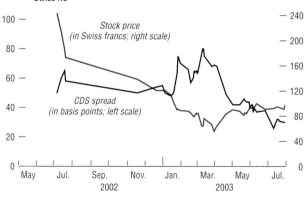

Source: CreditTrade.
[1]Spreads on CDS on euro-denominated senior debt with five-year maturities. The stock prices are plotted for dates matching CDS quotes in the CreditTrade database.

their positions more closely as volatility increased, adding further to the sales into a falling market.

In summary, the more volatile market environment for the agencies, potential difficulties for the market in absorbing their hedging needs, and possible lower profit margins all argue for regulators to examine closely whether the agencies' capital base is large enough to absorb the risks on their growing balance sheet. The narrowness of the safety margin provided by their capital has increased the need for them to maintain precise hedges on a continuous basis. The continuous, nondiscretionary hedging by the agencies and others in the mortgage market could amplify the size of any future increase in interest rates and add to market volatility. The amplifying effects of dynamic hedging are similar to those seen during some previous well-known spikes in market volatility, which are described in the case studies in Chapter III. But how powerful the amplification might be will depend on the speed and size of any interest rate rise and the not yet fully tested ability of the rest of the market to absorb the increasingly large duration needs of the hedgers.

Financial Conditions in the Insurance Industry Stabilized But Problems Remain

Previous GFSRs have emphasized the risks to the insurance sector from lower equity and bond markets. In recent months, the pressure from equity markets has eased slightly, but interest rates on fixed-income assets remain below those on liabilities in many cases, and the sector continues to face challenges.

Equity prices of insurance companies, particularly in Europe, recovered in the second quarter of 2003 and credit default spreads for key insurers narrowed from their peak levels in the first quarter (Figure 2.14). Credit downgrades of insurers slowed. In the first quarter of 2003, Moody's, for example, downgraded 1 percent of life insurers and 8 percent of non-life insurers, compared with 16 percent and

28 percent in the fourth quarter of 2002 (see Moody's, 2003b).

The improvement in balance sheets from the recent equity market rally will be limited. Many insurers have reduced their equity exposures substantially during the past 18 months. In Germany, for example, the portfolio share of equities has declined from a peak of almost 20 percent in 2001 to about 10 percent in the first quarter of 2003, according to the German Insurance Association, though the largest insurers have tended to maintain higher equity exposures.[3] Reported balance sheets may deteriorate further, notwithstanding the improved equity prices, since earlier losses on equity holdings have not yet been fully recognized in some countries. New statutory valuation rules introduced in Germany in 2001 allowed insurers to value their end-2002 equity holdings in their reported accounts at the average value of 2002 plus a premium of 10 percent (see Fitch, 2003a). Broadly speaking, they were able to value the DAX at about 4600 in their end-2002 accounts, compared with a level of about 3300 in early August, but nevertheless had to write down the value if losses are foreseeably permanent.[4]

More generally, the low interest rate environment continues to put pressure on insurers' financial conditions. The drop in long-term yields has exacerbated the squeeze of insurance companies between low-yielding assets and relatively high guaranteed returns on existing life insurance policies. Negative yield spreads in some countries, including Japan, have compressed solvency margins. Observers report asset returns of Japanese insurers of about 1 percent, while average guaranteed yields on existing policies are 3 percent to 4 percent and on newly issued policies are 1 percent to 2 percent (see Fitch, 2003d). Even in countries such as France,

where guaranteed returns are tied to market rates, profit margins have been compressed in part because of competitive pressures (see Fitch, 2003c). To alleviate the financial strains on life insurers, in recent months several countries, including Japan and the United States, have launched or passed new legislation to lower guaranteed returns on insurance policies (see Appendix I).

The strained financial conditions, particularly of some smaller European insurers, have led to a flight to quality as new funds have increasingly been flowing to large, presumably more stable, insurance companies. And they have caused the first failure of an insurance company in 50 years in Germany. In late June, assets and liabilities of Mannheimer Lebensversicherung, a small life insurer, were transferred to the industry-funded guarantee fund Protektor after bailout attempts by the German Insurance Association failed. Protektor was established only late last year and will continue to pay policyholders the minimum guaranteed rate of return.

Overall, the insurance industry remains troubled by negative spread problems. The reduced exposure to equities and the rising equity prices have reduced the risk that widespread equity sales into declining markets by insurers could further accentuate renewed equity price declines. But negative spread problems still need to be addressed in many countries to put life insurance underwriting on a sustainable footing in the current low interest rate environment. If, by contrast, long-term interest rates were to rise markedly, the gains to insurance companies from lower present values of their long-term liabilities would outweigh the capital losses on their bond portfolios, and over time they would benefit from higher returns on their fixed-interest investments.

---

[3]Some of the reduction in the share of equity investments was, of course, caused by lower equity values (see Moody's, 2003a).

[4]The average value of the DAX in 2002 was about 4200.

Credit Derivatives Performed Reasonably Well But the Risks Remain Unclear

Credit derivatives weathered the wave of corporate defaults in 2001–2002 reasonably well. Disputes over credit events were fewer than feared, but the defaults heightened the awareness of risk among market participants. Credit risk transfer markets merit close attention because the distribution of risks is opaque, legal standards need to be refined further, and activity is concentrated among a few of the largest global financial institutions. The lower-yield environment since the peak in defaults may also motivate some market participants to use credit derivatives to reach for yield without fully understanding the risks.

From a financial stability perspective, key questions are the extent to which credit derivatives concentrate risks in a few key financial institutions or disperse risks widely, and whether market participants can adequately price and manage the risks. The market for credit derivatives continues to grow rapidly. Gross outstanding credit derivatives contracts held by U.S. banks grew by 60 percent in the year to March 2003 to $710 billion (see U.S. Office of the Comptroller of the Currency, 2003). As with many over-the-counter derivative products, the structure of the market remains highly concentrated in a small number of dealers, commercial banks, and investment banks, primarily in London and New York. The Office of the Comptroller of the Currency survey reports that the largest participating bank accounts for 58 percent of U.S. bank activity in credit derivatives. Concentration to this degree brings the risk that a failure or withdrawal from the market by one of the major participants could cause extensive disruption, although netting and collateralization agreements reduce this risk.

In the wake of the credit stresses in 2002, concerns have been raised about the ability of credit protection sellers to manage the risk they have taken on. As some traditional sellers of credit protection (particularly insurers and German Landesbanken) have reportedly scaled back their operations in response to losses, some banks that have taken on more of the role of sellers are reportedly hedging the credit risk directly through trading in the underlying corporate bonds. A widening in the range of sellers of protection would help deepen the credit markets, but increasing use of corporate bonds for hedging could make their spreads more volatile, since liquidity in the corporate bond market is sometimes insufficient for taking short positions (see Tierney and Nassar, 2003). Nonetheless, credit default spreads continued to narrow from their peak in August 2002 broadly in line with corporate bond spreads, and the overall returns from taking on credit exposure have been high compared with other financial markets.

Despite considerable legal uncertainties involved in credit derivatives, most disputes have thus far been settled cooperatively, possibly because the financial costs of doing so are small while the market is still growing, compared with the damage to reputation and counterparty relationships from a protracted dispute. But as the amounts outstanding expand, disputes may be less easy to settle and so greater legal certainty and standardization is desirable. In May 2003, the International Swaps and Derivatives Association (ISDA) published new global standard documentation for credit default swaps. Among other measures, the new standard more clearly defines the types of credit events, including debt restructuring, that could trigger default (see ISDA, 2003). (The Basel II proposals would allow regulatory capital reductions for credit derivatives with certain restructuring clauses.) Although standardizing complex contracts is difficult, standard documentation is essential to reduce legal risks and facilitate deep and liquid markets.

Underfunding of Defined-Benefit Corporate Pension Plans

As noted in the March 2003 GFSR, the decline in interest rates (which raised the present value of pension obligations) and the drop in equity prices have created sizable funding shortfalls in corporate defined-benefit pension funds in the few countries (such as the United States, United Kingdom, and the Netherlands) that require firms to fund their pension obligations. In the United States, the aggregate pension underfunding of firms in the S&P 500 grew to $216 billion in 2002 (having had a surplus of $250 billion as recently as 1999), and funding levels declined to 82 percent of projected pension benefits. Nearly half of the deterioration in funding levels since 2000 resulted from stock market losses, with the balance stemming from increases in discounted pension obligations as interest rates fell and from net payouts. Funding problems are concentrated in a few large companies in older manufacturing industries, with fewer than 20 firms accounting for half of the aggregate funding shortfall of corporations in the S&P 500. One estimate for the United Kingdom (by financial consulting firm, Watson Wyatt LLP) has put the total pension funding gap for the corporate sector at about £55 billion.

Other countries that have no short-term funding requirements, where corporate pensions instead operate on a "pay as you go" basis, face perhaps even greater long-term funding shortfalls. Companies not subject to external funding requirements tend to hold financial assets in anticipation of these obligations, but there is concern that these provisions may be inadequate, particularly as populations age. In February 2003, Standard and Poor's downgraded 12 European firms specifically because of their pension obligations. Furthermore, without funding requirements, pensioners' incomes are more exposed to the financial health of their former employers.

While the current U.S. funding gaps are substantial, they cannot be blamed entirely on the equity market decline. In the late 1990s, U.S. corporations enjoyed larger gains from equity holdings than their current losses, averaging $200 billion per year according to Flow of Funds figures, and cumulative capital gains since 1994 are still $700 billion (Figure 2.15). As the capital gains ensured an overfunding, most corporations stopped contributing to their pension plans and relied instead entirely on investment income to pay benefits.

The overall funding situation could improve rapidly if financial markets recovered during an economic upswing. Equity returns near the long-run historical average of 7 to 8 percent would cause a notable improvement in funding positions. A rise in long-term interest rates would have an even more powerful effect on funding levels than an increase in equity prices. According to one estimate, each 50 basis point increase in interest rates reduces the projected benefit obligations for S&P 500 firms by $60 billion (see Credit Suisse First Boston, 2003).

Nevertheless, higher interest rates and equity prices alone may not fill the largest pension funding shortfalls. Many firms in the S&P 500 will need to increase their pension fund contributions. Already in 2002, firms in the S&P 500 tripled their pension contributions to $46 billion, subtracting 5 percentage points from the growth rate of economic profits (see Credit Suisse First Boston, 2002). If equity prices and interest rates remain unchanged for the year 2003, contributions would need to rise by a similar amount this year just to prevent underfunding from growing larger.[5]

Defined benefit plans typically invest in equities, corporate and government bonds, and money market instruments. In the late 1990s, U.S. pension plans allowed stock market gains to increase the share of equity investments to more than 50 percent, while reducing the share of government bonds.

[5]In June 2003, General Motors announced a $17.5 billion bond issue to reduce its $25 billion pension fund gap end-2002 data—the largest in the S&P 500 by a wide margin.

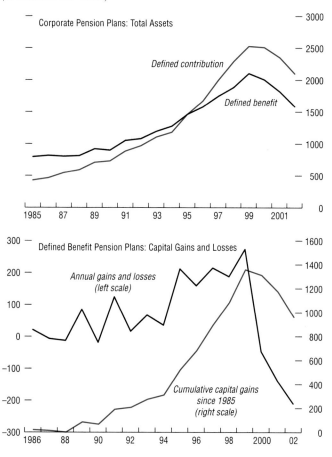

Figure 2.15. United States: Corporate Pension Plans
(In billions of U.S. dollars)

Source: Board of Governors of the Federal Reserve System, *Flow of Funds.*

Since pension liabilities share certain characteristics with long-term bond obligations—future liabilities tend to be relatively predictable over long time horizons—the greater use of equities increased the risk of potential financial mismatches and funding shortfalls.

To limit the impact of short-term asset price movements on operating earnings that result from these mismatches, current U.S. accounting rules allow firms to calculate pension plan earnings using an expected return in place of actual returns. But these rules can obscure firms' underlying financial position. Indeed, while over a long period average reported income from pension plans more or less matched actual returns, with the overreporting in 2000–02 being matched by the underreporting in 1995–99, the lack of transparent accounting had distortive short-term effects on reported profits that may have influenced stock market valuations (see Coronado and Sharpe, forthcoming). Accounting changes are underway in some countries to address this issue. In the United Kingdom, for example, new rules that will take effect in 2005 would require that pension assets are valued at market prices and any deficits (and surpluses) are reflected in reported earnings.

The choice of the discount factor for pension obligations has a large impact on the reported funding status of pension plans. The record low long-term yields on U.S. treasury securities have prompted a debate in the United States on the appropriate discount factor. In early July, the U.S. Treasury issued a series of proposals aimed at improving the accuracy of the present value of pension obligations and increasing the transparency of pension plans. They propose that pension liabilities should be discounted with rates drawn from a corporate bond yield curve that takes into account the term structure of a pension plan's liabilities. According to the proposals, companies should also improve the disclosure of pension fund assets and liabilities in their annual reporting and the government should disclose information on severely underfunded pension plans.

More generally, pension fund accounting and regulation worldwide are in need of reform to increase transparency and improve risk controls, including speeding the recognition of shortfalls and surpluses. But it is important not to create disincentives for companies to build up prudent pension fund surpluses to guard against future financial risks. For instance, in the United States current tax rules only allow deductions for contributions to underfunded plans. These rules discourage firms from building up surpluses in their pension plans to act as a buffer during strong financial conditions. The U.S. Treasury Department has proposed the helpful step of reviewing the limits on deductible contributions as an encouragement for firms to build surpluses.

Corporate Earnings Begin to Recover

Evidence is accumulating of stable to rising corporate earnings, even if current economic conditions do not improve. More stable earnings expectations have made equity dividend payments increasingly attractive compared with low fixed-income yields. So, a long and traumatic period of declining equity values may be coming to an end, and with it some of the balance sheet risks to pension funds and insurance companies.

Earnings Recovery

After deep declines in earnings, even deeper reductions in expectations, and several large revisions of audited results, especially in the United States, business earnings appear to be recovering despite a sluggish economic recovery. In the United States, operating earnings for the S&P 500 companies were up 12 percent in the first quarter compared with a year before, after stagnating in 2002. Earnings gains were concentrated in the previously weak energy and information technology (IT) sectors. Gains so far in the second quarter are

smaller, mostly because of a strong period the year before. But stronger and more broadly based gains are widely expected in the second half, depending on how strong a U.S. recovery emerges.

At a time when the accuracy of audited earnings statements remains a lingering issue for investors and analysts, reports using companies' own definitions of operating earnings will be subject to scrutiny. Other measures of earnings show weaker figures to date. U.S. national income accounts estimate underlying domestic business earnings were up 7 percent in the first quarter of 2003 compared with a year earlier.

Earnings in the euro area appear also to be showing early signs of improvement, although still lagging the recovery in the United States. Subdued domestic consumption and the weak export prospects resulting from the euro's high exchange rate continue to keep earnings prospects uncertain. Nevertheless, confidence indicators suggest some potential improvement in the retail trade and service sectors.

In Japan, progress has been made in improving company earnings in the face of deflationary pressures. The June Tankan survey showed a 16 percent corporate earnings increase in the year ending March 2003, and a 10 percent projected increase for the following year, helped by a strong export sector and lower oil prices. Nevertheless, sales revenues have continued to fall, suggesting that the burden of adjustment will still fall on cost-cutting. Costs have mainly been cut on the labor side. However, market observers are skeptical whether profitability can continue to be maintained in this way, especially when the current wave of early retirements is completed, and particularly if prices begin to fall more quickly.

Debt service costs have fallen sharply with lower interest rates. But debt levels remain high, and are increased in real terms by deflation. Japanese companies, in aggregate, have not paid off the surge in debt incurred during the bubble years. The persistence of

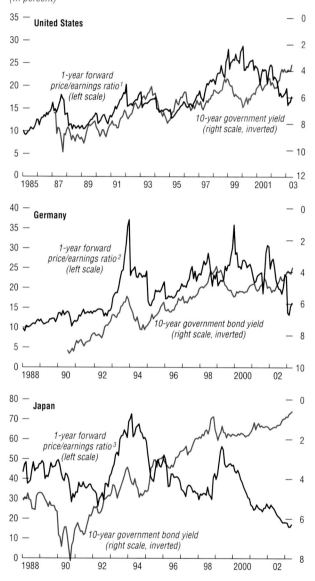

Figure 2.16. Forward Price/Earnings Ratios
(In percent)

Sources: I/B/E/S; and Bloomberg L.P.
[1]For S&P 500 index.
[2]For DAX index.
[3]For Topix index.

this debt burden remains a continued source of vulnerability for both companies and banks, and action to recognize and deal with nonperforming loans remains as important as ever.

Even bearing in mind possible overestimation, the earnings gains expected by market participants imply average U.S. forward price/earnings ratios are more sustainable at around 18, a level that is close to its historical average and down from the peak of 30 in 2000 (Figure 2.16). In Japan ratios are also around 18, compared with a peak of 50, and in Europe they are around 16, down from 25. The relatively low worldwide level of the alternative yields available on bonds increases the probability that these price/earnings ratios can be sustained, but a further steepening of the yield curve might put pressure on equity prices if not accompanied by a stronger earnings outlook.

Market Expectations

Expectations of corporate earnings derived by collating the forecasts of equity analysts can provide a useful assessment of prospects. Such analysts have been accused by observers of being persistently too optimistic on average in the past.[6] But tracking the changes over time in projections of earnings for a particular year provides a useful indicator of changes in overall market view as information becomes available.

Projections of U.S. company earnings for 2003 have remained stable through July 2003, in contrast with recent years when earnings projections for the then-current year were revised down continually during the year (Figure 2.17). Expectations for 2003 had already been revised down by 11 percent in 2001 and a further 16 percent in 2002 from the elevated level at the height of the technol-

---

[6]Quarterly earnings forecasts are collated by Thomson Financial's I/B/E/S service, using the definition of earnings most frequently used by analysts covering each individual company.

ogy boom. Now, as actual quarterly performance begins to bear out the new more conservative projections, despite continued doubts about the strength of economic recovery, it may suggest that the assumptions underlying equity valuations have become more realistic than in the past.

Longer-term, generally five-year, earnings growth expectations have also been reduced by analysts, from 18 percent growth forecast in 1999 to around 12 percent today (Figure 2.18). Nevertheless, analysts still hold higher long-term earnings expectations than those prevailing before 1996, indicating that views on underlying productivity growth remain relatively bullish. The standard deviation of analyst expectations around each long-run growth estimate is a little larger than before 1999, perhaps reflecting greater uncertainty over the accuracy of reported earnings figures as well as the uncertainty over the economic cycle.

With interest rates at low levels, dividend yields on equities have become more attractive relative to fixed-income securities. Companies and analysts have been increasingly focused on cash flow as a measure of performance, given the accounting concerns about earnings reports, and companies have increased their payments of dividends to demonstrate the solidity of their returns in a period when investors are less confident of future capital gains. The use of dividends will likely increase given the recent dividend tax reduction.

In Europe, strong earnings improvements in 2003 are expected from last year's weak levels. But the dispersion of analysts' projections of average earnings growth has become wider in the last few months, at the same time as median long-term earnings growth rates have been scaled back below 10 percent (Figure 2.19). The continuing low economic growth rate in Europe may be partly responsible for this volatility in expectations (see the discussion of volatility and economic activity in Chapter III).

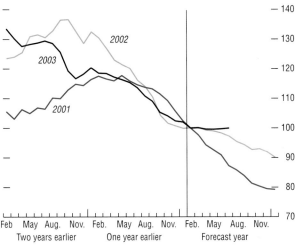

Figure 2.17. United States: Earnings Expectations for Recent Years[1]
(Forecast in February of the forecast year = 100)

Source: I/B/E/S.
[1]For S&P 500 index.

Figure 2.18. United States: Analysts' Long-Term Earnings Expectations[1]
(In percent)

Source: I/B/E/S.
[1]For S&P 500 index.

Figure 2.19. Euro Area: Analysts' Long-Term Earnings Expectations[1]
(In percent)

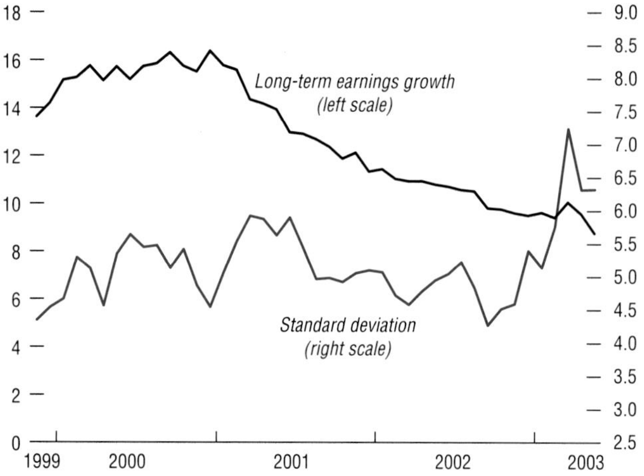

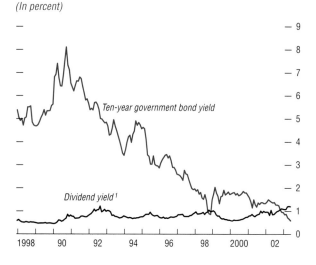

Source: I/B/E/S.
[1]For Euro Stoxx price index.

Figure 2.20. Japan: Dividend and Government Bond Yields
(In percent)

Source: I/B/E/S.
[1]For Morgan Stanley Capital International (MSCI) Japan equity index.

Dividend yields in Europe are rising, as in the United States. Combined with the fall in government bond yields, this has reached a point where the dividend income from equities almost matches the return on risk-free bonds. This unusual situation suggests that equity earnings, if they turn out to be sustainable, may provide strong support to equity prices as long as further rises in long-term interest rates remain moderate.

In Japan, dividend yields have already risen above government bond yields (Figure 2.20). Equity prices therefore seem well supported in current market conditions, but at the same time could be vulnerable to further large increases in bond yields.

In sum, projections of future earnings in major markets appear to have become more consistent with plausible future increases in productivity and economic activity since 2000. Meanwhile, equity yields have become more attractive relative to government bonds, notwithstanding the recent bond yield increases. If, indeed, this will be enough to sustainably reverse the long slide in global equity values, the improvement in company pension fund investments would provide a second round boost to company earnings. While equity values appear to be well supported under current market conditions, a sudden rise in interest rates that is not accompanied by a stronger economic outlook could change this position.

Favorable External Environment Helped Push Emerging Bond Yields Lower

Policy interest rates and government bond yields in the major financial centers that reached near historic lows and improved economic fundamentals in many emerging markets attracted sizable funds into the emerging bond markets during most of the first half of 2003. The resulting rally was led by higher-yielding bonds, particularly those of Brazil—which accounts for one-fifth of the international emerging bond market—as investor attitudes to the new administration there improved. However, the impressive performance gave way to this year's first major consolidation in emerging bond markets following the sharp yield increase in mature bond markets. The global quest for yield abated mid-year as renewed investor appetite for equities triggered outflows from bond funds. Yield spreads on emerging market bonds remained in many cases still well below historical averages, raising concerns about valuation levels, reduced investor discrimination between credit names, and, in particular, the risk of further weakness in emerging bond markets, if yields in the major financial centers were to increase further.

Strong Inflows Contribute to Emerging Market Bond Rally

Flows to the secondary emerging bond market were supported by a global quest for yield that pushed investors out along the credit spectrum (Figure 2.21). This impetus was accentuated through mid-March by the tendency of investors to shun equities. As a result, flows into U.S.-based emerging market bond mutual funds surged during most of the first half of 2003. This surge was largely at the expense of money market mutual funds and, through mid-March, equity mutual funds. In addition, institutional investors—notably U.S. and European pension funds—continued to increase their portfolio allocations. Crossover investors, including managers of corporate bond mutual funds, also stepped up their holdings of emerging market bonds, especially in the second quarter. A high level of coupon and amortization payments provided further technical support to emerging debt markets. By mid-year, emerging market mutual funds, however, began to experience redemptions.

This broad investor interest fueled a strong rally in the emerging bond market. Spreads on the EMBI+ narrowed substan-

Figure 2.21. Cumulative Net Flows to U.S. Mutual Funds
(In millions of U.S. dollars)

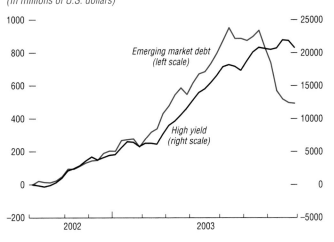

Source: AMG Data Services.

Figure 2.22. Sovereign Spreads
(In basis points)

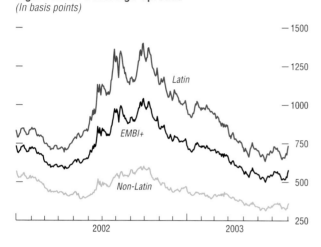

Source: Capital Data.

Figure 2.23. EMBI+ Total Returns, First Half of 2003
(In percent)

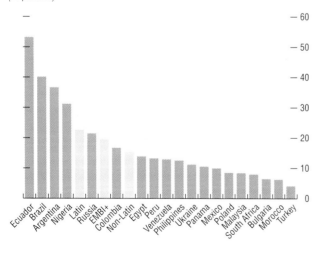

Source: J.P. Morgan Chase.

tially to 547 basis points in the first six months of the year, and the EMBI+ generated a total return of 19 percent (Figure 2.22). The rally that started in October 2002, however, was followed by a consolidation toward the middle of 2003, triggered by concerns over the extraordinary pace of spread compression and the sharp rise in U.S. treasury yields. The sell-off was broad-based, affecting sovereigns with fundamentals as diverse as those of Russia and Brazil. Nevertheless, returns on emerging market bonds during the first seven months of the year continued to compare favorably to other asset classes.

High-yielding credits and the Latin American sub-index outperformed (Figure 2.23) during the first half of 2003. This was indicative of expectations that investors' quest for yield would compress yield spreads of issuers with ratings at the lower end of the credit spectrum faster than spreads of more highly rated issuers. The latter had already fallen in many cases to near-historic lows.

The marked improvement in investor sentiment in Brazil and the stabilization of macroeconomic fundamentals across many emerging market countries helped underpin the broader rally in the emerging bond market. As concerns over the risk of default waned, credit spreads on Brazilian sovereign bonds narrowed sharply and the yield curve disinverted. With the decline in secondary market yield spreads, many emerging market countries regained access to external bond markets.

Global Quest for Yield Extends to Local Emerging Markets

Buoyed by a recovery in risk appetite and scope for policy rates to fall, high-yielding local currency debt markets increasingly attracted foreign inflows. As a result, the ELMI+ index—which measures total returns for local-currency-denominated money market

instruments in 24 emerging markets—rose
9 percent during the first half of 2003. Local
bonds, however, experienced a consolidation
mid-year in tandem with external debt
markets.

Local debt markets in Latin America
attracted considerable interest, especially in
Brazil and Argentina (Figure 2.24). The *real*
appreciated 25 percent against the dollar in
the first half of 2003. Prudent monetary policy
and the stronger currency helped to reduce
inflationary pressure, allowing the central
bank to begin cutting policy rates in June. At
the same time, the differential between
onshore and offshore interest rates on U.S.
dollar financing narrowed, as Brazilian banks
borrowed abroad to take advantage of arbitrage opportunities. The spread between offshore and onshore foreign exchange forward
contracts also declined considerably, in a further indication of easing concerns over convertibility risk.

In emerging Europe, the Middle East, and
Africa, steady declines and the prospects of a
significant easing of policy rates attracted
considerable inflows into the local currency
markets of Turkey and South Africa. In
central Europe, expectations for eventual
convergence with the European Union have
triggered a secular broadening of the investor
base, from both crossover investors and dedicated convergence funds. While increasing
foreign portfolio inflows allowed governments in central Europe to finance wide fiscal
deficits, it also increased the risk of sudden
capital outflows and elevated interest rate
and exchange rate volatility, underscoring
the urgency of fiscal consolidation (see
Appendix II).

Outlook Clouded by High Valuations and Prospect of Rising U.S. Interest Rates

An extended period of strong demand for
emerging market bonds has left the asset class
susceptible to consolidation. From October
2002 through the end of June 2003, the

Figure 2.24. Currency Performance Versus the Dollar, First Half of 2003
(In percent)

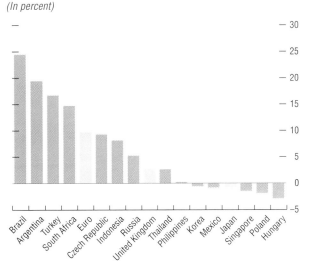

Source: Bloomberg L.P.

Figure 2.25. Sovereign Spreads Versus Historical Lows
(In basis points)

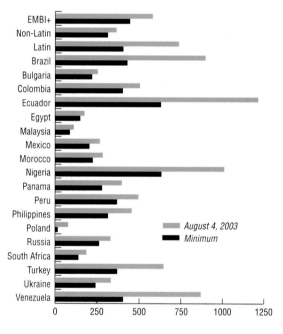

August 4, 2003
Minimum

Source: J.P. Morgan Chase.

spread on the EMBI+ index declined substantially by over 500 basis points. As a result, the spreads on most constituents of the EMBI+ were well below historical averages, and in many cases spreads had reached all time lows at the time of the correction that set in mid-year (Figure 2.25).

In light of the risk that yields of mature market bonds may rise further, following the increases observed in the second half of June and July, net flows into emerging market mutual funds and new dedicated emerging market mandates could dry up. Foreshadowing these risks, both emerging market and global bond mutual funds experienced outflows in late June and July.

Dedicated emerging market funds remained overweight in their bond holdings while carrying below average cash positions. Mutual funds appeared to remain optimistic about return prospects and maintained relatively high-beta portfolios, in an attempt to link their returns to broad market movements.[7] This suggests that there remains scope for managers to reduce market exposure should sentiment deteriorate (Figure 2.26), a process that began in July when overweight positions were scaled back.

The vulnerability of the asset class is accentuated by the concentration of crossover allocations to Brazilian bonds. Given the importance of Brazilian bonds for the overall market, a sentiment shift with respect to Brazilian fundamentals could trigger a sizable adjustment for the entire asset class.

The sharp increase in the correlations between the U.S. treasury and emerging bond markets following the spike in U.S. treasury yields mid-year illustrates the risk of

---

[7]The beta index aims to capture the degree of market exposure of U.S.-based emerging market mutual fund managers. It is a measure of the sensitivity of the portfolio to changes in the market as a whole as proxied by the benchmark index. Exposure can be increased (decreased) by lowering (raising) cash holdings or choosing assets that are more (less) correlated with the underlying benchmark.

Table 2.5. Emerging Market Spread: Coefficients of Variation

	Oct. 31, 2002	Jul. 31, 2003
Mean of EMBI Global (basis points)	611	368
Standard deviation	571	294
Coefficient of variation	0.93	0.80

Sources: J.P. Morgan Chase; and IMF staff estimates.
Note: Data exclude Argentina and Côte d'Ivoire.

a sell-off in emerging markets, if yields in the major financial centers were to rise further. (Figure 2.27).

As crossover investors began to reduce their exposure mid-year, the impact of higher U.S. treasury yields weighed disproportionately on higher-rated emerging market bonds, which are perceived as closer substitutes of mature market bonds. But even if mature bond market yields were not to rise further, the steepening of yield curves could result in a shift by emerging market issuers toward more shorter-dated financing in the future, adversely affecting vulnerabilities.

The strong rally in emerging bond markets was driven in large measure by a quest for yield and benefited issuers in an increasingly uniform way, as illustrated by the sharp rise in the average cross-correlation of individual country returns in the EMBI+ (Figure 2.28). The rise in the cross-correlation measure suggests that investors have emphasized asset-class considerations rather than country-specific factors when allocating funds to emerging markets. This is confirmed by the decrease in spread dispersion of emerging market issuers. Between the end of October 2002 and the end of July 2003 the standard deviation of emerging market spreads across issuers fell faster than average spreads, leading to a marked decline in the respective coefficient of variation (Table 2.5). If sentiment were to deteriorate suddenly, emerging markets would therefore face the risk of investors withdrawing from the asset class as uniformly as they entered it.

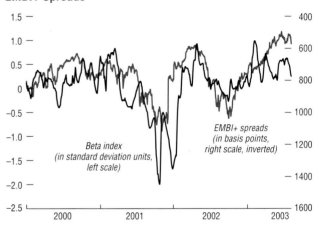

Figure 2.26. Emerging Bond Fund Beta Index and EMBI+ Spreads

Beta index (in standard deviation units, left scale)

EMBI+ spreads (in basis points, right scale, inverted)

Sources: Bloomberg L.P.; J.P. Morgan Chase; and IMF staff estimates.

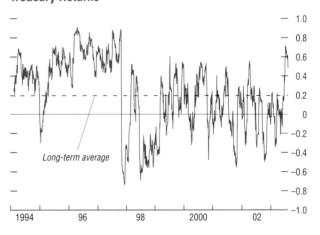

Figure 2.27. Correlations of EMBI+ with U.S. 10-Year Treasury Returns

Long-term average

Sources: J.P. Morgan Chase; Merrill Lynch; and IMF staff estimates.

Emerging Market Access Improves

Funding for emerging market countries on international capital markets rebounded in the first half of 2003 from last year's lows (Table 2.6). The rebound was largely driven by the marked pickup in bond financing. Bond issuance was strong in the first half of 2003, save for the six-week period surrounding the Iraq war, enabling more than two-thirds of sovereigns to complete their issuance plans for the year. While gross issuance was boosted by sizable liability management operations, net bond issuance also rebounded noticeably. Bank lending to emerging markets recovered in the first half of 2003. In contrast, equity issuance remained negligible, with cumulative placements through mid-year at levels last seen in the early 1990s. Foreign direct investment (FDI) flows to emerging markets continued to weaken in the first quarter this year.

Emerging Market Bond Issuance

Following the reopening of primary bond markets in November 2002, primary market activity remained brisk in the first half of 2003, with uncertainties stemming from the Iraq war dampening primary market activity only temporarily. The pace of issuance quickened, supported by investors' quest for yield and hefty amortization and interest payments, especially in the first quarter.

In all, emerging market bond issuance almost doubled from the low levels that resulted from the drought during most of the second half of 2002. Issuance rose to $45.1 billion in the first half 2003, up from $38.1 billion in the same period last year (Figures 2.29 and 2.30). While the rebound in bond issuance was supported by sizable liability management operations, net issuance also rebounded markedly from last year's depressed values. Preliminary market estimates suggest that net issuance through July 2003 has increased some 14 percent from the same period last year.

Figure 2.28. Emerging Market Debt Cross-Correlations

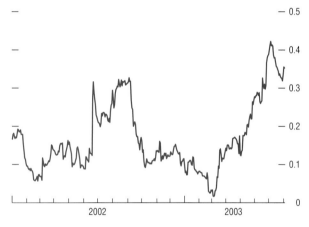

Sources: J.P. Morgan Chase; and IMF staff estimates.

Table 2.6. Emerging Market Financing Overview

				2001		2002		2003				
	2000	2001	2002	1st half	2nd half	1st half	2nd half	1st half	Apr	May	Jun	Year to date[1]
						(In billions of U.S. dollars)						
Issuance	**216.4**	**162.1**	**135.6**	**92.7**	**69.4**	**69.9**	**65.7**	**78.1**	**11.9**	**11.1**	**19.1**	**80.5**
Bonds	80.5	89.0	61.6	55.6	33.4	38.1	23.5	45.1	4.8	7.4	12.7	47.2
Equities	41.8	11.2	16.4	7.6	3.7	8.4	7.9	3.1	0.3	0.7	0.9	3.4
Loans	94.2	61.9	57.6	29.5	32.4	23.4	34.2	29.9	6.8	3.0	5.5	29.9
Issuance by Region	**216.4**	**162.1**	**135.6**	**92.7**	**69.4**	**69.9**	**65.7**	**78.1**	**11.9**	**11.1**	**19.1**	**80.5**
Asia	85.9	67.5	53.9	42.4	25.1	25.2	28.7	28.6	2.2	6.0	7.5	30.1
Latin America	69.1	53.9	33.4	30.6	23.3	20.2	13.2	19.6	7.7	0.4	3.2	20.3
Europe, Middle East, Africa	61.4	40.8	48.3	19.8	21.0	24.6	23.8	30.0	2.1	4.7	8.5	30.0
Secondary Markets (end-period)												
Bonds												
EMBI+ (spread in basis points)[2]	756	731	765	766	731	799	765	547	576	553	547	577
Merrill Lynch High Yield (spread in basis points)	871	734	802	736	734	809	802	554	576	612	554	507
Salomon Broad Inv Grade (spread in basis points)	89	78	62	80	78	73	62	51	49	57	51	70
U.S. 10 yr. Treasury Yield (yield in %)	5.12	5.07	3.83	4.93	5.07	4.86	3.83	3.54	3.89	3.37	3.52	4.29
						(In percentage change)						
Dow Jones	−6.2	−7.1	−16.8	−2.6	−4.6	−7.8	−9.8	7.7	6.1	4.4	1.5	10.1
NASDAQ	−39.3	−21.1	−31.5	−12.5	−9.8	−25.0	−8.7	21.5	9.2	9.0	1.7	28.3
MSCI Emerging Market Free	−31.8	−4.9	−8.0	−3.3	−1.7	0.7	−8.7	13.9	8.4	6.9	5.5	20.5
Asia	−42.5	4.2	−6.2	−1.7	6.1	7.7	−12.9	10.0	4.1	8.4	7.6	21.0
Latin America	−18.4	−4.3	−24.8	3.3	−7.4	−16.5	−10.0	21.4	16.9	2.6	2.2	22.6
Europe/Middle East	−23.4	−17.7	−9.1	−18.5	1.1	−10.8	2.0	33.2	17.6	10.7	3.8	28.3

Sources: Bloomberg L.P.; Capital Data; Merrill Lynch; Salomon Smith Barney; and IMF staff estimates.

[1]Issuance data are as of July 9, 2003 close-of-business London and secondary markets data are as of August 4, 2003 close-of-business New York.

[2]On April 14, 2000 the EMBI+ was adjusted for the London Club agreement for Russia. This resulted in a one-off (131 basis points) decline in average measured spreads.

Official data for the first quarter 2003 shows that European issuers had accounted for 57 percent of all emerging market net issuance, which compares to a share of 10 percent in 2001 and 22 percent in 2002. While Latin American net issuance of international bonds and notes in the first quarter of the year ($2.5 billion) rebounded sharply from the previous quarter ($200 million), this rebound masked a sharp divergence between countries according to credit ratings. Higher-rated credits like Mexico and Chile were net issuers while several lower-rated countries recorded negative net issuance. Asian bond issuers saw a sharp fall in first quarter net issuance from last year. While the region accounted for some 56 percent of all net issues last year, this share dropped to a mere 12 percent in the first quarter. With net issuance accounting only for some 11 percent of all announced bond issues, compared with 26 percent in the previous quarter, it appears that Asian issuers were particularly active in liability management operations.

Liability management operations increased in first half of the year. Notably, Mexico announced the retirement of its entire stock of outstanding Brady bonds, partly through the issuance of $3.4 billion in three separate bond deals. Poland repurchased more than $1 billion of its PDI Brady bonds in April, cutting its Brady exposure by almost 40 percent. In both instances, the countries reduced their external debt burden, generated net present value savings, and released the collateral underlying the bonds. These operations were

Figure 2.29. Cumulative Gross Annual Issuance of Bonds, Loans, and Equity
(In billions of U.S. dollars)

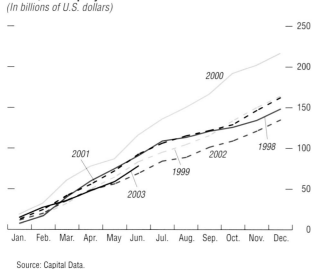

Source: Capital Data.

Figure 2.30. Cumulative Gross Annual Issuance of Bonds
(In billions of U.S. dollars)

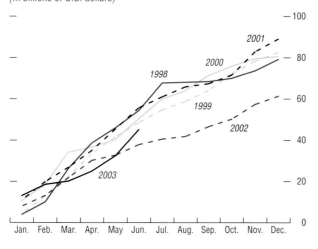

Source: Capital Data.
Note: Bonds adjusted for Brady exchanges.

followed by exchange offers for Brady debt by both Brazil and Venezuela in July.

Apart from Brady debt exchanges, Uruguay successfully exchanged most of its external debt for bonds with longer maturities at roughly unchanged interest rates, after warning investors it may not be able to continue to service its debt without the proposed exchange. Colombia issued with a view to retiring some of its more expensive dollar-denominated debt, although in small amounts. South Africa used part of the proceeds from a 10-year Eurobond issue in May to retire short-term debt and to eliminate the Reserve Bank's net open forward position. In local markets, Venezuela carried out several exchanges for longer-term bonds to extend the maturity profile of the domestic debt stock.

High-grade borrowers dominated activity in the earlier part of the year, but sub-investment-grade issuers were gradually able to access international capital markets as market conditions improved. Notwithstanding Brazil's return to international capital markets, Latin American borrowers accounted for roughly 30 percent of total issuance during the first half ($13.9 billion), a smaller share of the total than in previous years. This underscored the access difficulties faced by some of the riskier credits.

Sovereign issuance in the first half amounted to $29.9 billion, some 35 percent above the comparable period of 2002 (Figure 2.31).

Supported by strong crossover investor demand, investment-grade borrowers dominated, accounting for 60 percent of the total in the first half. Among the biggest borrowers in the year to date have been Mexico and Poland, which completed their financing requirements for the year and engaged in liability management operations aimed at retiring outstanding Brady bonds.

As the top-tier sovereigns completed their issuance plans, amid an improvement in both emerging market fundamentals and market conditions—including ongoing inflows into the asset class by dedicated investors—some of the lower-rated credits launched successful issues. After a notable one-year absence, Brazil returned to the market, with a $1 billion issue in April and a $1.25 billion placement in May; both were heavily oversubscribed. Turkey secured $4 billion in financing, with investors paying little attention to political events and delays in completing the IMF program reviews.

Issuance by emerging market corporates proved disappointing, despite the continued improvement in credit quality and the easing in corporate default ratios in mature markets. Corporate issuance accounted for just over 20 percent of total emerging market bond issuance during the first half of 2003. Financial institutions have accounted for the lion's share of corporate issuance. Banks in Brazil tended to raise short-term financing with a view to take advantage of high onshore interest rates for dollar-denominated financing. Benefiting from strong local investor interest, Russian corporates have been particularly active borrowers, with some "lesser-known" issuers gaining market access. In some of these instances, however, issuance by corporates was viewed as premature.

Euro-denominated issuance revived in 2003, in large part reflecting the comeback of the European retail investor base after an 18-month absence following the Argentine default. Of total issuance in the first half, over 25 percent has been euro-denominated, with the latter part of the second quarter seeing the greatest pickup after Latin sovereigns, which typically issue into the dollar market (Table 2.7).

Another salient development was the much wider inclusion of collective action clauses in sovereign bonds issued under New York law during the first half of 2003. Investment-grade credits—including Mexico, Korea, and South Africa—blazed the trail, followed by some of the sub-investment-grade credits—including Brazil and Uruguay (Box 2.2).

Figure 2.31. Share of Bond Issues
(In percent)

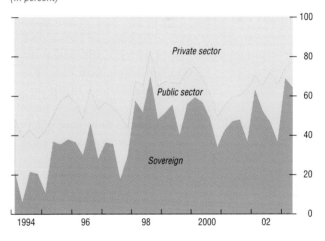

Source: Capital Data.

Table 2.7. Currency of Issuance
(Shares in percent)

	1999				2000				2001				2002				2003	
	Q1	Q2	Q3	Q4	Q1	Q2	Q3	Q4	Q1	Q2	Q3	Q4	Q1	Q2	Q3	Q4	Q1	Q2
U.S. dollars	62	67	59	53	62	51	65	60	57	72	63	72	77	84	83	83	69	70
Euro	26	28	36	37	33	28	18	21	31	17	7	20	16	13	9	6	28	24
Deutsche mark	2	0	2	0	0	0	0	0	0	0	0	0	0	0	0	0	0	0
Yen	2	1	1	8	3	17	14	13	7	6	19	6	1	1	5	6	2	5

Source: Capital Data.

International Equity Issuance

International equity issuance by emerging market companies fell to its lowest level in nearly a decade. The decline reflected relatively low valuations, which persisted in the first half of this year, and continued sluggish equity issuance in mature markets. Issuance in the first half of 2003 totaled just $3.1 billion, less than half that in the same period of 2002. China represented 27 percent of total equity issuance in emerging markets, with the privatization of Sinotrans being the only big-ticket item ($502 million).

Overall, Asia continued to dominate placements, accounting for 70 percent of the total. Notwithstanding, SARS-related worries played a constraining role, with June seeing a pickup in equity issuance amid signs the epidemic appeared under control. Latin corporates have been absent from primary markets this year, except for the sale of a 10 percent stake in Brazilian steelmaker Cia. Siderurgica Nacional for the equivalent of $134 million. Elsewhere, the sale of equity in South Africa's Telkom raised the equivalent of roughly $500 million.

Syndicated Lending

Syndicated lending to emerging markets rebounded modestly from the first half of 2002, with total loan volumes reaching $29.9 billion in the first half of 2003 (Figure 2.32). Concerns about SARS and the global slowdown notwithstanding, lending to Asia rose in the first half of the year to $13.8 billion, fur-

ther buoying the region's share (Figure 2.33) in lending to emerging markets. In contrast, lending to Latin America remained subdued, while lending to emerging Europe, the Middle East, and Africa declined.

Discrimination according to credit quality remained a prominent feature of the loan market in the first half of 2003. This contrasted with the synchronized reduction in sovereign spreads in secondary bond markets but was in line with the difficulties of some of the riskier issuers in accessing primary markets. While there was little activity by lenders in Argentina and Brazil, investment-grade-rated Mexico and Chile received substantial loan commitments. In Asia, a wide range of Korean, Singaporean, and Malaysian corporates accessed the market at thin margins, while the bulk of financing extended to the Philippines and Indonesia was to public institutions. In central Europe, corporate demand for cross-border funding has risen modestly despite lackluster activity in the euro area and abundant liquidity in local markets. Borrowers have taken advantage of the fine margins offered by international banks. Further afield, banks have been increasingly reluctant to lend cross-border to Turkey's corporates.

Sovereigns were prominent in the loan markets, particularly in the second quarter (Figure 2.34); these included the Dominican Republic (€4 million), Hungary (€500 million), Mexico ($2 billion), Romania (€50 million), and South Africa ($1 billion).

Among corporates, the range of borrowers gaining access to international finance expanded. Until recently, over 90 percent of syndicated lending had been to a small number of top-tier corporates in the energy sector. In a marked shift, however, companies outside the energy sector accessed the loan market with terms beginning to resemble those of the top-tier corporates.

Foreign Direct Investment

Preliminary statistics indicate that FDI flows to emerging market economies declined in the first quarter of this year, continuing a downtrend that began in 2000. The decline was in large part driven by reductions in flows to Latin America, while FDI to Asia and emerging Europe were broadly stable (Figure 2.35). The downtrend is largely explained by cyclical movements reflecting growth trends in the world economy, the fallout from the bursting of the technology and telecommunications bubble, and diminished regional and local growth prospects.

Nevertheless, it also reflects higher perceived risks, in particular unanticipated changes in regulations and contractual arrangements. In the context of a survey conducted by a working group of the Capital Markets Consultative Group (see CMCG, forthcoming). FDI investors underscore that predictable rules for investment and a sound legal framework are important determinants of FDI in emerging market countries. In this context, investors note that the abrogation of contracts in Argentina and a variety of regulatory difficulties in a number of countries have somewhat undermined their FDI prospects, notably in the banking and utilities sectors.

In Latin America, FDI flows fell in the first quarter this year compared with 2002 in all the larger countries with the exception of Chile. The declines ranged from a modest 1 percent in Mexico to about 80 percent in Columbia. Of particular concern was the 57 percent reduction in FDI flows to Brazil. Although FDI in Argentina declined by 60 percent in the first quarter compared with

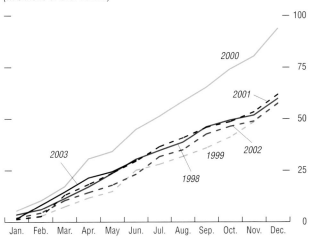

Figure 2.32. Cumulative Gross Annual Loan Issuance
(In billions of U.S. dollars)

Source: Capital Data.

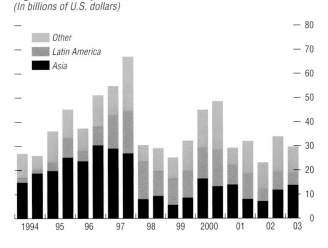

Figure 2.33. Syndicated Loan Commitments
(In billions of U.S. dollars)

Source: Capital Data.

Figure 2.34. Share of Loan Issues
(In percent)

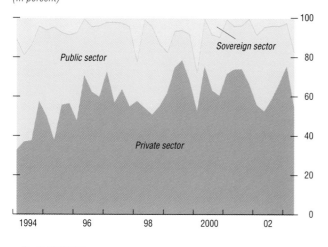

Source: Capital Data.

Figure 2.35. Quarterly FDI Inflows for Selected Emerging Market Countries
(In billions of U.S. dollars)

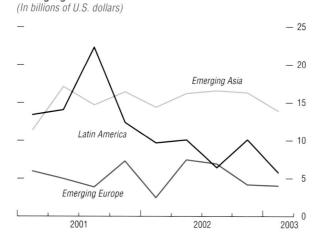

Source: World Bank.

a year ago, this represents something of an upturn since it was about 100 percent above the total for the entire second half of last year.

Asia continues to receive the major share of FDI to emerging markets, and aggregate flows have remained quite stable in recent years. However, this masks the rising importance of China, which received more than half of all FDI to emerging markets in the first quarter this year. Despite the outbreak of SARS, FDI to China remained strong in the first quarter. Elsewhere in Asia, first quarter FDI flows were less than half the levels recorded a year earlier in India, Korea, Malaysia, and the Philippines.

FDI flows to emerging Europe were somewhat higher in the first quarter this year than in the same period last year. Particularly noteworthy was the 300 percent increase of FDI to Russia, notably in the oil sector.

Emerging Market Banking Sector Performance and Risks

The distress in banking systems in some emerging markets has eased since the March 2003 GFSR. The instability stemming from shifts in confidence and contagion has subsided, but financial systems in several countries remain vulnerable to adverse macroeconomic developments. Economic slowdown is straining sectoral balance sheets in some countries, and in others rapid credit growth is raising concerns about potential credit quality problems. Deep-seated structural problems persist, especially where public sector institutions suffer from impaired asset quality and operational inefficiencies dominate. These inefficiencies are of particular concern in countries characterized by poor governance and weak public sector finances.

The global picture masks wide inter- and intraregional variations in developments in financial soundness indicators, financial strength ratings, market valuation measures,

Box 2.2. Collective Action Clauses—Recent Developments

The first half of 2003 has seen a shift in the use of collective action clauses (CACs) in international sovereign bonds. Most new issues of bonds governed by New York law, which traditionally used majority enforcement provisions but not majority restructuring provisions, have now included both types of CACs, as has been the market practice for English and Japanese law governed bonds (see the Table).[1] In March and April 2003 Mexico was the first major emerging market country to issue bonds governed by New York law with CACs. It was followed by Brazil, South Africa, and the Republic of Korea. All these issues were successful in that they were oversubscribed, and analysis provided no evidence that the price, either at the launch or in secondary market trading, included a yield premium for the inclusion of CACs. By the time Korea issued, market analysts virtually ignored the inclusion of CACs, instead focusing on Korea's economic fundamentals and the scarcity of Korean paper in the markets. Subsequently, Belize issued also with CACs and Mexico and Brazil followed with subsequent issues using CACs. Investment bank representatives have indicated that they expect new sovereign issues in New York to include CACs. CACs have also been included in the new bonds governed by New York law resulting from Uruguay's recent debt exchange.

[1]An exception was a bond issued by the Philippines under New York law without CACs.

A number of mature market countries have also taken steps to introduce CACs in their international sovereign bonds. Most recently, the EU member countries committed to include, beginning in June 2003, in bonds issued in foreign jurisdictions CACs that reflect the recommendations of the G-10 Working Group on Contractual Clauses. Italy has already issued such bonds.

The main features of the CACs in the bonds issued recently under New York law are as follows: the voting threshold for an amendment of payment terms is set at 75 percent of outstanding principal for the Mexican, South African, Korean, and Italian issues, and at 85 percent for those of Brazil and Belize; and the voting threshold for acceleration is set at 25 percent and for de-acceleration at 50 to 66⅔ percent. With the exception of the new bonds resulting from the Uruguay debt exchange, which use a trust structure, the others are issued under a fiscal agency agreement. Uruguay's new bond instruments also contain an aggregate voting clause.

During the same period, a number of bond issues using CACs took place under English and Japanese law, as has been traditional market practice in these jurisdictions. The emerging market countries among these issuers included Bahrain, Croatia, Hungary, Lithuania, the Philippines, Poland, Romania, the Slovak Republic, Thailand, Tunisia, and Ukraine.

Emerging Markets Sovereign Bond Issuance by Jurisdiction

	2001				2002				2003[1]		
	Q1	Q2	Q3	Q4	Q1	Q2	Q3	Q4	Q1	Q2	Q3
With CACs[2]											
Number of issues	14	10	2	10	6	5	2	4	9	15	0
Volume of issues (in billions of U.S. dollars)	5.6	4.8	1.8	2.2	2.6	1.9	0.9	1.4	5.6	11.6	0.0
of which: New York law		1.5							1.0	5.9	
Without CACs[2]											
Number of issues	16	17	6	18	17	12	5	10	14	5	3
Volume of issues (in billions of U.S. dollars)	6.7	8.5	3.8	6.1	11.6	6.4	3.3	4.4	8.1	3.4	1.0

Source: Capital Data.
[1]Data for 2003:Q3 are as of July 15, 2003.
[2]With CACs are English and Japanese law bonds, and New York law bonds where relevant. Without CACs are German and New York law bonds.

Box 2.3. Basel Core Principles Compliance and Banking System Financial Strength

Effective regulation and supervision are critical for the health of a banking system. An analysis of broad measures of supervisory compliance with international norms and indicators of institutions' financial strength points to a strong correlation between the two. The analysis gauges banks' soundness by the Moody's Financial Strength Index and the degree of compliance with the Basel Core Principles (BCP) of Effective Bank Supervision by a BCP Compliance Index. The BCP Compliance Index is constructed by assigning a numerical score to each of the 25 BCPs. The overall score equals 100.

The analysis is based on BCP assessments for 46 emerging market and industrialized countries undertaken mostly as part of the IMF's Financial Sector Assessment Program. The countries are grouped geographically by regions (see the Figure). The index for Western Europe reveals a high degree of compliance, meaning that on average, the supervisory frameworks and practice of many countries assessed thus far adhere to the Basel Core Principles. For other regions, deficiencies exist. Standard deviations of the assessments were similar across the regions with the exception of Asia, which shows a

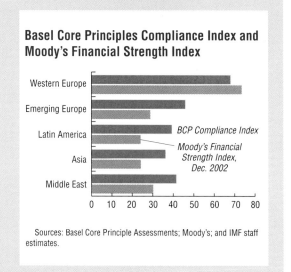

Basel Core Principles Compliance Index and Moody's Financial Strength Index

Sources: Basel Core Principle Assessments; Moody's; and IMF staff estimates.

higher heterogeneity of the individual assessments.

Although there are some noticeable differences for individual countries, the two indices have a correlation as high as 0.72, while the regional averages of the BCP Compliance Index and Moody's Financial Strength Index have a correlation of 0.97. These results underscore the importance of the quality of bank supervision for the health of the banking sector.

and credit to GDP growth (Box 2.3).[8] Notable differences in average performance persist across regions. In particular, financial soundness indicators continue to improve in Asia and Eastern Europe, while structural weaknesses remain in the banking systems in several countries in Latin America. Intraregional variations in performance remain high in all regions except in Eastern Europe, where

improvements have continued in the past six months, albeit at a slower pace than previously.

Latin America. Recent indicators of financial soundness and market valuations in the region show moderate improvement, dominated by developments in a few countries. While a degree of stability has returned to the banking systems that were rocked by collapse

[8]Financial soundness indicators refer to aggregate information on financial institutions, including indicators of profitability, measured by return on assets (ROA); loan quality, given by the ratio of nonperforming to total loans (NPLs); capitalization, measured by the ratio of shareholders' equity to total assets (EA). Financial strength ratings (FSR) are based on analysts' evaluation of the financial health and prospects of institutions, and market valuation (MV) is derived as the ratio of banks' stock index to broader market index.

of confidence and contagion, a more fundamental strengthening of financial positions
has not yet taken place, in part reflecting the
challenges posed by dollarization. In
Argentina, the liquidity situation of banks has
improved, but there is little progress in the
implementation of a bank restructuring strategy, and the solvency situation of the system
continues to be uncertain in the absence of
meaningful data on financial soundness indicators. The banking system in Venezuela
remains susceptible to instability in the context of worsening of profitability and loan
quality. Significant weaknesses also remain in
the banking systems in Bolivia, Ecuador,
Paraguay, and Uruguay, where loan portfolios
and profitability continue to suffer from high
proportions of nonperforming loans.

By contrast, the situation in Brazil remains
sound, in part supported by the recovery in
asset prices as a result of favorable sentiment
in international capital markets and greater
confidence in the economic policies of the
new government. Indicators of profitability,
loan quality, capital adequacy, and relative
market valuation of bank stocks improved in
2002 compared with the year before. Also,
despite pressures on profitability due to a
weakening economic environment, financial
systems in Chile and Mexico remain sufficiently robust.

Among some of the smaller countries in the
regions, concerns have emerged due to the
high exposure to government debt of banks in
Jamaica, in view of an exceptionally high and
rising public debt ratio. In the Dominican
Republic, pressures stemming from the incidence of fraud at one bank have highlighted
supervisory weaknesses and undermined confidence in the health of the banking system.

Europe. Financial soundness and market valuation indicators point to a pause as recent
improvements in the banking systems in
Eastern Europe are consolidated. In some
countries rapid credit expansion in the context of a weaker global economic environment
and a high degree of dollarization is raising

concerns about increasing credit risks. Turkey
has made significant progress in bank restructuring since the crisis, and the vulnerability of
its system now seems less pronounced,
although financial strength ratings have
slightly declined. In Israel and Poland, banks'
profitability and loan quality have been under
pressure, but their capital positions seem
adequate.

Asia. A generally improving trend is evident
in financial systems in the emerging markets
in the region, although significant weaknesses
remain in some countries. Indicators of profitability, loan quality, and capital adequacy on
average have been strengthening steadily and
financial strength ratings have improved. In
particular, financial soundness indicators have
stabilized in Indonesia in recent months,
while reform priorities are focused on bank
divestment and restructuring and strengthening of banking supervision and the regulatory
framework. In the Philippines, despite the
improvements in profitability, loan quality,
and capital adequacy indicated by recent data,
the banking system still faces substantial structural, governance, and supervisory weaknesses.

Financial indicators remained broadly
unchanged in Korea, with moderate improvement in the nonperforming loan ratio. Some
nervousness in the financial system was evident early this year with the revelation of
accounting fraud at one institution, which
affected the relative market valuation of
Korean banks. The problem has since been
contained. Banking systems in Thailand and
Malaysia are benefiting from progress in
restructuring and reforms, although this is not
as yet fully reflected in aggregate indicators.
Bank profitability in Thailand shows some
improvement, but banks' balance sheets
remain weak. The rehabilitation of banks' balance sheets and reforms are more advanced
in Malaysia, which achieved better profitability
and loan quality as well as a higher financial
strength rating.

In India, financial indicators for the banking system have generally strengthened. The

system remains exposed to significant credit and interest rate risk, however, in the context of long-standing asset quality problems at public sector banks. Analysis of banking trends in China is hampered by a paucity of data. Generally, state-owned financial institutions remain burdened by poor profitability and weak balance sheets. Weak economic conditions, partly reflecting the effects of SARS, are undermining the financial performance of otherwise strong and resilient financial systems in Hong Kong SAR and Singapore. Banks in these countries continue to be well capitalized and the quality of their loan portfolio has steadily strengthened in recent years.

Middle East. Banking systems in a number of countries in the region are faced with structural weaknesses, although near-term stability is not threatened. Despite recent efforts to recapitalize public sector banks in Egypt, banks' capital adequacy and earnings performance could be strengthened. The financial situation of both banks and the government has improved in Lebanon. However, banks remain significantly exposed to sovereign risk and nonperforming loans have recently increased, but so has provisioning coverage. Banks' profitability remains high. In Morocco, while financial soundness indicators of commercial banks are generally strong, the balance sheets of two state-owned specialized banks could be strengthened even though these do not raise systemic concerns. The privatization and restructuring of balance sheets of public sector banks in Pakistan are planned, but remain to be fully implemented. These problems, however, are long-standing and are not likely to be a source of systemic instability in the near term. The banking systems in Saudi Arabia and other oil rich states of the Gulf Cooperation Council remain highly liquid, profitable, and well capitalized. This generally robust picture is clouded only by the risk of an economic slowdown and geopolitical uncertainties.

Africa. Data limitations, distortions related to the rapid growth in banks' assets and high inflation in some countries, and differences in loan classification criteria in others make developments in financial soundness indicators for the region difficult to interpret. Recent measures of banks' profitability show some improvement in South Africa, where the quality of data is of lesser concern. Loan quality and capital adequacy of banks in the country stabilized in early 2003 and their financial strength ratings and relative market valuation improved. Turbulence due to insolvency and liquidity problems in some of the smaller banks in 2002 has subsided following the prompt actions taken by the authorities.

Appendix I: Regulatory and Supervisory Challenges and Initiatives

The blurring of the boundaries between insurance companies and other financial institutions and insurers' (and reinsurers') increased participation in complex financial markets have heightened the importance of the insurance industry for systemic stability.[9] The resulting regulatory and supervisory challenges for the insurance and reinsurance industry are outlined in the first part of this Appendix. In the second part, the Appendix more broadly reports on the recent regulatory responses to market developments, such as the equity market decline and the rapid growth of the credit risk transfer market, and describes initiatives to strengthen international regulatory standards and best practices. While regulators have begun to move their focus from individual institutions to a more systemic view, a stronger policy response is still required.

Insurance: Regulatory and Supervisory Challenges

Insurance and Systemic Issues

Financial problems in the insurance industry, particularly life insurance, have tradition-

---

[9]This Appendix was prepared by the IMF's Monetary and Financial Systems Department.

ally been viewed as unlikely to jeopardize systemic stability. However, as insurers intensify their financial market activities and build up considerable counterparty relationships with banks, they are becoming increasingly important to systemic stability. This comes at a time when solvency margins are under pressure from several sources, including the increased frequency and severity of catastrophic claims, escalation of asbestos liabilities, and the depressed stock markets. This calls for a stronger supervisory focus on insurer's financial risks, in addition to traditional underwriting risks.

The increased importance to financial stability mainly arises from three factors: (1) increased investment by insurers in equities; (2) consolidation between banks and insurers; and (3) insurers' role as intermediaries of credit and market risk.[10] As a major source of long-term capital, the industry can be viewed as a stabilizing element. It funds its relatively long-term liabilities with long-term investments (mostly bonds and loans, and also equities). In some countries, however, there was a tendency to cover a greater proportion of long-term liabilities with equity investments. Recent developments have demonstrated that life insurers may be prompted—in part by regulations—to sell equities into declining markets, possibly amplifying the effect of equity price declines.

The traditional view that the primary cause of insurer failure is due to underwriting losses is also changing. Recent events have shown that asset price shocks can rapidly pose a severe threat to solvency. EU supervisors have, however, identified poor corporate governance as the most common cause of insurer failure because it generates weaknesses, including poor pricing or investment

strategies.[11] Triggers may be sudden, such as a catastrophic event or a sharp dip in equity values, or slower acting, such as the cumulative effects of underpricing or underreserving risks. Supervisors should therefore examine the strength of internal controls and the susceptibility to triggers. For example, underpricing could be detected by comparing prices on a range of similar products between companies and between jurisdictions.

The increasing importance of insurance for financial stability puts greater emphasis on insurance regulation and supervision. Supervisors need to make sure that insurers are well equipped to manage the new financial risks they assume, that they understand the international exposures they take on, and that the negative effects of regulatory arbitrage are prevented. Trigger events are becoming gradually more severe—for example, surges in asbestos claims and equity price volatility. If these trends persist, underlying weaknesses are likely to become exposed more frequently. Supervisors and insurers alike need to take effective measures to prevent more frequent insolvencies.

This Appendix explores insurance regulatory and supervisory vulnerabilities identified by recent assessments of major insurance markets under the IMF's Financial Sector Assessment Program (FSAP), as well as the current work in strengthening insurance regulation at the international level. It identifies gaps in regulatory or supervisory policy and suggests priority actions. While a number of these issues are being dealt with at the national level and within the International Association of Insurance Supervisors (IAIS), a stronger and a more cohesive regulatory policy response is required.

---

[10]For more details of the systemic implications of insurance, as well as an overview of recent insurance failures, see Das, Davies, and Podpiera (2003), who point out the need for more work on preventing and managing insurance insolvency, especially cross-border.

[11]See the report of the Conference of the Insurance Supervisory Services of the Member States of the European Union (2002).

*Principal Regulatory and Supervisory
Vulnerabilities*

The assessments carried out under the
FSAP provide oversight and a means of peer
review of regulatory and supervisory regimes.
Analysis of the assessment findings and recommendations for a selected group of countries
indicates that the most frequent supervisory
concerns relate to prudential rules (covering
the valuations of assets and liabilities that
underpin solvency and the vulnerabilities arising from asset price shocks), solvency calculations, corporate governance, and organization
of the insurance supervisor. Three other common issues are the need for greater cooperation between supervisors of conglomerates,
improvements to financial reporting, and regulation and supervision of reinsurers.[12]

Prudential Rules

Prudential rules for the holding and valuation of assets need to be strengthened. The
decline in the value of equities has hurt insurers' balance sheets in some countries, threatening the ability of many companies to meet
solvency requirements. Additionally, some
national life markets provide guaranteed rate
products and in recent years companies have
not been able to achieve a return sufficient to
meet these guarantees. The negative spread
has caused insurers to consume capital.

The situation is being dealt with in different
ways. In the United Kingdom, the Financial
Services Authority (FSA) temporarily relaxed
the application of its resilience tests on life
insurers. In Japan, legislation has been passed
that will allow life companies to cut payouts
below the level originally contracted. In
Switzerland and Germany, where life insurers
pay a guaranteed minimum payout on life
policies, regulators have proposed lowering

the guaranteed payouts to below government
bond yields on new contracts. Also in
Germany, insurers have been allowed to value
equities (subject to certain conditions) at
their estimated ultimate realizable value.
Changes in valuation methods and suspension
of resilience tests can be seen as forms of for-
bearance that do not address the underlying
increased vulnerabilities due to more complex
risk profiles.

Moreover, stock market volatility is leading
insurance companies to reduce their equity
investment.[13] If this process continues, then
there may be a knock-on effect to stock
exchange activity and liquidity.

The market for long-term savings and
investment products is increasing in many
countries in response to the increasing need
to self-finance retirement income. This places
new demands on life insurance companies to
supply attractive products in competition with
other types of suppliers—notably, equity-
linked products. However, the decline in
share prices is causing insurance companies
and capital markets to rethink some of the
basic design and pricing features of these
investment products. The prudential rules for
the holding and valuation of assets therefore
need to be revisited to ensure the robustness
of insurers' balance sheets to equity price
fluctuations.

Reform of Solvency Regime

Insurance regulation lacks a detailed internationally accepted standard for setting the
level of required capital and solvency for
insurance companies. Assessments reveal a
large diversity in regulations. There are no
detailed standards for valuing assets or policy
and other liabilities that underpin solvency
calculations. Furthermore, capital adequacy

---

[12]The current version of the Insurance Core Principles issued by the IAIS does not cover the supervision of reinsurers. The FSAP reporting of this issue has therefore been marginal. The revised Insurance Core Principles, due
for adoption later in 2003, apply to reinsurers, whose financial strength is relevant for stability.

[13]The OECD estimates that insurers' equity investment as a percentage of total assets declined from 32 percent
to 21 percent between end-1999 and end-2002. In countries with high equity investment (Sweden and the United
Kingdom) the drop was from 53 percent to 29 percent.

requirements in many jurisdictions almost exclusively reflect insurance risks—the liability side of the balance sheet—ignoring the growing investment risks.[14]

In an effort to address this problem, the IAIS issued a paper on the principles of capital adequacy and solvency (IAIS, 2002a). This paper has provided more detailed criteria but still does not define the specific details of a required capital formula and this leaves scope for countries to adopt a regime that meets the general requirements of the principle without achieving consistency between countries. The European Union is revising its solvency regime and, as input to the process, has studied risk-based solvency systems in other jurisdictions and sectors.

Setting a uniform capital and solvency standard for insurance companies does pose several difficulties. Such a standard would need to take into account the diversity of insurance risk contained within the underwriting process, in addition to asset, credit, market, operational, and other risks. Despite the difficulties, the IAIS should press on with these tasks vigorously to ensure that companies have enough capital to meet the normal range of contingencies and volatility that arise as a result of each firm's profile.

Organization of the Insurance Supervisor

The organization and staffing of insurance supervisory authorities is a pervasive concern. The assessments continue to emphasize the need to increase the independence of the authority and to enhance levels of expertise. The organization of supervisory authorities, including their independence and accountability, is improving slowly, but accountability without susceptibility to political influence is sometimes difficult to achieve, and work is

needed (say, by the IAIS) to devise a model terms of reference for a supervisory authority. In a great many jurisdictions, including some of the major ones, the need to increase staffing and expertise is being highlighted in most assessments. Without sufficient resources, there is a risk that corporate governance and other prudential requirements may not be properly implemented and enforced.

Risk Management Practices

Several deficiencies remain in the risk management practices within the insurance sector. Many insurers rely on the underwriting expertise of internationally active reinsurance companies. But in several markets they are not required to adopt sound practices for underwriting or other forms of risk management. In some markets, regulation of internal controls and corporate governance concepts are not well established within the insurance sector. In some cases, this is because they have been developed for closely held and publicly traded insurance companies (Germany provides a good example of the latter). The involvement of external auditors does, however, provide some comfort that internal controls work effectively, although it could lead to concerns about overreliance on external auditors on the part of some insurance authorities.

In several markets, insurance companies are getting more actively involved in nontraditional business activities, such as products that transfer the credit risk from banks to the insurance sector. While innovation and competition can improve efficiency and spread risk, some of the innovations are a challenge to measure, manage, and supervise. This is a particular concern in companies and markets that do not have sound risk management practices in place. Innovative transactions are

---

[14]A small number of major jurisdictions (Australia, Canada, and the United States) have, however, developed sophisticated risk-based solvency systems. A comparative qualitative study indicates that they are quite dissimilar, dealing with risks in different levels of detail, partly because each is directed toward the particular features of the local market. A detailed quantitative study of companies under the various systems might reveal a greater level of convergence than is evident from a qualitative study and could be used as a starting point for gathering consensus on quantitative best practices.

often routed through jurisdictions with a relatively light supervisory touch. To address this, standards have also been developed for offshore insurance activities through solvency requirements for captive insurers and exchange of information among offshore insurance supervisors.

Insurance supervisors are implementing corporate governance practices for insurance companies, but progress has been slow. Strong corporate governance is an overarching control and its development within the insurance sector should be prioritized. The IAIS needs to develop a model regime.

Financial Conglomerates and Supervisory Cooperation

Financial conglomerates represent a supervisory challenge for insurance (and banking) supervisory authorities in many countries. In countries where there are strict supervisory rules limiting intercompany transactions between related parties, these risks can be controlled. Likewise, such risks can be monitored by risk-based supervision, and a cross-sectoral regulatory approach. However, not all countries have rules or integrated approaches of these types. Whereas there is an emerging trend toward the development of unitary supervisory authorities, frameworks for cross-border supervisory cooperation and information exchange have yet to fully develop. Cooperation between EU supervisors, under the Insurance Groups Directive, is an example of increased regional coordination and is a good example of what can be achieved given the correct framework. Such cooperation will be extended to financial conglomerates with the EU Financial Conglomerates Directive.

Cooperation between supervisory authorities in different countries has improved, with more insurance supervisors entering into memoranda of understanding with their foreign counterparts. Other initiatives

include the IAIS Standard on Exchange of Information and the OECD Decision of the Council on the Exchange of Information on Reinsurers.

There has been a trend toward greater cooperation between banking and insurance supervisors and increased harmonization of supervisory practices. In some important financial markets (Germany, Japan, and the United Kingdom), the banking and insurance supervisory functions have been combined into a single authority. In other cases, this type of consideration has resulted in a formalization of interagency relations.

Insurance supervisors generally share experiences and good practices with other supervisors more than they did a few years ago and this benefits many supervisors as they work to strengthen the regime in their country. This does, however, place a burden on supervisory authorities in the major markets. As an alternative, a formal body could be set up to provide information and training to supervisors of all jurisdictions.

Financial Reporting and Disclosure

In general, much less is known about the financial activities of insurance and reinsurance companies than that of commercial and investment banks.[15] This is in part because the regulatory and supervisory framework for insurance has traditionally been oriented toward policyholder protection and less focused on how insurance companies manage their financial risks. As these risks gain importance, the focus of insurance supervision needs to shift toward their assessment. Also, disclosure and transparency of financial market activities of insurance companies at present appears to be insufficient given their increased financial activities. The increasing role of insurers as intermediaries of financial risk should go hand in hand with increased disclosure of their financial and underwriting

---

[15]See the June 2002 issue of the *Global Financial Stability Report* (IMF, 2002).

risks—both for on- and off-balance-sheet exposures.

Accounting and financial reporting standards for insurance enterprises continue to vary significantly between countries. The IAIS issued a Guidance Paper on Public Disclosure by Insurers (IAIS, 2002b) that calls for supervisors to ensure that companies disclose relevant and timely information on the financial position of the company. This guidance in turn would lead to a greater level of consistency and scope in reporting that would provide FSAP assessors a better opportunity to identify vulnerabilities and recommend improvements.

Likewise, supervisory reporting standards and formats vary greatly. This may contribute to the relatively low volume of information exchange. Assessors sometimes receive comments from internationally active companies that the lack of standardization of supervisory reporting is a bureaucratic barrier to cross-border business. In addition, the International Accounting Standards Board (IASB) insurance project, whose phased implementation begins in 2005, applies primarily to annual reports and will not necessarily assist in harmonizing supervisory reporting. No work is currently under way to harmonize supervisory reporting.

Reinsurance

Reinsurers are systemically important to insurers, they provide protection by covering peak exposures, and are often parts (or even the dominant business) of conglomerates. In addition to the same risks faced by primary insurers, reinsurers face two additional risks.

First, reinsurers protect the peak exposures of the primary market and consequently experience greater volatility in results and therefore need greater capitalization. Second, reinsurers often are the top trading company in a group structure and hold the group's capital. In such a position, they may be called upon to support ailing insurance or noninsurance subsidiaries, and thus may transmit systemic shocks within or between sectors.[16]

In many jurisdictions, including some of the major ones, reinsurers are supervised with a lighter touch than primary insurers despite their more complex risk profile. Yet their financial health can only be assessed by detailed risk-based supervision, and the potential for contagion assessed during both the licensing process and ongoing supervision.

The IAIS Reinsurance Subcommittee has drafted a standard on the supervision of internationally active reinsurers, including effective supervisory coordination. The IAIS and Financial Stability Forum Task Force on Transparency and Disclosure in Reinsurance is currently formulating a supervisory reporting package designed to enable supervisors to better understand concentrations of risk and conduits for systemic contagion.

Regulatory Response to Market Developments

In addition to addressing the specific insurance issues discussed above, regulatory and supervisory agencies have responded to recent trends in other financial products and markets, including the role of financial analysts and audit firms, securities market fragmentation in the European Union, and

---

[16]The 2002 report of the Conference of the Insurance Supervisory Services of the Member States of the European Union cited earlier argues that companies rarely fail unless the major shareholder withdraws support. Worryingly, it reports that "we sense changing shareholder attitudes, with a tendency to prefer higher returns on capital in the short term and to have less concern for the long-term impact on their reputation of withdrawing support from a firm in trouble, increasing the risk of the firm's failure."

As an example of the range of pressures reinsurers can face, a large European reinsurer, Gerling Global Re, recently ceased underwriting due to three triggers—increased U.S. asbestos liabilities, increased claims on credit insurance business, and claims from the September 11 attacks. Despite raising capital, the group's primary insurers were downgraded and a major banking shareholder wrote off the value of its investment in the group.

cross-sector (banking and insurance) issues, including the growth of credit risk transfers. Supervisory practices are being strengthened as a result of regional convergence, greater cooperation, and the dissemination of guidance on good practices by standard setters. This has been visible across financial sectors, as well as in accounting and auditing.

Securities Markets and Regulation

Accounting and auditing standards are under review by securities regulators, particularly in the United States and Europe. The International Organization of Securities Commissions (IOSCO) and the International Federation of Accountants (the body responsible for standards on auditing) are discussing the structure of the audit industry—in particular, the concentration of audits in the big four accounting firms.

IOSCO has also developed a methodology for the assessment of the Objectives and Principles of Securities Regulation (the original Principles were published in 1998). The final methodology, which has not yet been approved by IOSCO's full membership, is a major undertaking that will add depth and detail to the international consensus on minimum standards of securities regulation.

Securities and investment analyst conflicts of interest are being addressed in the United States following the decision to take criminal action against several large investment banks. That action has resulted in large global financial settlements and in changes in internal structures of research at investment banks. There has also been pressure to improve governance structures of companies and stock exchanges, including over conflicts of interest.

The European Union is finalizing an amended Investment Services Directive (ISD), which is aimed at strengthening and harmonizing the European regulatory framework for securities markets. The ISD has raised a number of important questions regarding market fragmentation and competition between markets for liquidity. There is an intense debate among member countries, with some countries favoring a greater protection of exchanges. The European Union has also finalized the new Market Abuse Directive, which members will begin implementing, and the Prospectus Directive is in place and is being implemented by member countries.

The debate is intensifying on the role of hedge funds in the financial system and whether they should be directly regulated. In most jurisdictions, hedge funds are exempt from requirements applicable to investment funds, primarily because they focus on sophisticated and institutional investors rather than the retail market. The U.K.'s FSA took the lead by issuing a discussion paper arguing that, while current regulation of hedge funds is sufficient, they should become more transparent to lenders, and lenders in turn should better account for the risks in extending credit to highly leveraged hedge funds.[17]

Credit Risk Transfers

Efforts are being made to gain a better understanding of the use and extent of credit risk transfers (CRTs) and risk management by banks and insurance firms.[18] Since transparency and data on the size of the CRT market are insufficient, information on the distribution of CRT risks is poor. It is widely acknowledged that the regulatory framework

[17]The discussion paper is available at http://www.fsa.gov.uk/pubs/discussion/dp16.pdf.
[18]See for example the Committee on the Global Financial System, *Credit Risk Transfer*, available on the Internet at http://www.bis.org/publ/cgfs20.pdf; also, the IAIS Paper on Credit Risk Transfer Between Insurance, Banking and Other Financial Sectors, available at http://www.iaisweb.org/content/03pub/03fsfcrt.pdf. In addition, an IAIS subgroup has been set up to follow developments on alternative risk transfer products. An issues paper on insurance securitization has been drafted, and the group has begun work on the effectiveness of hedging.

and supervisory skills for assessing financial institutions' risk management systems and controls on CRT activities are not sufficiently developed. One concern is that use of CRTs may partly reflect differences in the regulatory treatment of credit risks between different types of financial institutions. Regulatory concerns would also increase considerably if information became available that suggested that use of CRTs was leading to undue concentration of risk, or was resulting in a significant fall in the amount of system-wide capital to support a given quantity of aggregate risk.

Work is being done on the involvement of EU banks in the credit risk transfer market and implications of structural relations between banking and insurance. This work follows from the EU Financial Conglomerates Directive.[19]

Financial Conglomerates

Prompted by consolidation in the financial sector, in particular between banking and insurance companies, the Joint Forum is examining the cross-sectoral implications of extreme exogenous shocks to financial conglomerates. Work is currently under way on risk aggregation across multiple businesses and risk categories; operational and credit risk management and the transfer of these risks; and the disclosure of financial risks (following up on the recommendations of the Multidisciplinary Working Group on Enhanced Disclosure—the Fisher Report—published by the Committee on the Global Financial System).

Banking Supervision—Further Convergence and Cooperation

In April 2003, the Basel Committee on Banking Supervision issued the third, and presumably final, consultative paper on the new Basel Capital Accord (Basel II). The new Accord is intended mainly to address interna-

tionally active banks in the G-10 countries, but is also expected to maintain its global reach as supervisory standard.

Even as national discussions have been focused on the implications of Basel II, the European Union has taken initiatives to promote regulatory convergence and efficiency. A major overhaul of European regulatory and supervisory structures is under way following the Ecofin Council's endorsement in December 2002 of a report on financial regulation, supervision, and stability in Europe. The Lamfalussy framework already in place in the securities sector will be extended to other financial sectors, including banking. It envisages the establishment of "level 2" (regulatory) and "level 3" (supervisory) committees. The reform aims at speeding up the European Union's legislative process, promoting convergence in supervisory practices, and increasing accountability.

Initiatives on information sharing have further underpinned convergence. Cooperation among banking supervisory authorities and the central banks of the European Union has been strengthened through additional Memoranda of Understanding on high-level principles of cooperation in crisis management situations and on the exchange of information among credit registers operated by EU central banks. Protocols on information sharing have been signed with EU accession countries. More generally, both EU and South East Asia, New Zealand and Australia (SEANZA) supervisors have been seeking to address concerns in establishing Memoranda of Understanding with third-party countries, including issues of confidentiality of information, the examination rights of home supervisors, and the legal ability to exchange information.

Outside the European Union, supervisors are also seeking to promote regional convergence. Efforts of Eastern and Southern

[19]Directive 2002/87/EC of December 16, 2002

African supervisors are focused on developing an onsite supervisory model for the region, standardizing licensing standards, and developing a unified approach to the supervision of microfinance institutions. Association of Supervisors of Banks of the Americas members have issued implementation guidelines for the Basel Core Principles of Effective Banking Supervision. At the same time, the Caribbean and Central American supervisory groups are working to harmonize regulations.

Accounting Standards and Practices

The evolution of accounting standards in recent years has reflected an emerging strategic focus on global convergence between national regulators and supranational bodies. Of key importance is the agreement reached between the IASB and the U.S. Financial Accounting Standards Board (FASB) on projects for eventual convergence of their respective financial reporting standards. Also, the European Union has decided that listed companies must prepare consolidated financial statements in accordance with International Financial Reporting Standards (IFRS)[20] by 2005. This follows IOSCO's endorsement of IAS as the accounting standard for companies listing on its member exchanges. The recent corporate failures and consequent investigations by national regulatory bodies also have given impetus to convergence, including through a reexamination of the relevant merits of rules-based versus principles-based standards.

The IASB has accelerated its work program. One of its key projects is to develop a comprehensive standard on financial instruments, which has seen wide-ranging consultation between the IASB and interested parties, including financial institutions and regulators. The IASB is also as a high priority addressing issues raised by corporate scandals, including treatment of off-balance-sheet vehicles and income and expense recognition.

In the United States, steady progress is being made in implementing the Sarbanes-Oxley Act. A Chairman for the Public Company Accounting Oversight Board established to oversee auditors was named in May 2003. The SEC concluded a staff study in July 2003 mandated by Sarbanes-Oxley on the possible adoption of a principles-based accounting system in the United States. The study favors a principles-based system, as it believes that rules-based systems encourage financial engineering aimed at avoidance. But it suggests that some principles-based systems provide too little guidance or structure. It therefore recommends that the FASB continue to move toward consistently developing an "objectives-oriented" approach, where the accounting objectives and model are sufficiently detailed to give managers and auditors a framework to apply the principles underlying standards. The SEC has reconfirmed FASB as the U.S. accounting standards setter, and the FASB is working actively on enhancing standards, including on accounting for stock options, accounting for defined-benefit pension plans, off-balance-sheet items, and consolidation of special purpose entities.

Accounting issues for the global insurance industry related to the implementation of "fair value" accounting remain highly contentious in work organized by the IASB. The IAIS has raised several issues relating, in particular, to the definition of insurance contracts, embedded derivatives, measurement of assets, credit insurance, and participating contracts. Issues have also been raised on assets backing insurance contracts and on disclosure.

The insurance industry is questioning the proposed changes, arguing that the volatility of reported earnings will increase with a consequent increase to the cost of capital. The

---

[20]IFRS includes International Accounting Standards (IAS) issued by the predecessor organization to the IASB.

accounting changes would involve most investments being valued at market prices and the elimination of claims-equalization reserves so that they would no longer be available as a profit smoothing mechanism. The increased earnings volatility will be largely due to fluctuating asset and liability valuations and will highlight the vulnerabilities associated with risk sharing over time. Risk sharing over time (as opposed to traditional risk pooling) is particularly relevant where life policyholders are given rates of return that are more stable over time than the investment returns of the insurer.

Appendix II: Convergence in Central Europe—Setbacks and Perspectives

Despite the devaluation of the Hungarian forint in June 2003 and a marked rise in risk premiums this year, Economic and Monetary Union (EMU) entry expectations for the Czech Republic, Hungary, Poland, and the Slovak Republic remain firmly embedded in market prices. Nevertheless, the scope for financial market volatility has risen. EMU entry is widely seen as delayed to the end of the decade, and reliance on foreign portfolio financing in Hungary and, to a lesser extent, in Poland has risen. These developments underscore the need for tightening the region's large fiscal deficits to support the conduct of monetary policy.

Fading Exuberance Amid Deteriorating Fundamentals

The passage of the Irish referendum on October 19, 2002, completed the ratification of the Nice Treaty, with markets anticipating European Union accession to occur on schedule on May 1, 2004. As a result, risk premiums—measured as the spread of local currency bond yields over German Bund yields—fell substantially across the region in 2002 (Figures 2.36 and 2.37). These premiums reflect a variety of risks, including

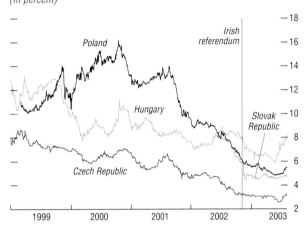

Figure 2.36. Five-Year Benchmark Yields
(In percent)

Source: Bloomberg L.P.

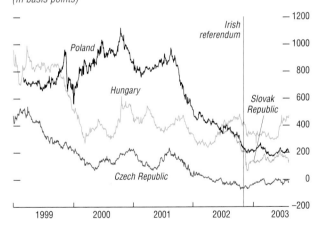

Figure 2.37. Five-Year Benchmark Spreads over Bunds
(In basis points)

Sources: Bloomberg L.P.; and IMF staff estimates.

exchange rate, interest rate, and sovereign risks.

Exuberance, however, gave way to concerns over fundamentals in 2003. The region's continued fiscal laxity, rapidly rising debt burden, and overall weak policy coordination raised doubts over the prospects for early EMU entry and the outlook for exchange rates. Against this background, yield spreads widened anew across central Europe during the first half of 2003. Hungarian yield spreads rose to levels not seen since the Irish referendum following the 2.26 percent devaluation of the forint on June 4 and two subsequent interest rate hikes of a cumulative 300 basis points. Nevertheless, spreads in Poland and the Slovak Republic at the end of June remained below the levels that preceded the referendum, while interest rates in the Czech Republic remained below those in Germany.

Nevertheless, most foreign and, to a lesser extent, domestic investors expect interest rate convergence to advance over the medium term. Investors emphasize that markets learned from the tightening of spreads triggered by the creation of the euro in 1999 as well as EMU entry by Greece in 2001.

EMU Entry Timing is Increasingly Viewed as Back-Loaded

Expectations for the timing of euro adoption have shifted toward the end of the decade from 2007/08 previously. By June 2003, market participants expected Hungary, Poland, and the Slovak Republic to adopt the euro in 2008 or 2009, with an increasing bias toward 2009. The Czech Republic was widely expected to adopt the common currency only in 2010. While investors have thus far been unperturbed by these "delays," the convergence process is widely viewed as far from complete. Box 2.4 discusses a simple econometric model in support of this view.

- The region's fiscal laxity is widely seen as clouding the prospects for early EMU entry. Investors are concerned that the region's

large structural deficits may not be sufficiently tightened near-term, with parliamentary elections scheduled in Poland for 2005 and in the Czech Republic, Hungary, and the Slovak Republic for 2006. Unless the bulk of the fiscal adjustment is undertaken in 2004, investors will tend to see little scope for early EMU entry. In this context, market participants tend to point to the fiscal slippage preceding Hungary's elections in 2002.

- Government debt levels pose another potential concern. The debt ratio of the Czech Republic has risen, albeit from a relatively low level, and there are concerns that the Maastricht ceiling on general government debt may be breached in Hungary and Poland (Figure 2.38). Citing concerns about reform fatigue, Standard and Poor's lowered in June 2003 its outlook on Poland's sovereign rating (BBB+) to negative, warning that that the debt-to-GDP ratio may rise above 60 percent by 2006.

- Investors are also concerned about inadequate policy coordination that risks clouding the exchange rate outlook and the eventual fulfillment of the stability criterion. The region's wide fiscal deficits are viewed as having overburdened monetary and exchange rate policy. Investors generally perceive the inflation target as having been subordinated to exchange rate considerations in Hungary, following the speculative attack in January and the June devaluation.

EU Entry Prospects, However, Unlock Access to Broader Pool of Portfolio Capital

The local currency debt markets in central Europe have experienced a secular broadening of their investor base. In the expectation that EU membership will trigger the inclusion of the accession countries in mature bond market indices, albeit at relatively small weightings, convergence countries have increasingly attracted investments from crossover investors, proprietary trading desks of investment banks, as well as hedge funds. Meanwhile, dedicated convergence and emerging market funds, which traditionally had provided most of the portfolio investments to the region, continued to experience steady and sizable inflows for most of the first half of 2003.

Foreign Investor Participation in Local Debt Markets Rises

Consequently, foreign investor participation in the region's local bond markets surged. The key beneficiaries have been Poland and Hungary, with investors underscoring the importance of the relatively larger size and liquidity offered by these markets. In Hungary, the foreign share in government bonds rose from 39 percent in December 2001 to 47.5 percent in May 2003 (Figure 2.39). The share of Polish government securities held by foreign investors is estimated to have risen to 18 percent in April from 13 percent in December 2001, notwithstanding the relatively higher volatility of the Polish zloty. The Slovak Republic's inverted yield curve continued to attract firm interest, but the market's limited liquidity deterred foreign inflows. In the Czech Republic, foreign investor involvement is also small, estimated near 7 percent, given that local currency bond yields are near Bund yields.

Signs of Overreliance on Foreign Portfolio Flows

Foreign portfolio flows have been the primary source of external financing in Hungary since 2001 and have begun to rival FDI flows in Poland in 2003 (Figure 2.40). Foreign direct investments slowed amid rising concerns over Hungary's competitiveness and political uncertainties in Poland. The dependence on portfolio flows has risen sharply in Hungary and, to a lesser extent, in Poland. Poland's external financing requirements have fallen, as the current account deficit has halved since 1999. In

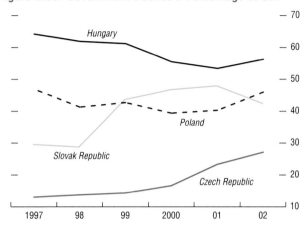

Figure 2.38. Government Debt as a Percentage of GDP

Sources: Eurostat; and IMF staff estimates.

Figure 2.39. Foreign Ownership of Government Securities
(In percent)

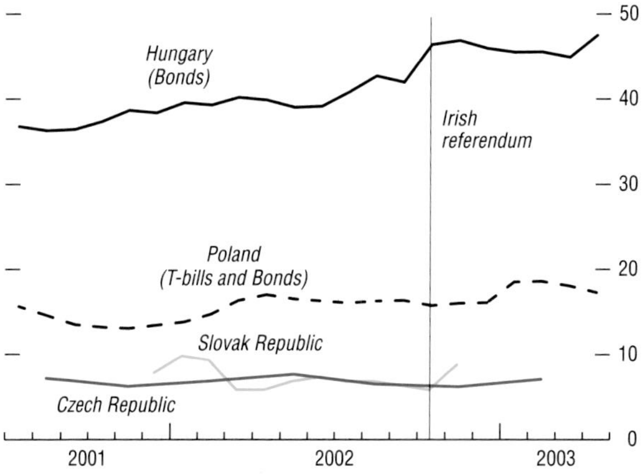

Sources: National authorities; and IMF staff estimates.

Box 2.4. Yield Compression in Central Europe: Convergence Expectations Versus Macroeconomic Fundamentals

The sharp decline of local currency bond yields in central Europe in recent years has been widely attributed to convergence expectations. We test this view with a simple econometric model. We find that domestic macroeconomic fundamentals and inflation, in particular, have remained the overriding driver of central Europe's recent yield compression. In contrast to the national bond markets in the euro area, we find little statistical evidence that Bund yields have significantly affected yields in the convergence countries. This provides further evidence that convergence is far from complete and emphasizes the need for prudent macroeconomic policies, including fiscal consolidation and improved policy coordination.

Bund Yields Versus Fundamentals

The convergence of interest rates has created strong linkages between the national bond markets in the euro area. National bond yields exhibit an almost perfect correlation with Bund yields and can be decomposed into in Bund yields and spreads over Bund yields. The latter can be positive or negative, depending on relative credit fundamentals.

The sharp decline of local currency bond yields in central Europe has been widely attributed to convergence expectations. Not unlike the experience of Greece in the run-up to EMU entry in 2001, the correlations of interest rates in central Europe with benchmark interest rates in the euro area have however remained highly volatile. This juxtaposition suggests that Bund yields have not yet become the primary driver of the local currency bond markets in the convergence countries. Such a finding would provide statistical evidence that convergence is far from complete, underscoring the vulnerabilities of the financial markets in the convergence countries to domestic policy shocks (see the Figures).

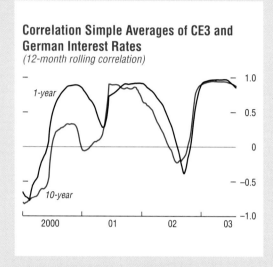

Correlation Simple Averages of CE3 and German Interest Rates
(12-month rolling correlation)

The Model

Against this backdrop, we present a simple econometric model to test whether Bund yields or domestic macroeconomic fundamentals have been the key drivers of yield developments in the Czech Republic, Hungary, and Poland (the CE-3). We approximate domestic fundamentals by inflation ($\overline{INFL}_t$) and retail sales ($\overline{RS}_t$), with the latter providing a proxy for consumption and

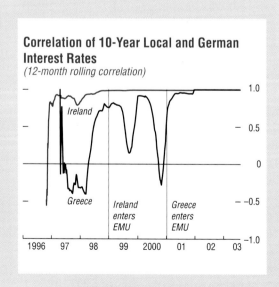

Correlation of 10-Year Local and German Interest Rates
(12-month rolling correlation)

Estimation Results
(*t*-values between parentheses)

	1-year rates	5-year rates	10-year rates
$\Delta INFL_t$	0.516 (13.4)	0.298 (8.93)	0.266 (11.0)
ΔRS_{t-3}	0.0692 (2.31)	0.0284 (1.15)	0.0491 (2.83)
R^2	0.82	0.57	0.67

domestic demand.[1] We regress local currency bond yields ($\bar{Y}_t$) on domestic fundamentals and Bund yields ($\bar{Y}_t^{GE}$).

$$\bar{Y}_t = \bar{\gamma} + \bar{\alpha} \cdot t + \beta^1 \cdot \overline{INFL}_t + \beta^2 \cdot \overline{RS}_{t-3} + \beta^3 \cdot \bar{Y}_t^{GE}, \quad (1)$$

Most of the series, however, exhibit unit roots. The model is therefore estimated on the basis of first differences for one-, five-, and ten-year maturities.

The Results

German yields are found to be either insignificant, or as having a negative coefficient when significant. A possible explanation for the latter phenomenon is that correla-

---

[1]For reasons of data availability, we use swap rates instead of bond yields for the Czech Republic and Poland. These are almost perfectly correlated with bond yields. The Slovak Republic is omitted from the analysis owing to data limitations. The estimations rely on three months lagged retails sales ($\overline{RS}_{t-3}$) rather than current sales. All trend variables were found to be negative.

tions between interest rates in central Europe and Germany have broken down at various stages, as illustrated in the Table. The data, therefore, do not appear to support the hypothesis that central European yields movements are primarily driven by Bund yields.[2] Coincidentally, bond traders confirmed that correlations tend to break down and that Bund yields tend to matter most during times of high volatility or times of little market specific news. German yields therefore are removed from the model and the model is re-estimated (setting $\beta^3 = 0$).

The results shown in the Table indicate that yields in central Europe remain largely driven by domestic macroeconomic fundamentals and, in particular, inflation. While cyclical developments had a statistically significant effect on bond yields, inflation was found to have been a much more powerful explanatory variable across the maturity spectrum. These findings emphasize the extent to which further interest rate convergence in central Europe hinges on prudent policies and price stability. Given the current policy mix, price stability depends upon fiscal consolidation as well as an improved policy coordination.

---

[2]A separate econometric analysis of Greek and Irish bond yields confirms these are driven by German Bund yields, with coefficients close to 1.

contrast, Hungary's external imbalances have begun to widen again in 2002, further raising the need for attracting foreign financing.

In contrast, FDI flows have been the primary source of external financing, and have overfinanced the current account deficits by a wide margin in the Czech Republic and the Slovak Republic in recent years. While privatization receipts have boosted FDI flows, the Czech Republic and, to a lesser extent, the Slovak Republic have also benefited from green field investments (Figure 2.41).

Financial Market Vulnerabilities and Policy Conclusions

• Expectations of EU accession in May 2004 have spurred a secular broadening of the investor base. While this has allowed governments in central Europe to finance wide fiscal deficits at favorable interest rates, the increasing reliance on foreign portfolio flows, especially in Hungary and, to a lesser extent, in Poland, has raised the risk of sudden capital outflows, and interest rate and exchange rate volatility. This underscores the urgency of fiscal consolidation in

Figure 2.40. Percentage of FDI and Bond Flows in Current Account
(In percent, 12-month moving totals)

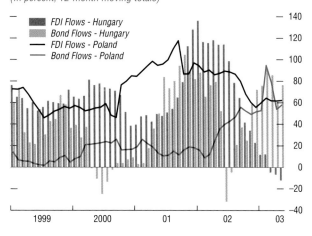

Sources: National authorities; and IMF staff estimates.

Figure 2.41. Percentage of FDI and Bond Flows in Current Account
(In percent, 12-month moving totals)

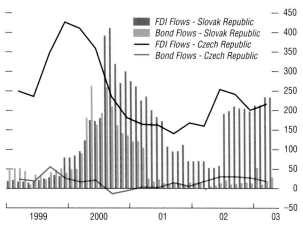

Sources: National authorities; and IMF staff estimates.

central Europe, regardless of the targeted EMU entry date.

- The scope for volatility has increased as a result of the changing investor base. Trading strategies of proprietary desks, crossover investors, and leveraged investors tend to be more focused on short-term developments than the strategies of dedicated investors, increasing the potential for volatility.

- With fiscal deficits deemed excessively large across the region, investor confidence has predominantly relied on the transparency of interest rate and exchange rate policies. The devaluation of the forint, however, has heightened market concerns that exchange rate policy might remain subordinated to inflation targeting in Hungary. In Poland, the need to reconstitute the Monetary Policy Council in early 2004 when the terms of all current members will expire is seen as creating policy uncertainty.

- The broadening of the investor base also leaves local bond markets in central Europe more vulnerable to global market forces, especially a continued weakening of mature government bond markets or a shift out of high-yielding currencies.

References

Capital Markets Consultative Group, forthcoming, *Foreign Direct Investment in Emerging Market Countries,* Report of the Working Group.

Conference of the Insurance Supervisory Services of the Member States of the European Union, 2002, *Prudential Supervision of Insurance Undertakings,* December 2002. Available via the Internet at http://www.fsa.gov.uk/pubs/occpapers/london_working_group_report.pdf.

Coronado, Julia Lynn, and Steven A. Sharpe, forthcoming, "Did Pension Plan Accounting Contribute to a Stock Market Bubble?", *Brookings Papers on Economic Activity,* Brookings Institution.

Credit Suisse First Boston, 2002, *The Magic of Pension Accounting* (New York, September 27).

———, 2003, *The Quarterly Report, Second Quarter 2003* (New York, April 14).

Das Udaibir S., Nigel Davies, and Richard Podpiera, 2003, "Insurance and Issues in Financial Soundness," IMF Working Paper No. 03/138 (Washington: International Monetary Fund).

Fitch, 2003a, *Special Report: German Life Insurers: Insurers May be Forced to Write Off Billions* (March 18).

———, 2003b, *Special Report: U.S. Life Insurance Industry 2002 Results: A Year of Living Dangerously* (April 25).

———, 2003c, *Special Report: Life Insurance in France: Prospects and Challenges* (May 16).

———, 2003d, *Japanese Life Insurance: Guaranteed Yield Cuts* (June 5).

International Association of Insurance Supervisors, 2002a, *Principles on Capital Adequacy and Solvency*, Principles No. 5 (Basel, January).

———, 2002b, *Guidance Paper on Public Disclosure by Insurers*, Guidance Paper No. 4 (Basel, January).

International Monetary Fund, 2002, *Global Financial Stability Report*, World Economic and Financial Surveys (Washington, June).

ISDA, 2003, *Master Agreement Amendments* (New York: International Swaps and Derivatives Association, May).

Modukuri, Srinivas, 2003, "Update on Mortgage Convexity Hedging," *Lehman Brothers Mortgage Strategy Weekly* (June 30).

Moody's, 2003a, *Special Comment: German Life Insurance Industry* (February).

———, 2003b, *Moody's Rating Actions and Reviews— Quarterly Update* (April).

Tierney, John, and Tarek Nassar, 2003, "Synthetic CDOs: Recent Market Developments," *Deutsche Bank Global Market Research* (April 29).

U.S. Office of the Comptroller of the Currency, 2003, *Bank Derivatives Report*, First Quarter.

FINANCIAL ASSET PRICE VOLATILITY:
A SOURCE OF INSTABILITY?

Financial asset price volatility, and its potential to undermine financial stability, has been a subject of concern in recent years. This chapter examines historical volatility and correlations between asset classes in the major mature markets. It discusses the links between volatility and instability, some of the policy lessons that have been learned during various crises, and the implications those lessons have today. The chapter focuses mostly on equity prices, as these have been unusually volatile in recent years, but also considers their relationship to the wider financial markets.

Asset price volatility is unavoidable and is not necessarily undesirable, since it reflects the process of pricing and transferring risk as underlying circumstances change. Indeed, if financial markets do not react to changing underlying conditions in the markets (policy changes or shocks, for example), misallocation of financial resources will occur. But if volatility leads to financial instability that too can impose real costs. Examination of past crises indicates that the biggest dangers to financial stability seem to have come not so much from a sustained high level of volatility as from sudden increases in volatility. This suggests that policymakers and market participants should focus more on reducing the instability that surrounds unexpectedly strong turbulence than on controlling the general level of volatility.

The empirical work in the chapter will show that most periods of high volatility in equity prices have been associated with negative shocks to the real economy. But there are several instances where the volatility was rooted more in financial market disturbances instead. These instances provide opportunities to look more specifically at the financial sector causes and consequences of volatility and instability. Four case studies are examined: the Black Monday crash of 1987; the bursting of the Japanese bubble in 1990; the Long-Term Capital Management (LTCM) crisis of 1998; and market conditions following the bursting of the recent technology, media, and telecommunications (TMT) equity bubble.

From these cases, policymakers and market participants could learn lessons about how volatility can become amplified in a crisis and how to control factors such as leverage, shortage of liquidity, and lack of transparency that can turn volatility into instability. This is inevitably an ongoing process, with lessons from each crisis and subsequent innovations by the market and by policymakers. An important continuing policy question is how to avoid creating circumstances where, in a crisis, participants' attempts to control their own risk by selling into falling markets make the overall system unstable in new ways.

Concepts: Financial Market Volatility and Financial System Instability

Since the terms "market volatility" and "financial instability" are often used interchangeably in the public debate, it may be useful first to define and distinguish these concepts. Volatility, simply put, refers to the degree to which prices vary over a certain length of time. (This chapter limits itself to discussing volatility of prices, rather than volatility of capital flows.) Most commonly—and this convention will be followed here—price volatility is defined as the standard deviation of changes in the log of asset prices.

Although there is no generally accepted definition of financial system instability or systemic risk, the following definition, which incorporates many of the elements in definitions put forward by other authors, may be useful:[1]

Periods of financial system instability entail severe market disruptions that—by impairing the system's ability to provide payment services, to price and transfer risks, and/or to allocate credit and liquidity—have the potential to cause a reduction in real activity.

Financial system instability is often linked to concerns about key financial institutions becoming illiquid or failing, although concerns about the overall liquidity and infrastructure of financial markets can also play a role. Although financial instability has the potential to damage the real economy, it will not always lead to an actual reduction in economic activity. Policy reactions by the authorities, for instance, may avert economic problems.

Periods of financial instability are nearly always accompanied by greater market volatility. However, market volatility need not imply financial instability (see Schwartz, 1985; and Crockett, 1997a). Volatility will often have benign consequences and need not be a concern to authorities. In efficient markets, where prices embody all available information, asset price volatility will reflect the volatility of economic fundamentals and is an inherent part of a well-functioning financial system. Even relatively large short-term volatility can be the result of a rational reaction by market participants to rapidly changing events and increased uncertainty about future returns. It is only when volatility becomes extreme (often referred to as "tail events"), is a potential source of strains on key financial institutions or markets, or results in self-perpetuating contagious price falls, that it is associated with financial instability and should be a concern for the authorities.

The financial system is continually subject to shocks (related to news or events) that cause participants to reevaluate the future value of, and the risks embodied in, assets or their perception of counterparty risks. There are generally two types of shocks: those that are broad or systematic, affecting large segments of the financial system, and those that are idiosyncratic, affecting the health of specific institutions or the price movements in specific markets. Broad shocks are often related to large changes in one or more countries' prospective macroeconomic performance, while examples of idiosyncratic shocks are a sudden drop in the prices of certain key assets—sometimes stemming from a correction of an earlier asset price misalignment (or bubble)—or the failure of a financial institution.

The degree to which shocks to the financial system are amplified and propagated across markets or across institutions is a key element of financial system instability. Because idiosyncratic shocks originate in one part of the market and could spread to others, they can often prove particularly useful case studies of the vulnerability of the financial system. Broad shocks, on the other hand, tend to affect the financial system in several areas simultaneously, making it more difficult to isolate individual systemic weaknesses. The four case studies presented later in this chapter therefore look at idiosyncratic financial shocks.

Factors That Can Turn Volatility into Instability

Among the factors that can amplify price volatility and turn it into instability are the following:

Incentive Structures

Peer-group performance measures or index-tracking can encourage herding and short-termism among institutional investors, leading to amplified or self-perpetuating price

---

[1]See Crockett (1997a and b), Davis (2002), and De Bandt and Hartmann (2000) and the references therein for various definitions of financial system stability and systemic risk.

movements. Pressures to meet short-term earnings targets, for instance, or structures that reward staff at intermediaries according to volume of business rather than risk-adjusted return can lead to underestimation of long-term risk and imprudent leveraging. Conflicts of interest at intermediaries can also lead to insufficient disclosure of risks to investors. Sudden changes in herd sentiment, amplified by any increase in leverage, could then create instability through contagious price falls and difficulty in repricing risks.

Lack of Robust Risk Management

Leverage increases the sensitivity of financial institutions and the system as a whole to economic downturns and to asset price declines more generally. Rare events and regime shifts that may not be factored into risk measurement models or stress tests may be sources of unappreciated risk. Currency mismatches can lead to systemic risks, especially under pegged exchange rate regimes where the possibility of a regime change may not be fully taken into account in risk management. Certain hedging strategies (delta hedging or "portfolio insurance") may lead to feedback mechanisms that amplify price movements. The unwinding of a concentration of leveraged positions (relating perhaps to a popular "carry trade" or asset bubble) can similarly increase volatility. A combination of extreme price movements and sudden realization of previously unappreciated market and credit risks could lead to heavy losses at key institutions and disruptions to market pricing.

Lack of Transparency

Lack of disclosure by individual firms makes risk management by others under volatile conditions more difficult. Inadequate initial disclosure of the true scale of positions or financial condition can lead to sudden changes in market sentiment when the existence of large exposures or weaknesses becomes known and to extreme price reac-

tions as market participants try to discern the facts and assess the implications amid partial information and rumors. Market uncertainty over the solvency of individual firms, and concerns (whether justified or not) about others that share some of the same characteristics, can impair the allocation of credit and functioning of payment systems.

Market Infrastructure Weaknesses

Payment, clearing, or settlement systems may not be adequate to allow participants to cope with large margin calls, doubts over counterparty risk, or heavy volumes of business. This could cause illiquidity and payments difficulties to spread rapidly through the system.

The appropriate balance between market discipline and regulation needs to be found. Otherwise deregulation can lead to an excessive buildup of debt as new investors in the market underestimate the risks in the newly deregulated segment of a market, while new regulatory and supervisory systems may not have been sufficiently calibrated to withstand an economic downturn or a burst of negative news. Alternatively, regulations that tighten risk limits during times of market instability can have procyclical effects that amplify market volatility. Regulation could also be excessive, hampering market innovation. All these are challenges that authorities unavoidably face and therefore need to be prepared to address.

The potential sources of instability just mentioned are illustrated by the case studies discussed later.

Empirical Evidence on Volatility, Correlations Between Markets, and Macroeconomic Factors

The empirical work that follows assesses historical trends in financial market volatility and aims to separate episodes of high volatility that reflect macroeconomic factors from those that stem more from financial shocks. The data examined relate to equity prices, foreign exchange rates, and bond returns in Germany, Japan, the United Kingdom, and the United States, representing the four major financial centers. Volatility is measured by the historical standard deviation of price changes, calculated as the moving average over a rolling sample.

Developments during the past 30 years suggest that equity volatility has recently picked up, while recent bond and foreign exchange volatility have remained within their typical historical bands (and indeed in a number of cases show less volatility than periods in, for example, the 1980s). The evidence also indicates that the major mature equity markets have become more integrated.

Econometric estimates suggest that, apart from in Germany, the connection between equity market volatility and domestic recessions is fairly close.[2] However, the periods of our four case studies are exceptions where volatility is elevated with little or no direct link to domestic recessions.

Historical Trends in Financial Market Volatility

Equity price volatility has trended up since the mid-1990s.[3] Equity volatility has been particularly high since 2000, except in Japan, as the TMT bubble burst, followed by shocks such as the events of September 11, 2001, the Enron and WorldCom accounting scandals, and geopolitical uncertainty (Figure 3.1). This pattern is consistent with an asymmetric "feedback" or "leverage effect" generally observed: equity volatility tends to rise when asset prices fall (Campbell, Lo, and

---

[2]It is important to note that these estimates examine the correlation between volatility and recessions, but do not attempt to test the causality between them.

[3]Volatility is calculated as the annualized standard deviation of percentage returns over a rolling sample. The standard deviations are calculated from an exponentially weighted moving average of past squared returns, where the weights decay by a factor of 0.94 for daily returns and 0.92 in the case of monthly data.

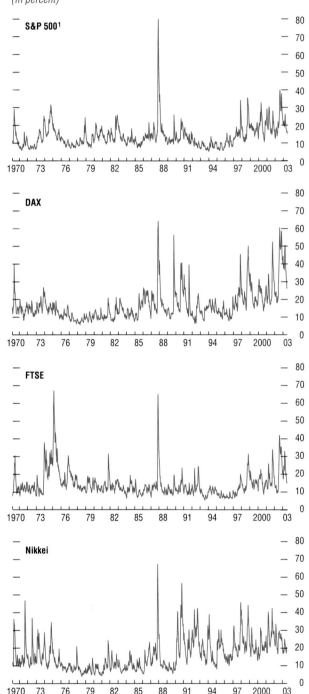

Figure 3.1. Equity Market Volatility
(In percent)

Sources: Datastream; and IMF staff estimates.
[1]The following figures are outside the scale of this figure: 94 percent on October 5, 1987; and 91 percent on November 1, 1987.

Figure 3.2. Bond Market Volatility[1]
(In percent)

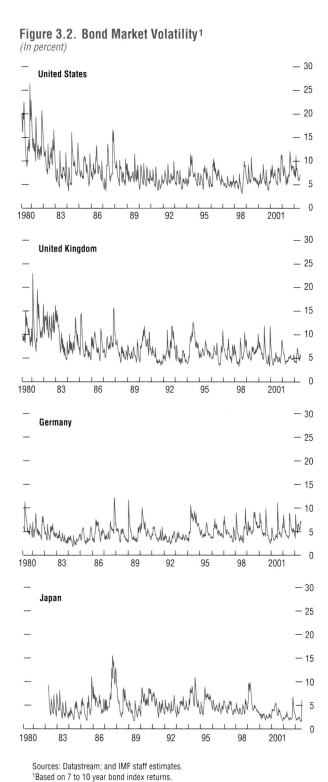

Sources: Datastream; and IMF staff estimates.
[1]Based on 7 to 10 year bond index returns.

MacKinlay, 1997, p. 497). All four equity markets analyzed exhibit brief intense spikes in volatility during periods of financial stress, such as the October 1987 crash and the LTCM crisis in 1998. Except for the 1987 crash, equity volatility in the United States and the United Kingdom until the mid-1990s had remained generally lower than during the oil crisis in the mid-1970s. Equity market volatility in Japan surged in the early 1990s following the bursting of the equity bubble, and in Germany volatility jumped at the time of reunification.

The volatility of returns on an index of 7 to 10 year government bonds in the United States, the United Kingdom, and Germany has moved in a relatively stable range since the 1987 crash (Figure 3.2), and for the United States and United Kingdom has remained considerably lower than during the high inflation of the early 1980s. Some simultaneous spikes in volatility can be identified in all four markets, including in 1994 when the U.S. Federal Reserve reversed its interest rate policy and the 1998 LTCM episode, but in general spikes are much less pronounced than for equities.

Like bonds, foreign exchange volatility does not show any rising trend (Figure 3.3). Foreign exchange volatility between the dollar, yen, pound, and euro has been high only at specific moments of policy uncertainty, most notably around the 1985 Plaza Agreement and the 1992 Exchange Rate Mechanism crisis. Since the early 1990s, the volatility of the dollar vis-à-vis the euro and pound has declined, with a peak in mid-2000 when the euro reversed its decline. The yen-dollar volatility jumped in the fall of 1998 when investors reduced their yen carry trades and associated hedging positions.

Extreme daily price changes (so-called tail events) have become more frequent for equity markets, while less frequent in bond markets and stayed close to average frequencies in foreign exchange markets (Table 3.1). Since October 1997, the percentage of days in which equity prices moved more than 3 percent was two to three times higher than in the overall period since 1970. By contrast, the number of large daily movements declined sharply in bond markets while it remained at about normal in foreign exchange markets. The frequency of tail events is a useful measure of market instability because standard deviation measures of volatility are a form of averaging that may mask occasional large price movements that can impose strains on the system.

Large equity tail events—though recently more frequent than average—have not been unusually common compared with past episodes of financial stress.[4] Monthly U.S. equity data that includes the Great Depression show how limited recent tail event counts have been by comparison with some other periods (Table 3.2).[5] For example, the 1973–74 recession, oil shocks, and the end of the Bretton Woods regime created deep uncertainty and a period of much more frequent large price moves.[6]

Correlations between national markets have been rising for equities and in some cases for bonds. As financial markets and underlying economies become increasingly integrated and companies' operations become more multinational, correlations would be expected to rise.[7] Indeed, correlations between national equity returns have risen substantially in several cases, generally

[4]Following the 1987 crash, U.S. stock markets introduced circuit breakers that cause trading to halt after an equity price decline reaches a certain threshold. However, these have been triggered only once and so have not directly significantly reduced the recent tail event count.

[5]Jorion (2002) comes to the same conclusion using similar data and technique.

[6]See Davis (2003), who compares the 1973–74 bear market in equities to the bear market that began in 2000.

[7]See Bordo, Eichengreen, and Irwin (1999), who show that, since the mid-1970s, globalization has led economies and financial markets to be more integrated.

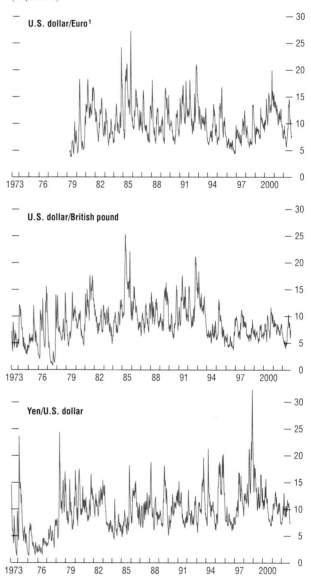

Figure 3.3. Historical Foreign Exchange Volatility
(In percent)

Sources: Datastream; European Central Bank; and IMF staff estimates.
[1]Prior to 1999, data refer to European Currency Unit.

Table 3.1. Frequency of Tail Events[1]
(In percent)

Equity	2000s	1973–74	1970–Sep. 1997	Oct. 1997–2003	Full Sample	Sample Standard Deviation
S&P 500	5.7	1.9	0.6	3.4	1.1	1.0
DAX	16.7	0.7	1.7	10.2	2.7	1.3
FTSE	4.4	4.4	1.3	2.6	1.5	1.0
Nikkei	9.7	9.1[2]	2.2	5.9	2.9	1.2

Bond returns	2000s	1990–92	1994	Oct. 1997–2003	Full Sample	Sample Standard Deviation
United States	1.4	1.3	1.2	0.9	1.9	0.5
Germany	2.0	1.7	3.8	1.1	1.5	0.3
United Kingdom	1.4	1.5	1.5	0.9	1.8	0.5
Japan	0.9	2.9	3.4	0.5	1.9	0.3

Foreign exchange	2000s	1990–92	1973–Sep. 1997	Oct. 1997–2003	Full Sample	Sample Standard Deviation
Euro	0.1	0.4	0.2	0.1	0.2	0.6
Sterling	0.0	0.0	0.1	0.0	0.1	0.6
Yen	0.7	0.0	0.3	0.4	0.3	0.7

[1]For equity and foreign exchange, the frequency is calculated as the number of trading sessions with 3 percent or greater returns as a percentage of the total number of trading sessions during the relevant period. For bonds the cut-off is calculated as 3 times the full sample standard deviation for each series of bond returns.

[2]Sample period is 1990 to 1992 for comparison purposes with the Japanese bursting bubble period.

involving a greater comovement with the S&P 500. An average of these correlations has varied substantially, but reached a new high in 2002 (Figure 3.4).[8] Cross-country bond return correlations between the United States, United Kingdom, and Germany have become increasingly positive recently, in line with increasingly integrated fixed-income markets as well as the convergence in business cycles. Only Japanese bond returns exhibited slightly declining correlation with those abroad, reflecting an increasingly isolated domestic financial system (Figure 3.5). The correlation of bond and equity returns within the United States, the United

Kingdom, and Germany has generally, and perhaps ominously (see below), been declining (Figure 3.6).[9]

Macroeconomic Factors and Equity Market Volatility

While the *level* of asset prices is related to macroeconomic activity, the relationship between asset return *volatility* and macroeconomic conditions is not so straightforward. Although studies have found that stock market volatility rises during economic contractions,[10] the explanations put forward for this empirical observation have

[8]Like the volatility measures, correlations are calculated using exponential weights with a decay factor of 0.94.

[9]One criticism of the correlation estimates used here is that they are biased upward during periods in which returns are more volatile (Forbes and Rigobon, 2001). However, Chakrabarti and Roll (2002) argue that correlations are not necessarily biased if the crisis is characterized by sharp asset price declines, which happen also to coincide with heightened volatility.

[10]Studies of U.S. equity market volatility and the business cycle date back to Officer (1973). Schwert (1989) shows that recessions are the single most important explanatory factor for volatility. Hamilton and Lin (1996) show that recessions account for about 60 percent of the variation in volatility, while Campbell and others (2001) find that volatility increases by a factor of two to three during recessions. There is also some limited empirical evidence that cross-country stock market correlations rise during recessions (see Erb, Harvey, and Viskanta, 1994).

Table 3.2. United States: Frequency of Monthly Equity Returns Greater Than 8 Percent

(In percent)

Periods	S&P 500
1871–1899	2.0
1900s	3.3
1910s	0.8
1920s	5.0
1930s	22.3
1940s	2.5
1950s	0.0
1960s	0.8
1970s	4.1
1980s	5.7
1990s	3.3
2000s	8.8
1871–2002	4.3
Periods	**S&P 500**
Oct. 1997–2002	6.6
Oct. 1997–Dec. 1999	3.7
1973–1974	10.8
1980–1982	10.8

Data Source: Robert Shiller's website: http://aida.econ.yale.edu/~shiller/data.htm.

The frequency is calculated as the number of 8 percent or greater monthly returns as a percentage of the total number of months during the relevant period.

received only weak support.[11] Recent research, however, has shown that larger investor uncertainty about asset fundamentals tends to increase volatility (and correlations) of asset returns and that this investor uncertainty in principle rises during recessions. This could explain the positive correlation between equity volatility and recessions that has been observed. On the other hand, periods of high market volatility that are unrelated to economic recessions may tend to indicate increases in investor uncertainty related to instability in the financial system rather than to macroeconomic factors.

Asset price volatility could increase even if the fundamentals themselves do not become more volatile. This could happen if investors become more uncertain about underlying

[11]One explanation for this is that firms become riskier during recessions because they tend to be more financially levered and as a result their share prices fluctuate more. Yet Schwert (1989) finds that U.S. recessions still explain a substantial part of U.S. equity market volatility even after controlling for firm leverage.

Figure 3.4. Average Cross-Country Stock Market Correlations[1]

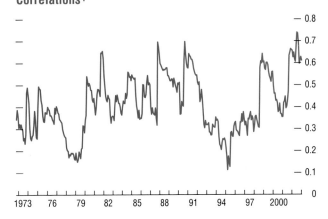

Sources: Datastream; and IMF staff estimates.
[1]Average of the bilateral correlations between S&P 500, FTSE, DAX, and Nikkei.

Table 3.3. Correlations Between Historical Volatility and Recessions

Market	Own Recessions	U.S. Recessions
S&P 500	0.28[1]	
FTSE	0.20[1]	0.17[1]
DAX	−0.27[1]	0.00
Nikkei	0.24[1]	−0.05

[1]Indicates estimates that are significant at the 5 percent level.

Figure 3.5. Bilateral Bond Market Correlations

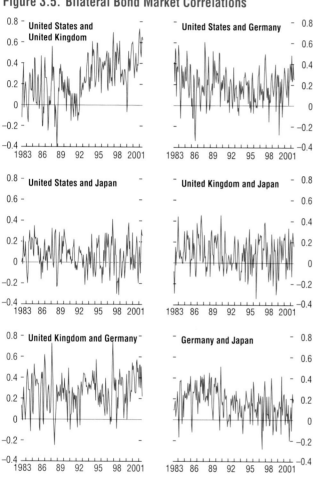

Sources: Datastream; and IMF staff estimates.

long-term economic and financial growth rates and trends and therefore attach large significance to relatively small pieces of news. This may explain why the volatility of macro-economic variables per se explains only a small amount of asset price volatility. (In the G-7 there has been a general decline in the volatility of many macroeconomic variables such as GDP growth or inflation during the 1990s, and yet there is no evidence that asset price volatility has declined concurrently.)

The behavior of return volatility in the various equity markets during business cycles suggests an interesting pattern (Table 3.3).[12] There is a fairly close positive correlation between equity market volatility and domestic recessions—except in Germany, where the correlation was negative. Meanwhile, the volatility in the FTSE was as almost as strongly correlated with U.S. recessions as with U.K. recessions.

High equity market volatility and domestic recessions were particularly closely synchronized in the United States and the United Kingdom (Table 3.4) when measured by a concordance statistic, which, unlike correlations, is not biased by a few large events. To

---

[12]To time recessions, for the United States, the National Bureau of Economic Research (NBER) recession dates are used. For the other countries, the recessions are dated based on the analysis presented in Chapter III of the April 2002 *World Economic Outlook* (IMF, 2002). There, business cycle turning points are identified based on peaks and troughs in real economic activity. Since the *World Economic Outlook* dates are at a quarterly frequency, while the analysis in this chapter is based on monthly data, we assume that the economy is in recession during all three months of a recession quarter.

Table 3.4. Concordance Statistics for High Equity Volatility Regimes and Recessions[1]

High Volatility Regime	Own Recessions	U.S. Recessions	High U.S. Volatility Regimes
United States	0.87[2]		
United Kingdom	0.82[2]	0.83[2]	0.80[2]
Germany	0.53	0.62[2]	0.65[2]
Japan	0.48	0.41	0.50

[1]The concordance statistic determines the number of periods, as a proportion of the number of periods in the sample, during which the two relevant variables are in the same state.

[2]Indicates estimates that are significant at the 5 percent level, implying that the respective regimes statistically coincide.

that end, an econometric model with two equity-volatility regimes—a high-volatility and a low-volatility regime—was used to estimate the probabilities that the observed equity returns fall into the high volatility regime (Figure 3.7).[13] Using this measure, German and U.K. volatility appear even more closely synchronized with U.S. recessions than with recessions in their own countries. By contrast, equity market volatility in Japan is relatively detached from domestic and international economic cycles.

U.S. recessions overlap with all but three periods when the model suggests that U.S. equity markets were in the high-volatility regime. The three episodes unrelated to recessions coincided with the 1987 stock market crash, the autumn of 1998, and the second volatility spike in 2002, and were likely triggered by financial stability concerns rather than macroeconomic factors. Meanwhile, the sustained period of the high-volatility regime in Japan begins when the 1990 bubble bursts and precedes recession by several years. These are our four case studies (see the Appendix to this chapter for details).

The correlations between equity markets rise during U.S. recessions (Table 3.5). These results suggest that global fundamental

[13]We use a Markov-switching regime econometric model, where recurring persistent regimes of heightened volatility are identified endogenously (see Hamilton, 1994, for details).

Figure 3.6. Correlations Between Stock and Bond Returns

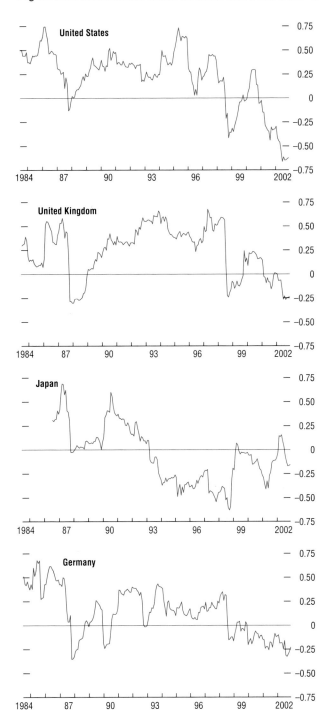

Sources: Datastream; and IMF staff estimates.

Table 3.5. Equity Market Correlations During U.S. Recessions and Expansions

	United States	Germany	United Kingdom	Japan
United States		0.51	0.55	0.34
Germany	0.64		0.44	0.30
United Kingdom	0.69	0.58		0.29
Japan	0.60	0.71	0.54	

Bottom part of matrix reports the estimated correlation coefficients during recession periods; top, during expansions.

Figure 3.7. Probability of High Equity Volatility State and Recession Dates[1]

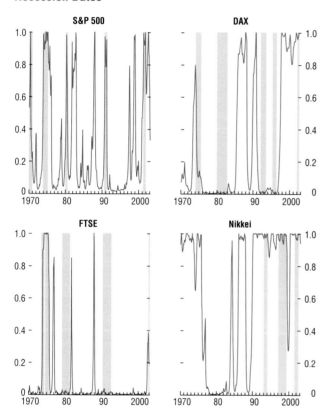

Sources: Datastream; and IMF staff estimates.
[1]Shaded areas show recession periods for each country.

uncertainty—proxied by U.S. recessionary periods—has not only an impact on the volatility of equity returns but also their correlation across countries.

U.S. recessions also overlap with all the periods when correlations between equity markets surged abruptly except the same three episodes identified above in the case of U.S. high-volatility regimes. These non-recession-related periods of heightened stock market volatility generally corresponded to times of greater systemic risk where flight-to-quality dynamics were prevalent, as described in the following section.

Episodes of Negative Correlation Between Bonds and Equities

While correlations between bond returns and equity returns in each country have typically been positive since the early 1980s, the correlations sometimes turn negative during periods of equity market volatility, suggesting flight-to-quality. The three episodes in this period coincide with the three U.S. high-volatility regimes identified above as not coinciding with recessions (Figure 3.8). As such, episodes of negative stock-bond correlations tend to coincide with, and can be a signal of, financial instability in mature markets, but generally do not arise in periods when high stock market volatility is related to economic recessions.

Negative correlations of equity and bond returns also tend to coincide with sharp increases in implied volatility in U.S. and

Table 3.6. Regime-Switching Model for Bond-Equity Correlations: Coefficient Estimates[1]
(In percent)

	United States	Germany
β_0	0.30	0.10
β_1	−0.10	−0.10
Correlation	0.53	0.64

The coefficient related to the negative (positive) regime is β_1 (β_0) for the U.S. and Germany. The negative values for β_1 imply a negative relationship between stock and bond returns when in this regime, and thus represent the flight-to-quality periods. The bottom row is the correlation estimate between estimated probability of being in the flight-to-quality regime and the implied volatility measures.

[1]All estimates are significant at the 5 percent level.

German equity markets, as measured by the volatility indexes VIX and VDAX.[14] Based on a regime-switching econometric model, the synchronization is measured by the correlation between periods of negative bond-equity correlations, on the one hand, and periods of high or low implied volatility, on the other hand (Table 3.6).[15] The results suggest a close mapping between the "flight-to-quality" periods and high levels of the VIX or VDAX (Figure 3.9). The flight-to-quality regimes coincided in the United States with the 1987 crash, the 1998 LTCM crisis, and the period since mid-2000. For Germany, flight-to-quality dynamics have been observed more or less since 1998.

Overall, the flight-to-quality analysis supports the hypothesis that periods of high equity market volatility that are unrelated to economic recessions tend to coincide with heightened perception of risk by market participants in response to increases in global financial instability. The period since 2000—when negative bond-equity correlations over-

Figure 3.8. Bond and Stock Return Correlations[1]

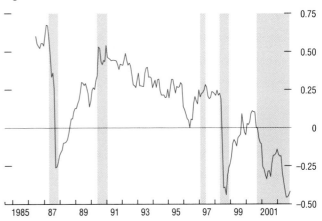

Sources: Datastream; and IMF staff estimates.
[1]Average of the stock and bond correlations for each country. Shaded areas indicate high equity volatility dates for the United States.

[14]In Whaley (2000) the VIX index is referred to as the "Investor Fear Gauge" because it tends to spike during times of market turmoil.

[15]Following Stivers, Sun, and Connolly (2002), an econometric Markov-switching model was estimated. Bond returns were regressed on stock returns (plus lagged bond returns and a regime-dependent constant), and the coefficient on the stock returns was allowed to take on one of two values—depending on the positive or negative correlation regime.

lapped with a mild recession and high equity volatility—is an exception, presenting a "hybrid" case where both recessionary and financial factors seem to have been at play.

Case Study Analysis of Periods of Recessionless Financial Stress

Although many spikes in financial asset price volatility are related to periods of stress in economic cycles, volatility can also spike at other times. For example, major market innovation, deregulation, or other structural changes can lead to financial bubbles that create volatility when they eventually burst. At the outset of the bubble, new business opportunities can prompt a sudden rise in risk appetite in financial markets, which is often accompanied by a buildup of leverage (whether explicitly, through direct borrowing, or implicitly, such as through use of derivatives). Unrealistic assumptions about long-term financial returns and beliefs in stable relationships in markets, combined with weak risk management, can encourage excessive risk-taking.

When market participants—in reaction to exogenous events—reevaluate underlying assumptions and curb their risk appetite, they start to unwind their financial positions. Those exogenous events may be the proximate causes of the bursting of the bubble, but are not necessarily the underlying causes, particularly if the market dynamics were unsustainable in the long run; if the particular events had not occurred, some other event in due course would likely have led to a similar reevaluation. Once the market decline begins, leverage heightens financial stability risks: it increases investors' losses from the falling asset prices; it tends to raise counterparty exposures; and it can force them to liquidate positions quickly. These sorts of factors can amplify the price declines.

Four particular episodes that involved spikes in volatility provide some lessons for financial stability and are discussed as case studies in the Appendix at the end of this

Figure 3.9. "Flight-to-Quality" Probabilities and Implied Volatility[1]

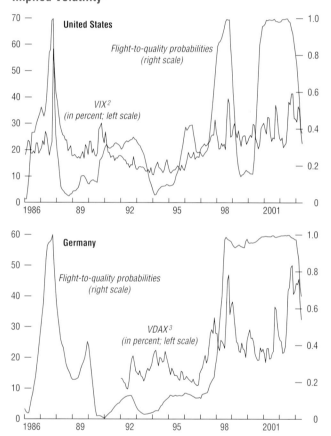

Sources: Datastream; and IMF staff estimates.
[1]"Flight-to-quality" probability represents the probability of being in a period when bond and stock returns are negatively correlated, based on a regime-switching model.
[2]VIX is Chicago Board Options Exchange volatility index. This index is calculated by taking a weighted average of implied volatility for the eight S&P 100 calls and puts.
[3]VDAX represents the implied volatility of the DAX.

chapter. These episodes were not accompanied by recessions, and so appear to have been less related to fundamental uncertainty about macroeconomic conditions. The four events, which all led to major concerns about financial instability, are:

- The Black Monday stock market crash of 1987;
- The bursting of the Japanese equity and real estate bubble in 1990;
- The LTCM crisis of 1998; and
- Market conditions following the collapse of the TMT equity bubble in 2000.[16]

A sharp reduction in risk appetite in a crisis, uncertainties over asset valuations, and the complex web of interlocking counterparty exposures may make it difficult for market participants to coordinate an orderly unwinding of positions without official intervention. These four financial instability cases suggest that financial authorities, particularly central banks, played a crucial role in restoring calm to the markets. The case studies focus less on the run-up to the crisis and more on the period of the crisis itself and its unwinding. Typically, asset price volatility is particularly high during and after the crisis, rather than in the run-up, and the factors that determine whether volatility leads to financial instability can often be seen most clearly at that point. In some ways, the periods of high volatility in the case studies are very different; some took place over days and others over years. Yet the lessons learned still show similarities.

Policy Implications

Is the Current Period of Market Volatility a Cause for Concern?

Although it is often stated that volatility has increased in recent years, within the mature markets a rise in volatility of asset prices and returns has only been evident in equity markets and not in other markets such as bonds or foreign exchange.[17] But in episodes of high equity market volatility, significant strains and flows have emerged in other markets as well. Although many of the details of the case studies have been specific to equity markets, the policy lessons are more widely applicable across the financial system.

The current period of high equity volatility, which includes the period following the collapse of the TMT equity bubble, is unusual for its length rather than its height. Most periods of volatility in recent decades have been short-lived spikes that corresponded to sharp share price falls followed by a steady return to stability. However, the current period of higher volatility has lasted much longer than previous episodes.

The unusual nature of the current period of volatility therefore makes it difficult to say whether it could evolve into financial instability. Previous crises have often arisen from periods of relatively modest volatility. Arguably, market participants became complacent about market risks, assuming for instance that existing exchange rate relationships would remain stable or that sustained asset price rallies would continue. An extended period of high volatility could, in fact, be less threatening to financial stability than one where volatility is low because a risk is not recognized by investors or because market mechanisms artificially dampen volatility. When volatility is in plain sight to market participants and to regulators, the awareness for risk management is sharpened, more likely guarding institutions and the system itself against potential financial instability.

Nevertheless, periods of high volatility always argue for enhanced caution. First, mar-

---

[16]Part of the period following the TMT bubble coincided with a U.S. recession, but the high volatility persisted after the recession ended.

[17]Although in recent months equity market volatility has fallen (see Chapter II), the average volatility over the last three years remains high.

kets may have adjusted to the risk arising from the existing level of volatility but may not be prepared for a further increase. Second, risk management systems may adequately protect intermediaries from solvency and liquidity problems, but perhaps at the cost of lower levels of financing for the economy than would be the case at lower volatility levels or of inefficient allocation of capital as intermediaries pursue profit opportunities arising from the volatility itself rather than from long-run investment. Third, the volatility may itself be an indicator of underlying market weaknesses, which can be harbingers of instability.

Policy measures should not aim at reducing asset price volatility for its own sake, but should instead attempt:

- to avoid conditions where excessive vulnerabilities to volatility build up (e.g., through excessive leverage or risk exposures); and
- to prevent volatility from triggering financial instability (if, for instance, there are market features that, during a crisis, would tend to artificially amplify volatility, put payments or settlement systems under strain, or induce the bankruptcy of a key intermediary).

The policy implications therefore often involve measures to reduce the weaknesses in behavior of institutions and systems that can lead to forced sales or otherwise amplify price volatility, rather than to directly control price volatility itself.

The case studies indicate policy lessons from past periods of financial stress aimed at limiting the *effects* of volatility by:

- breaking the cycle of amplifying volatility;
- strengthening risk management practices;
- aligning incentive structures;
- enhancing transparency;
- improving market infrastructure; and
- finding the balance between leaving risk control to market discipline and regulation.

These topics are discussed in turn below.

Breaking the Cycle of Amplifying Volatility

Most of the case studies showed that, once a crisis had begun, the provision of liquidity by central banks was a key factor in easing the funding constraints that were amplifying volatility. Liquidity injections allowed transactions to be settled smoothly and boosted the confidence of market participants that the authorities would proactively address the wider crisis. They also helped to improve the relative yield return of other assets compared with cash. Conversely, in Japan, even after the asset bubble had burst, high interest rates were maintained for wider policy reasons and monetary policy thus could not soften the impact of falling asset prices.

As another important step, officials and market participants can establish a forum for finding collective means to resolve short-term liquidity problems. The agreement brokered by the Federal Reserve Bank of New York, for example, permitted creditors to unwind LTCM's positions in an orderly fashion, without the official sector providing liquidity. In other cases, private sector groupings—such as stock exchanges, clearinghouses, or more informal crisis groups—may be able to reach similar agreements.

Features of the market structure can also aim to stop the market's fall. Following Black Monday, circuit breakers were devised to slow the transmission mechanisms between equity and futures markets once a market fall begins. If circuit breakers, however, are not well designed, they could themselves be a source of amplified volatility.

In principle, and if possible, policy measures to avoid the amplification of volatility should best be taken before a crisis happens, so as to address underlying causes rather than symptoms. The remaining policy lessons address aspects that are more preventive. However, finding the right balance is not always easy. In particular, the debate remains unresolved as to how to strike an appropriate balance between two important goals for controlling the effects of volatility:

- setting rigorous and consistent standards for limiting participants' exposures and disclosing information on mark-to-market positions, thereby avoiding the buildup of leverage and potentially unsustainable positions that amplify volatility; and
- preventing these standards from simply amplifying volatility in another way, for example, by forcing or encouraging asset sales into falling markets at fire-sale prices to control risks.

There are a number of areas, described below, where this policy dilemma exists.

Strengthening Risk Management

Striking this balance is particularly pertinent in risk management, both for regulators and for the market itself.

The degree of leverage is a crucial factor in the extent to which volatility turns into instability, as it can increase both market risk and counterparty risk. Even a small number of leveraged players can cause major problems for the market as a whole, as the portfolio insurers of Black Monday, the hedge funds and other arbitrageurs of the LTCM crisis, and the telecom and energy firms of the TMT equity bubble showed. Their leverage creates the potential for large margin calls and even for insolvency and can greatly accentuate the original price fall as they attempt to rapidly close out their large and sometimes highly risky positions. Continually more sophisticated measurement of leverage—including leverage embedded in off-balance-sheet exposures—is needed as new financial instruments and strategies evolve.

During Black Monday, the severe limitations of portfolio insurance in coping with tail events of extreme volatility were exposed. While this kind of formalized computer trading was better controlled afterwards, the risks associated with arbitrage were exposed again

during the LTCM crisis. The need to adjust exposures rapidly (such as on swap spreads and on options) exaggerated the breaking down of the normal price relationships between instruments, thus increasing losses and the need for participants to close positions at fire-sale prices. Strict Value-at-Risk exposure limits and simple stop-loss rules also tend to provoke sales in a price-insensitive manner, and this experience has led some risk managers to reassess the need for flexibility in the application of such rules (or at least in their timing).[18]

The control of counterparty exposures can exacerbate developments during a crisis. Black Monday focused attention on counterparty exposures in equity markets and exchange-traded futures contracts, as well as in bank clearing systems. It helped launch initiatives for wider use of collateral and netting. Meanwhile, in the LTCM crisis, counterparty exposure problems surfaced in a new range of markets, such as over-the-counter (OTC) derivatives and in transactions with hedge funds. This has led to tighter collateral and netting practices, such as larger haircuts, and greater emphasis on "know-your-customer" procedures. It is important not to use collateral as the only safeguard; in Japan, the widespread use of real estate and equity collateral, on the assumption that valuations were robust, gave false comfort.

Notwithstanding improvements in risk management, several questions are unresolved, carrying the potential to amplify volatilities during crises:
- Banks and other financial institutions (including particularly large and complex institutions) have greatly strengthened the measurement and management of consolidated counterparty and other credit exposures, including their monitoring of hedge funds. But the official sector needs to continue to identify remaining gaps (such as in

---

[18]For a dissenting view, see Jorion (2002).

consolidated supervision of banking and insurance operations), and vulnerabilities, some of which can result from differences or lack of coordination and information-sharing between national supervisory systems.

• The highly concentrated nature of the OTC derivatives business exposes the market to the risk of failure of a major dealer, although market participants contend that collateralization and netting agreements cover most of the risk. In the absence of public information about derivatives exposures, it is unclear how quickly exposures could grow in the event of a major market movement.

• In the current low-yield environment, historical volatilities of fixed-income returns have been relatively modest, and participants may have been tempted to move to riskier assets to improve yield. Market risk measurement, including through Value at Risk (VaR), has become much more sophisticated. But participants must not rely too heavily on historical relationships, such as volatilities and correlations, for risk management, because a sudden shift to a higher-yield environment is unlikely to follow historical statistical patterns. Appropriate stress tests should be conducted because, if VaR limits are rigidly applied, many participants using similar VaR techniques could simultaneously try to close their positions in a falling market.

• The focus on internal and external ratings in the Basel II proposals, while generally helpful, carries the risk of procyclical increases in lending during a boom and reductions in lending if the credit environment deteriorates. As with market risk measures, too abrupt an implementation of tighter limits risks increasing volatility during a downturn.

• While banks and securities firms have improved their risk management, including dispersing risks by selling them to others, there are potential questions about the sophistication of risk management elsewhere in the system. Some have suggested that insurance companies have taken on credit risk from banks because, by using different risk methodologies, insurers estimate credit risks as being lower than banks do, and because their regulatory capital requirements for investment risks may be less demanding. A buildup of credit risk leverage in the insurance and other sectors could amplify volatility in the event of a rapid reevaluation of risks—these concerns are related to the debate about fair-value accounting (see below).

Aligning Incentive Structures

The bursting of the TMT equity bubble demonstrated the importance of aligning market participants' incentives with the goals of stable and efficient markets and avoiding short-termism. Compensation packages for corporate managers often encouraged short-termism, including bonuses and stock options tied to near-term performance. Practices are now changing (partly because of changes in accounting treatment). For instance, some companies have started instead to issue shares with long-term lock-up provisions to executives. Possible conflicts of interest by stock market analysts and other participants undoubtedly accentuated the bubble and the resulting crash and have contributed to the lingering uncertainty about underlying company performance that is helping to keep equity volatility high. The corporate governance issues this raised have started to be addressed. Index-tracking by institutional investors and the short-term focus on meeting quarterly earnings targets by corporate managers, analysts, and fund managers can lead to herd behavior, leading investors not to question the majority market view during a boom and thus heightening the risk of an abrupt change in market views.

Looking ahead, a number of issues still need to be addressed:

- More needs to be done to encourage longer-term incentive structures for corporate managers. For instance, greater use of executive compensation packages that are vested only after, say, a three-year performance record would help to reduce short-termism. But the underlying tendency for markets to focus excessively on quarterly earnings figures remains a difficulty.
- While corporate governance is being strengthened in the wake of the TMT equity bubble, the process of agreeing new standards both within countries and internationally will inevitably be complex (especially when relating to accounting) and will last a number of years. The sharper focus on underlying earnings, removing some of the distortions of profit-smoothing, and recognizing previously hidden factors such as stock options and pension fund valuation changes, will be helpful. However, a balance needs to be found between avoiding artificial smoothing and creating spurious volatility through rigid application of fair-value accounting.[19]
- The prevalence of index-tracking and benchmarking among portfolio managers could be seen as reducing the risk of amplifying sales into falling markets, by leading investors to continue to hold their positions during downturns. However, it could also amplify volatility. First, it could lead institutional investors not to conduct due diligence during market rallies (for instance, the sharp gains of TMT stocks forced index-trackers to hold heavy weightings in those sectors). Second, there could be a sudden shift away from pure index-tracking when the market turns down, for instance if investors simultaneously shift portfolios into cash, reinforced by fund managers trying to match asset allocations in their peer group. It remains unclear, however, whether there is much the official sector can (or should) do to address this.

- It is now better recognized that conflicts of interest within investment banks can amplify volatilities by encouraging investment booms and hampering full risk assessment. The public attention suggests that conflicts of interest will be dampened at least for a while, not only through regulation but through banks' desire to protect their reputations. But standards have by no means been raised uniformly and the risk that these conflicts could shift to less heavily regulated companies exists.

Enhancing Transparency

The need for transparency was a particular lesson from the 1998 crisis. Globally this was reflected in the new international financial architecture, and of particular importance to the mature markets were topics such as increased disclosure by hedge funds, at least to their counterparties. The other episodes also raised transparency issues. The Japanese and TMT equity bubbles highlighted the need for bank and corporate sector balance sheet transparency and accuracy, not just so that counterparties and analysts have meaningful information but also so that the reporting institutions themselves operate under the right economic incentives.

Transparency could be further strengthened in several areas:

- Measuring risk concentrations and leverage during normal market times reduces the danger that a sudden realization of the scale of positions during a crisis could lead to destructive simultaneous attempts to unwind exposures. While reporting and disclosure in OTC markets are being improved, more needs to be done to the market's ability to assess aggregate levels of exposures in the related areas of derivatives, offshore centers, Special Purpose Vehicles, and hedge funds.

---

[19]A Banque de France discussion paper (2001) suggested that full fair-value accounting, in particular of banking books, would further amplify credit cycles.

- More broadly, the process of making corporate balance sheets more transparent and meaningful involves complex issues. One area where difficult judgments need to be made is "fair-value" accounting, and particularly how it relates to longer-term investments by financial institutions such as insurance firms and pension funds. It is important to give the public a transparent measure of institutions' financial situations in existing market conditions, while avoiding excessive focus on the balance sheet impact from short-term volatility. Moving to fair-value accounting for insurance companies could likely harden minimum capital requirements, for example, and could risk amplifying volatility.

- There may be scope for some middle ground in the fair-value accounting debate to achieve an appropriate level of transparency, while smoothing the more extreme effects of marking to market. This could avoid unwarranted market reactions from disclosures or premature supervisory requirements to sell assets during market downturns. Ways could be sought to make "fair values" more stable, help analysts interpret the sensitivity of the results to market values, or use appropriately gradual periods for adjusting holdings to stay within regulatory standards. For instance, market prices could be averaged over a relatively short period, supplemental accounting information could illustrate the dependence of headline data on the assumptions made—particularly on the liability side—or regulatory limits could use more stable valuation measures or appropriately long adjustment periods.

Improving Market Infrastructure

Lessons about financial infrastructure have tended to progress from formal, centralized, markets to less formal markets, such as over-the-counter transactions. The 1987 crash and Japanese bubble highlighted the importance of collateralization, netting, and other aspects of payments and settlement systems in stock markets, exchange-traded derivatives markets, and banking systems. By 1998, similar issues were highlighted in the OTC international bond and derivative markets, resulting in tightening of practices and contractual standards. By contrast (or perhaps, rather, as a consequence) these topics were less of an issue in the aftermath of the TMT equity bubble. Currently work continues in such areas as derivatives documentation, refinement of payments and settlement systems, and central clearinghouses.

Finding the Balance Between Market Discipline and Regulation

In many respects markets functioned reasonably well during the case studies illustrated. Indeed it could be argued that the financial instability in mature markets in the 1987 stock market crash and the LTCM crisis was encouragingly short-lived. In the Japanese and TMT equity bubbles, it was perhaps not the speed but the size of the market fall that caused the main problems.

In considering the degree to which new policy efforts are needed, it is important to strike a balance between regulation and allowing market forces to work. The predisposition should perhaps be not to impose extra restrictions or requirements unless a solid case is made that there is a market failure to be addressed. But the markets will continue to innovate, and regulators need to innovate with them. Some innovations will be direct responses by participants seeking less regulated alternatives as regulators become more sophisticated in monitoring existing markets and controlling leverage and risk. The challenge for regulators is to reach the optimum trade-off between regulation and market discipline. Experience shows that in many areas, self-regulation is not enough. Participants are often too close to events and insufficiently independent to be able to see what is needed for the big picture of stability. At the same time, regulators need to work with participants to think through the likely changes in market behavior that would result from new regulations.

Future Work

Of all the areas of debate described above, the question of "fair-value" accounting perhaps best crystallizes the need to balance the requirement for continuously updated risk measurement and control against not inducing price-insensitive sales of positions to stay within limits during a crisis. There are no easy answers, but policymakers and market participants should find a solution that considers the systemic need to avoid amplifying market volatility, while still keeping close and timely control of risks at individual institutions. It would be preferable to learn the lessons on finding this middle ground from past financial crises rather than from the next one.

Future editions of the GFSR will return to other aspects of volatility and the policy reform agenda. Potential topics for examination include:

- the volatility of flows in mature markets, to complement this analysis of price volatility;
- the balance between regulation and market discipline, and possible trade-offs between transparency of mark-to-market values and volatility; and
- the implications of these subjects for the current reform agenda, including potential procyclical effects associated with Basel II and with "fair-value" accounting for the insurance and pension fund industry.

Appendix: Case Studies

The "Black Monday" Stock Market Crash of 1987

Initial Macroeconomic and Business Conditions

A dollar stabilization policy set out by the Plaza Accord in 1985 and Louvre Accord in early 1987, combined with steady growth in U.S. economic activity, led to increased confidence in U.S. financial assets, which fueled the stock market boom. Leveraged M&A activity led to stock retirements and takeover premiums, which strongly promoted the upsurge in stock prices. At the same time, however, the United States was running increasingly large trade and fiscal deficits. Financial deregulation in other countries, especially Japan, helped finance the U.S. trade deficit. In the first half of 1987, foreign institutions bought as large a volume of U.S. equities as domestic institutions. Many of these foreign investors had weak risk management capabilities and relied on U.S. institutions to manage their funds.

Crisis Trigger

In early October 1987 a disagreement between G-5 authorities on the appropriate stance of monetary policy unsettled markets and led to market speculation that the Louvre Accord was breaking down. On October 14, 1987, the announcement of the unexpectedly large August trade deficit depressed the dollar and sent U.S. bond yields up. Equities thus became less attractive to foreign investors and also less attractive relative to bonds. On the same day, legislation was filed in Congress to eliminate tax benefits from the financing of corporate takeovers. In response, arbitrage traders started to sell shares in takeover candidates, which had led the earlier market rally.

Market Price Reaction

In the seven days after October 14 the Dow Jones Industrial Average fell by 31 percent, including 23 percent on October 19, 1987, the largest one-day fall in its history. The correlation between U.S. bond and stock prices turned suddenly negative amid a flight to quality. Bid-ask spreads widened, and at times liquidity evaporated altogether. The equity price falls and overall volatility rapidly spread around the world, as correlations between national stock markets rose sharply.

Amplifying Factors

The use of *portfolio insurance* strategies by a number of major institutional investors amplified the speed of stock price falls. Portfolio insurance uses computer models to protect equity portfolio values in a falling market by selling stock index futures automatically. This selling drove stock index futures prices down and created price gaps between futures and the underlying stocks, which gave index arbitrageurs an opportunity to profit by simultaneously buying futures and selling stocks. This arbitrage transferred the selling pressure from the futures market back to the stock market. The ensuing stock price falls triggered further programmed selling of index futures, with additional pressure on spot equity prices. Only a handful of large market players were responsible for much of the selling pressure.

Foreign investors also amplified the market decline as the dollar's fall prompted them to close U.S. equity positions.

Complexity and fragmentation of clearing systems for stocks, futures, and options created delay and confusion over payments of margin calls triggered by stock price falls, raising concern over the solvency of securities brokers and the ability of exchange clearinghouses to make payments. Banks quickly restricted lending to brokers. The consequent illiquidity and worries that participants would make forced sales to meet margin payments further amplified the market price falls and increased the flight to quality.

Responses by the Market and by the Official Sector

In response to mounting fear of a systemic breakdown, the Federal Reserve announced that it was ready to provide ample liquidity to the U.S. financial system. The Fed's action helped restore banks' confidence and thus maintain the supply of funding to brokers and market makers and avoid payments failures. Banks, which had little direct exposure to equities and therefore remained strong,

worked as a conduit for the Fed to coordinate orderly securities clearings. As a result, market functions were recovered rapidly. Nevertheless, the "flight to quality" shift of investments from stocks to bonds persisted for some time after the crash. Authorities in other countries also supplied short-term liquidity in response to the spillover to their own financial systems, but in more limited fashion than in the United States. Continental European central banks, in particular, kept monetary policy on a more even keel.

Large investors moved away from computer-generated portfolio insurance as a hedging tool, as they learned of its limitations during large market movements.

The Fed improved payment systems and stocks, futures, and option clearing systems were integrated, introducing delivery versus payment and the use of collateral. Since then, market participants as well as official bodies have developed more extensive collateralization and netting systems throughout the financial markets that could reduce the need for large margin calls in the midst of market turbulence. The Fed was also empowered to lend directly to securities brokers in case of emergency.

The securities regulators introduced circuit breaker mechanisms such as price limits, position limits, volume limits, and trading halts.

Recommendations for greater disclosure focused on payment systems positions. Although portfolio insurance standing orders had been large and undisclosed, there was no real move to try to encourage extra disclosure of participants' positions.

Although market confidence was temporarily damaged, the steady recovery in equity prices after the crash (within two years the Dow Jones index was back above its pre-crash level) restored many institutional investors' belief that equities were the highest returning asset in the long run. Incentives, based on past performance, to weight long-term portfolios toward equities therefore remained in place, especially in the United

States, United Kingdom, and a number of other countries.

Bursting of Japan's Equity and Real Estate Bubble in 1990

Initial Macroeconomic and Business Conditions

In the aftermath of the Louvre Accord, the Bank of Japan kept interest rates down to support the value of the dollar and to boost Japan's domestic economy, stimulating demand for equities. Easy monetary conditions encouraged leveraged investment, aggressive equity financing, and excessive borrowing based on inflated land collateral. Restrictions on land sales limited the supply of land and drove up land prices, and banks took greater risks, mostly through real-estate-related lending. Rapid bank credit expansion, supported by bank equity issues that increased lending capacity and by unrealized gains from banks' stockholdings, further fueled the stock and real-estate market boom. Cross-shareholdings (i.e., double-gearing), historical cost accounting, and insufficient disclosure contributed to weakening market discipline in an atmosphere of widespread optimism. Starting in May 1989, concerns over inflation led the Bank of Japan to progressively increase the official discount rate.

Crisis Trigger

Excessive price-earnings ratios and the successive official discount rate rises during 1989 started to concern the equity market. As long-term interest rates spiked up in early 1990, and equity futures began to fall, arbitrage between cash stocks and futures transmitted the downward pressure to the stock market.

Market Price Reaction

From February 20 to April 5, 1990, the Nikkei index dropped 23 percent, even though the S&P and European indices rose, then fell further, this time in line with other markets. From December 31, 1989 to its low in October 1990, the index fell almost 50 per-cent, and continued to drift down in the decade that followed. Neither bond yields nor any cross-market correlations responded immediately. Land prices continued to rise for a while, but reacted sharply to the lending limits on real-estate-related industries set by the Ministry of Finance in April 1990. By the fall of 1990, land prices were falling nation-wide. Bond-equity correlations remained positive until 1993. Lack of liquidity and infrequent settlement cycles, as well as inflation concerns, inhibited the use of government bonds as a safe haven.

Amplifying Factors

The stock market falls were amplified by portfolio insurance products and by arbitrage activities between stock and futures markets—the same mechanism as in Black Monday—as well as by unwinding of margin trading.

Lending based on land and, to a lesser extent, equities as collateral amplified Japan's financial bubble and the subsequent burst. When equity prices began falling, initially investors shifted their funds out of the stock market into land investments and bank deposits, which boosted banks' lending against land collateral. The "land myth" that land prices would never fall and "bank myth" that banks would never fail created a widespread false belief that land and banks were a safe haven, even after the stock market collapse began.

Financial risks started to accumulate in banks' balance sheets. Due to long-term relationships, banks did not wind down stock-holdings or, after land prices began falling, loans collateralized on land. Historical cost accounting and inadequate disclosure allowed banks to defer losses stemming from stock falls and recognition of nonperforming loans. Nevertheless, the continued slide in land and stock prices gradually eroded banks' economic capital. Ineffective unwinding of impaired assets aggravated the crisis by leading to credit contraction and contributing to recession and deflation.

*Responses by the Market and by
the Official Sector*

Initially, the continued strong economic and monetary growth led the Bank of Japan to continue tightening monetary policy even though stock prices were collapsing. The Bank of Japan eventually began easing monetary policy in August 1991 but a substantial amount of funds flowed into the government bond market for safety. Continued land and stock price declines further weakened the balance sheets of the banks and corporations despite further monetary easing and fiscal expansion. Eventually in February 1999, to abate deflationary pressures, the Bank of Japan adopted the zero interest rate policy.

On the structural front, a series of deregulations was introduced to improve the efficiency of the financial system and the government promoted financial consolidation. Mark-to-market accounting was introduced and several agencies were established by the government to purchase nonperforming loans (NPLs) and shares held by banks.

But, amid weak capital and low profitability, low interest rates and deposit guarantees allowed banks to delay costly debt restructuring. Delays in debt restructuring created more NPLs than banks' operating profits can absorb. Cross-shareholdings also made it difficult for banks to sell devalued stocks, and thus left banks highly vulnerable to equity prices. Consequently, the financial system became more fragile to the point that some banks required injections of public capital.

Failure of LTCM in 1998[20]

Initial Macroeconomic and Business Conditions

In the mid-to-late 1990s, most mature economies, especially the United States, grew steadily in a low inflationary environment. The belief that the U.S. economy had entered a new age of high productivity growth, financial globalization and the successful process toward EMU, and continued flows of funds into the United States and other mature equity and bond markets supported a long-lasting appreciation of asset prices. However, weakening counterparty credit standards, complacent risk management, and lack of disclosure by hedge funds allowed firms such as LTCM to build up highly leveraged positions that were not appreciated by the market and that in some areas amplified the asset price appreciation. Instead of controlling the size of their positions with hedge funds, counterparties relied heavily on collateralization of mark-to-market exposures to control risks.

Crisis Trigger

In August 1998, Russia's unilateral debt restructuring triggered a global reversal of the excessive narrowing in credit spreads. Unwinding convergence plays put selling pressures on mature market securities that had been used as collateral in leveraged positions in GKOs and other emerging market asset positions. By mid-September, the rapidly mounting margin requirements pushed LTCM to the brink of collapse.

Market Price Reaction

Market stories of LTCM's weakness contributed to the swap spread widening in the week of August 17 and equity option volatility increases in the week of August 24. Spreads between older ("off-the-run") and benchmark treasuries widened by up to 35 basis points as the sell-off of off-the-run issues caused their liquidity to evaporate, while there was a flight-to-quality into benchmark bonds. U.S. and other government yields dropped from September 29 to October 6. The principal equity markets sold off jointly and bond-equity correlations turned negative in the United

---

[20]See IMF (1998) for more details.

States, United Kingdom, and Germany, reflecting further flight-to-quality. As margin calls spread to other hedge fund positions, the dollar dropped by 17 percent against the yen from October 6 to 8.

Amplifying Factors

The key amplifier in the LTCM episode was leverage. LTCM engaged in credit spread plays based on the leveraging of on- and off-balance-sheet positions (though reportedly later also took some directional positions, particularly on equity volatility). LTCM levered up its positions by short-selling lower-yielding high-quality assets and using the proceeds to take long positions in riskier assets (mortgage-backed securities, mature market junk bonds). It also repoed assets and invested the proceeds in other relatively high-yield assets, including derivative contracts. LTCM's balance sheet positions totaled about $120 billion at the beginning of 1998, compared with a capital base of $4.8 billion. At the same time, LTCM held $1.3 trillion gross notional value of off-balance-sheet derivative positions.

Major counterparties, because of competitive pressures, did not require initial margins for derivative contracts and took no haircut on repo transactions, and this allowed LTCM to build up high leverage with relatively little capital. Lack of transparency about hedge fund activities and failure by many other market participants to adequately monitor counterparty and market risks further allowed LTCM and others to build up leverage.

Once the crisis began, LTCM's attempts to unwind its positions amplified the volatility. The Russian crisis, at first, widened credit spreads. LTCM responded to the resulting margin calls by liquidating some of its most liquid positions. However, the selling pressure pushed down the prices of underlying assets and widened credit spreads further. This spiral gradually forced LTCM to liquidate less liquid positions at losses. The unwinding process was also accentuated by the fact that many of

its counterparties, and other market participants, took on similar leveraged positions and also faced selling pressures.

Responses by the Market and by the Official Sector

Concerned that a forced liquidation of LTCM's complex positions could produce major market disruptions and possible counterparty failures among systemically important institutions, the Federal Reserve orchestrated a coordinated resolution of LTCM by its creditors. Fourteen major creditors and counterparties of LTCM agreed to take over its management and inject $3.6 billion to manage its orderly unwinding. This coordinated effort prevented a chain reaction of distressed sales of positions and possible failures that could have further disrupted U.S. and international capital markets. The Fed did not contribute funds to LTCM's resolution, and instead provided liquidity to the wider money market to ensure orderly clearing of securities transactions and deter panic sales.

Learning from these lessons, financial supervisors in the United States and elsewhere put more emphasis on internal risk controls and risk assessment, and encouraged banks to intensify monitoring of their borrowers' financial status (see IMF, 1999). Many mature market supervisors have intensified market surveillance. Due to the global repercussions of the LTCM incident and related problems from the financial crisis, the G-7 established the Financial Stability Forum to improve cross-border and cross-market cooperation of official agencies in identifying incipient vulnerabilities. The Basel Committee on Bank Supervision published guidance on sound practice for banks' interaction with highly leveraged institutions (HLIs). Internationally active banks strengthened monitoring of HLIs and improved counterparty risk and collateral management. The growing understanding of the need to diversify credit risks also spurred the growth of new financial products, such as credit derivatives.

Market Conditions Following the TMT Equity Bubble Collapse

Macroeconomic and Business Conditions

The long period of global economic growth in the 1990s supported strong investment and consumption spending—financed to a large extent by debt—and the surge in equity prices. Information technology (IT) innovation led to euphoria about the "new economy," strong sustained productivity gains, and exuberant expectations of long-term growth in demand and profits, especially in the TMT sector. Deregulated energy and communications markets created opportunities for rapid business growth. The dotcom boom was also fuelled by the prospect of lucrative initial public offerings or takeovers by established companies.

Crisis Trigger

A developing investment and inventory overhang and overcapacities, particularly in the fast-rising telecom and IT industries, gave rise to a reassessment of business models and of projections for long-term earnings. Against this background, a sharp drop in profits for companies in these sectors in early 2002 combined with increasing nervousness about valuation levels of stocks led TMT stocks to begin falling.

Market Price Reaction

A far slower process of risk aversion has emerged through the process of unwinding the TMT equity bubble. The NASDAQ fell 32 percent from its open on March 27 to its close on April 14, 2000, the start of a long slide that ultimately took this technology-related index down 78 percent from early 2000 to late 2002. Deepening and widening interactions included a decline in the broader U.S. and European indices starting in the second half of 2000. Successive equity lows created deeper uncertainty, culminating in the equity lows of mid-to-late 2002 (for the broader markets, the largest cumulative equity decline since the mid-1970s) when equity volatilities peaked, and credit spreads reached highs not seen in over a decade. Bond-equity correlations in the United States and the United Kingdom turned negative and remained so from early in 2000, reflecting flight-to-quality. In Germany and Japan bond-equity correlations turned sharply negative in the fall.

Amplifying Factors

Leverage taken on, particularly by energy and telecommunications companies, amplified the TMT equity bubble. Many issuers in these newly deregulated sectors were able to remain highly rated and raise large amounts of debt. Meanwhile others were able to raise large amounts in the high-yield market.

Moreover, attempts were made by others in the corporate sector to match the apparent equity results of high-tech sectors by financial leverage, including venture capital investments in dotcom companies and telecom companies. Weak corporate governance and internal controls allowed many companies to reward their managers with stock options and other benefits, sometimes tempting managers to manipulate short-term earnings. Conflicts of interest and governance problems at investment banks led to abuses, such as misleadingly optimistic analyst reports and allocations of IPO stock to insiders.

During the boom, many insurance and pension fund investors tended to automatically purchase equity and debt in proportion to the market to remain close to index weightings. This helped to sustain the boom, although these investors were not highly leveraged and therefore did not come under pressure to sell quickly once the bubble burst.

Nevertheless, during the post-bubble period, gradual sales of equities by insurers to preserve their capital strength and meet regulatory requirements as their asset portfolio values fell contributed to equity market declines.

Bank lending began to decline, reflecting the shared assessment by syndicated lenders in late 2000 that some lending had been excessive. The commercial paper market contracted sharply, cutting off new funding and requiring repayments in response to market rumors, starting in 2001. Subsequently, headline bankruptcies at Enron (2001) and WorldCom (2002) led to large investor losses and a loss of confidence in the accuracy of reported corporate results. During this later period lower corporate investment and GDP growth, combined with the events of September 11, 2001, and the uncertainties leading up to the Iraq war, kept the equity falls going.

Responses by the Market and by the Official Sector

The robust banking system worked as a conduit of liquidity to securities brokers. Although banks had facilitated corporate fund-raising, they had managed to control their risks, including by taking a cautious attitude toward equity investments, selling credit products on to other investors, or by otherwise reducing exposure through devices such as credit derivatives.

Businesses themselves, facing a cash squeeze, began aggressively improving their cash flow starting in early 2001. Investment spending dropped precipitously, liquidity cushions were built up, and the maturity of borrowing extended. Corporate bond markets were willing to fund companies based on case-by-case examination of the names, resulting in a surge in bond issues in 2001.

As longer-term policy responses, authorities in the United States and other financial centers took measures to strengthen corporate governance and accounting and auditing standards. The Sarbanes-Oxley Act of 2002 created the Public Company Accounting Oversight Board, required new rules dealing with analyst conflicts of interest, strengthened corporate governance and disclosure, and limited insider transactions and loans to executives. The New York Stock Exchange and NASDAQ are taking steps to tighten corporate governance standards and place more empha-sis on independent directors. The U.S. financial supervisors now require financial conglomerates to separate research and investment banking.

References

Banque de France, 2001, "Financial Cycle: Factors of Amplification and Policy Implications," Banque de France Bulletin No. 95 (Paris, November).

Bordo, Michael D., Barry Eichengreen, and Douglas Irwin, 1999, "Is Globalization Today Really Different Than Globalization a Hundred Years Ago?" NBER Working Paper No. 7195 (Cambridge, Mass.: National Bureau of Economic Research).

Campbell, John, Martin Lettau, Burton G. Malkiel, and Yexiao Xu, 2001, "Have Individual Stocks Become More Volatile? An Empirical Explorations of Idiosyncratic Risk," *Journal of Finance*, Vol. 56 (February), pp. 1–43.

Campbell, John, Andrew Lo, and A. Craig MacKinlay, 1997, *The Econometrics of Financial Markets* (Princeton: Princeton University Press).

Chakrabarti, Rajesh, and Richard Roll, 2002, "East Asia and Europe during the 1997 Asian Collapse: A Clinical Study of a Financial Crisis," *Journal of Financial Markets*, Vol. 5 (January), pp. 1–30.

Crockett, Andrew, 1997a, "The Theory and Practice of Financial Stability," Essays in International Finance No. 203 (Princeton: Princeton University, Department of Economics).

———, 1997b, "Why Is Financial Stability a Goal of Public Policy?" in *Maintaining Financial Stability in a Global Economy: A Symposium Sponsored by the Federal Reserve Bank of Kansas City* (Federal Reserve Bank of Kansas City), pp. 7–36.

Davis, E. Philip, 2002, "A Typology of Financial Instability," *Financial Stability Review 2* (Vienna: Osterreichische Nationalbank), pp. 92–110.

———, 2003, "Comparing Bear Markets—1973 and 2000," *National Institute Economic Review*, No. 183 (January), pp. 78–89.

De Bandt, Olivier, and Philipp Hartmann, 2000, "Systemic Risk: A Survey," European Central Bank Working Paper No. 35 (Frankfurt: ECB).

Erb, Claude, Campbell R. Harvey, and Tadas E. Viskanta, 1994, "Forecasting International Equity

Correlations," *Financial Analysts Journal*, Vol. 50 (November–December), pp. 32–45.

Forbes, Kristin, and Roberto Rigobon, 2001, "Measuring Contagion: Conceptual and Empirical Issues" in *International Financial Contagion*, ed. by S. Claessens and K. Forbes (Boston: Kluwer Academic Publishers).

Hamilton, James, 1994, *Time Series Analysis* (Princeton: Princeton University Press) .

———, and Gang Lin, 1996, "Stock Market Volatility and the Business Cycle," *Journal of Applied Econometrics*, Vol. 11 (Sept.–Oct.) pp. 573–93.

IMF, 1998, *World Economic Outlook and International Capital Markets Interim Assessment*, World Economic and Financial Surveys (Washington).

———, 1999, *International Capital Markets: Developments, Prospects and Key Policy Issues*, World Economic and Financial Surveys (Washington).

———, 2002, *World Economic Outlook*, World Economic and Financial Surveys (Washington, April).

Jorion, Philippe, 2002, "Fallacies About the Effects of Market Risk Management Systems," *Financial Stability Review*, Issue No. 13, December (London: Bank of England).

Officer, Robert R., 1973, "The Variability of the Market Factor of the New York Stock Exchange," *Journal of Business*, Vol. 46, pp. 434–53.

Schwartz, Anna, 1985, "Real and Pseudo-Financial Crises," in *Financial Crises and the World Banking System*, ed. by Forrest Capie and Geoffrey Wood (New York: St. Martin's).

Schwert, G. William, 1989, "Why Does Stock Market Volatility Change Over Time?" *Journal of Finance*, Vol. 44 (December) pp. 1129–55.

Stivers, Chris, Licheng Sun, and Robert Connolly, 2002, "Stock Implied Volatility, Stock Turnover, and the Stock-Bond Return Relation," Federal Reserve Bank of Atlanta Working Paper No. 2002–3a (Atlanta).

Whaley, Robert, 2000, "The Investor Fear Gauge" *Journal of Portfolio Management*, Vol. 26 (Spring) pp. 12–17.

CHAPTER IV

VOLATILITY OF PRIVATE CAPITAL FLOWS TO EMERGING MARKETS

Since 1990, private capital flows have far exceeded official loans and grants to became the dominant source of external funding for many emerging market countries. The terms and conditions under which these countries access international capital markets thus weigh heavily on economic performance. This chapter focuses on one key aspect of the relationship between emerging markets and international capital markets—namely, the degree of stability of access to international capital markets as measured by the volatility of capital flows. As discussed in Chapter III, volatility is an inherent feature of capital markets and is not necessarily undesirable. Some measured volatility in capital flows can be expected in the presence of, for example, a seasonal pattern in trade financing. However, there were periods in the 1990s when the volatility of capital flows was associated with a sudden loss of access to international capital markets by many emerging markets countries. This loss of access was at times associated with political and economic forces in individual emerging markets. Sometimes, however, it has been developments in mature markets that resulted in restricted market access for many emerging markets. An unexpected and sustained loss of market access can naturally impose high costs in terms of adjustments of policies and incomes.

The experience with volatility in private capital flows to emerging markets has raised a number of questions. Exactly how volatile have private capital flows been since 1990, and how does this volatility compare with that in other periods of large private capital flows? Which countries and regions have been most affected by such volatility, and how have emerging markets responded to it? What have been the key factors in both emerging and mature markets that have contributed to the volatility of capital flows? Are these factors likely to persist in the near term and how would they affect emerging markets as an asset class?

This chapter provides some answers to these questions. The chapter first characterizes the pattern and volatility of capital flows to emerging markets, showing the coexistence of low-frequency swings (or boom-bust cycles) in some components of flows with higher frequency fluctuations in other components. A notable feature of the behavior of the low-frequency analysis is the fact that emerging markets have become net capital exporters since 1999, and that the volatility of net flows in the 1990s has been much lower than that of the previous historical period of financial integration—the classical gold standard era. We also show that the high-frequency volatility of flows increased in the second half of the 1990s as compared to the first half. A second section of the chapter focuses on some of the key structural determinants of the boom-bust pattern and higher volatility of capital flows, in particular the changing role of international banks and the investor base for emerging market securities. The chapter concludes with an assessment of whether these structural changes in the behavior of the main suppliers of funds to emerging markets are likely to be permanent—hence causing the current bust phase of flows to persist—or transitory. It also discusses the main policies that borrowing countries have adopted to cope with the changing pattern and volatility of capital flows.

Pattern and Volatility of Flows

The pattern and volatility of private capital flows can be examined by using data on either

Figure 4.1. Net Private Capital Flows to Emerging Markets
(In billions of U.S. dollars)

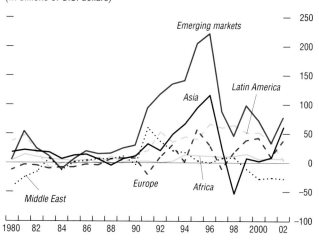

Source: IMF, *World Economic Outlook.*

Figure 4.2. Emerging Markets: Net Private Capital Flows by Component
(In billions of U.S. dollars)

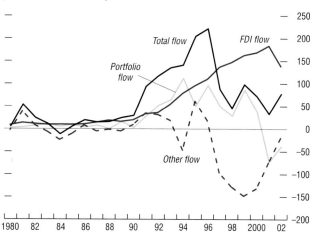

Source: IMF, *World Economic Outlook.*

net capital flows to emerging markets or gross issuance of international bonds, equities, and syndicated loans by these countries. Net capital flows are most representative of the net transfer of resources to emerging markets through the capital account of the balance of payments. However, the data on net capital flows from the IMF's *World Economic Outlook* are available only on an annual frequency. While such annual data can be used to identify major trends and cycles in capital flows, this data cannot be used to determine exactly when "sudden stops" in capital flows have occurred within any given year. Nevertheless, the analysis of such sudden stops can be undertaken using higher frequency, complementary data on gross issuance of international bonds, equities, and syndicated loans by emerging markets; these data are available on a weekly basis.

Net Private Capital Flows

The volatility of net private capital flows to emerging markets since 1990 can be examined from the perspective of the overall level of the flows, the various subcomponents (such as foreign direct investment), and the regional distribution of the flows. Starting from their lowest level of the 1990s, overall net private capital flows experienced a sharp cyclical upswing until 1996—peaking at about $222 billion in that year. Subsequently, private flows declined and fluctuated around $70 billion annually (Figure 4.1). Overall net private capital flows during 1990–96 were over five times the level of flows for the whole of the 1980s.

The hump-shaped pattern of overall flows, however, masked important differences in the volatility of the regional flows and of the various components of total flows. Asia received most of the capital inflows up to 1996 but then suffered a large decline after the financial crisis of 1997. Although inflows to Latin America were relatively stable during the Asian and the Russian crises, they declined sharply in 2002 following the Argentina default. While European emerging markets

Table 4.1. Changes in Bank Exposures to Emerging Markets
(In billions of U.S. dollars)

	1990	1991	1992	1993	1994	1995	1996	1997	1998	1999	2000	2001	2002
Developing countries	17.7	8.1	51.1	0.3	47.2	112.9	109.8	72.7	−53.2	−66.1	−33.0	−30.8	8.7
Africa and Middle East	3.6	−12.1	11.5	−10.8	5.9	−6.4	−3.3	18.3	25.5	−3.4	−10.6	8.6	2.2
Asia and Pacific	36.3	16.2	23.4	17.1	50.9	88.4	74.8	1.7	−81.7	−48.0	−36.3	−16.8	−3.3
Europe	2.5	1.6	3.8	−6.2	−13.7	13.3	11.4	22.6	9.5	−0.6	9.4	−18.2	21.1
Latin America/Caribbean	−24.7	2.4	12.4	0.1	4.1	17.6	26.9	30.0	−6.6	−14.2	4.5	−4.4	−11.3

Source: Bank for International Settlements (BIS).

had more limited but volatile inflows, Africa experienced the smallest inflows of any region. Inflows to the Middle East were strong in the beginning of the decade but then declined and, beginning in 1999, turned into a capital outflow, possibly because of the uncertain security situation in the region or the investment of oil revenues offshore.

The volatility of the individual components of net capital flows varied greatly (Figure 4.2). A prominent feature of flows in the 1990s was the resilience of foreign direct investment (FDI) even during periods of major crises. FDI to emerging markets rose from $19 billion in 1990 to its peak of about $183 billion in 2001. However, FDI fell by about 25 percent in 2002. Almost 70 percent of the decline was due to reduced flows to Latin America, where recessions plagued several countries and the pace of privatization slowed. Moreover, only a few countries (Brazil, China, the Czech Republic, India, and Mexico) accounted for more than half of total FDI flows between 1990 and 2002.

Net portfolio investment, consisting of net equity and bond flows, was the second most important source of financing for emerging markets from 1990 through 2002 but it too remained volatile. In contrast, net bank lending (the main component of "other flows" in Figure 4.2) has been contracting since the Asian crisis (Table 4.1). While the decline in net bank lending was most pronounced for Asia, owing to the retrenchment by Japanese

banks, it was evident in varying degrees in all other emerging markets as well.

Another notable feature of net flows between emerging markets and international capital markets is that emerging markets as a whole have become capital exporters since 1999 (Table 4.2). The reduced level of net private capital flows to emerging markets has resulted in a more than offsetting increase in current account surpluses, as countries increased their foreign exchange reserves (Figure 4.3). Indeed, only Latin America remained a capital-importing region, albeit on a much reduced scale. As a result of the net capital exports in 1999–2002, the net resources transferred to emerging markets throughout the period since 1990 have been rather limited. For example, if net resources invested are defined as equal to total net capital inflows to a country less any reserve accumulation, then the cumulative resource invested in emerging markets since 1990 totals about $100 billion, about 1 percent of emerging markets' GDP in 2002 (Figure 4.3).

Given this experience, one key issue is whether net private capital flows have been "excessively" volatile since 1990. As one means of explaining this issue, Table 4.3 provides the coefficients of variation for overall net private capital and the main subcomponents of total flows for four time periods.[1] The time periods are the "1990s" (1991–2002), the "1980s" (1980–1990), the "1970s" (1970–79), and the "classical gold standard period" (1880–1913).

[1]The coefficient of variation equals the standard deviation of the flows during a given period divided by the mean level of the flows.

Table 4.2. Balance of Payments: All Emerging Markets
(In billions of U.S. dollars)

	1990	1991	1992	1993	1994	1995	1996	1997	1998	1999	2000	2001	2002
Emerging markets													
Current account	−24.9	−85.9	−70.2	−110.8	−73.3	−102.7	−94.8	−78.2	−47.4	44.8	134.5	96.1	132.7
Net private flows	29.6	93.7	117.0	135.0	140.9	204.7	221.6	87.7	45.6	98.1	72.0	32.9	77.4
Net official flows	28.5	35.8	25.2	47.7	5.4	28.4	−2.8	56.3	83.0	13.9	−3.9	38.7	25.8
Change in reserves	69.0	74.5	27.5	83.6	92.3	126.0	109.8	69.7	61.0	87.2	98.7	109.1	248.8
Africa													
Current account	−5.6	−6.9	−10.0	−10.8	−11.3	−16.6	−6.2	−6.4	−18.6	−15.6	5.1	−0.3	−8.0
Net private flows	1.3	1.5	−0.6	1.6	12.4	11.3	10.0	8.9	10.4	13.7	4.7	6.0	5.4
Net official flows	5.3	7.0	9.5	6.0	5.1	5.7	−2.2	3.2	4.2	2.0	3.0	1.6	2.2
Change in reserves	4.7	3.6	−3.1	1.5	4.9	2.7	5.4	11.7	−2.2	0.9	12.7	10.2	7.8
Asia													
Current account	0.4	0.7	0.5	−15.1	−5.7	−39.3	−41.5	16.0	115.3	106.3	88.3	90.1	121.0
Net private flows	11.5	32.3	20.8	48.8	66.7	94.9	116.1	23.6	−53.3	7.3	2.4	8.9	60.7
Net official flows	5.1	11.9	10.3	10.1	3.2	4.3	−12.7	17.2	26.1	4.2	3.2	−6.0	−10.1
Change in reserves	47.8	46.4	7.9	44.1	79.3	49.3	61.9	23.9	63.7	80.0	52.0	79.7	182.0
Europe													
Current account	−21.1	3.3	−5.0	−14.1	5.3	−6.2	−15.5	−29.1	−28.5	−4.1	14.1	14.9	8.1
Net private flows	7.5	−20.0	8.5	29.7	0.9	56.1	30.3	−11.1	16.6	37.9	42.1	9.3	36.8
Net official flows	8.2	11.2	2.0	−2.0	−12.3	−6.3	1.3	14.9	32.3	2.1	0.9	22.0	9.0
Change in reserves	2.7	0.8	−1.0	13.4	9.8	41.1	3.0	8.3	5.4	7.0	18.8	13.4	47.5
Middle East													
Current account	2.5	−66.0	−21.1	−24.7	−9.3	−3.2	8.2	8.3	−25.1	14.5	74.6	44.8	28.4
Net private flows	−3.1	60.0	36.7	20.6	17.5	3.4	−0.2	7.6	8.7	−11.0	−27.8	−25.9	−27.6
Net official flows	5.1	−2.0	0.1	2.1	4.4	4.6	6.8	6.4	4.8	5.1	−6.6	−2.5	6.2
Change in reserves	−1.6	5.8	1.0	4.3	2.6	7.8	12.8	11.9	2.7	6.5	12.4	3.5	9.4
Western Hemisphere													
Current account	−1.1	−17.0	−34.6	−46.0	−52.3	−37.4	−39.9	−67.0	−90.5	−56.2	−47.7	−53.3	−16.8
Net private flows	12.4	19.8	51.7	34.2	43.4	39.1	65.3	58.7	63.3	50.2	50.5	34.7	2.1
Net official flows	4.8	7.7	3.2	31.4	5.0	20.0	3.9	14.6	15.5	0.7	−4.3	23.7	18.4
Change in reserves	15.4	17.9	22.7	20.3	−4.2	25.0	26.7	13.8	−8.7	−7.2	2.8	2.3	2.1

Sources: IMF, *International Financial Statistics and World Economic Outlook.*

The 1970s represented the first period since World War II in which net private capital flows played an important role in the external financing of emerging markets. The syndicated bank loan was the principal financing instrument, and major international banks were heavily involved in the recycling of oil revenues. Capital flows during the 1980s were much more limited in scope than in either the 1970s or 1990s and were depressed by the lingering effects of the 1982 debt crisis. The classical gold standard, which lasted roughly from 1880 to 1913, is typically regarded as the longest period of high capital mobility between a set of major capital exporting countries (the United Kingdom and to a lesser extent France and Germany) and a set of "emerging markets."[2]

Owing to data limitations, the regional distribution of net private capital flows during the gold standard period in Table 4.3 is defined as Asia (Australia), the Western Hemisphere (Canada and the United States), and Europe (Italy, Norway, and Sweden). Bonds were the principal instrument of international finance during this period.

Our results suggest that the 1990s were not the most volatile period (Table 4.3). Indeed,

[2]There were two principal capital importing groups. One group—consisting of countries in North America, Latin America (primarily Argentina, Brazil, and Mexico), and Oceania (Australia)—received most of its capital from the United Kingdom. The other group, consisting of countries in central and eastern Europe, Scandinavia, the Middle East, and Africa, was financed by France and Germany.

Table 4.3. Coefficient of Variation of Net Private Capital Flows to Emerging Markets

	1880–1913	1970–1979	1980–1990	1991–2002
Total net private capital flows	1.71	0.29	0.94	0.52
Asia	1.65	0.67	0.65	1.27
Western Hemisphere	1.97	0.67	1.88	0.43
Europe	7.04	−1.12	−2.34	1.16
Africa and Middle East	n.a.	−7.50	−36.61	3.06
Net foreign direct investment	. . .	0.63	0.33	0.47
Net portfolio investment	. . .	0.88	0.88	1.33
Bank loans and other	. . .	0.41	67.51	−1.82

Sources: Bloomfield (1968); and International Monetary Fund, *World Economic Outlook.*

overall net private capital flows in the 1990s were only about one-third as volatile as flows during the classical gold standard era.[3] A similar result holds for the regional flows. As for the subcomponents of net private capital flows, foreign direct investment was the least volatile inflow during both the 1980s and 1990s. A direct comparison with the gold standard era is not possible because of the absence of data. But anecdotal evidence suggests that most of the net private capital flows during that era were bond issues.[4] Thus, to the extent that the volatility of total net private capital flows to emerging markets in the gold standard era can serve as a proxy for the volatility of net portfolio flows, the volatility of net portfolio flows in the 1990s was also less than that of the earlier era.

Volatility of Gross Capital Flows

While net private capital flows data can be used to analyze the general pattern and volatility of capital flows, their annual frequency does not allow for an examination of what many analysts regard as a key source of volatility during the 1990s—namely, that

[3]The same conclusions are reached if the coefficients of variation are calculated on the basis of capital flows relative to GDP.

[4]Bloomfield (1968) reports that during 1870–1914, only 10 percent of U.K. foreign investments involved direct investments.

Figure 4.3. Emerging Markets: Net Private Capital Flows and Current Account Balance
(In billions of U.S. dollars)

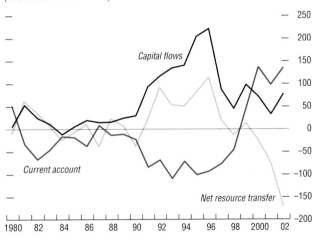

Source: IMF, *World Economic Outlook.*

Table 4.4. Coefficient of Variation of Private Gross Issuance to Emerging Markets

	1980–1990	1991–2002
Total Gross Issuance	0.31	0.42
Asia	0.38	0.48
Western Hemisphere	0.66	0.49
Europe	0.86	0.47
Africa and Middle East	0.57	0.53
Bonds	0.57	0.46
Equities	1.34	0.61
Loans	0.26	0.41

Sources: Dealogic; and IMF staff estimates.

Figure 4.4. Emerging Markets Gross Financing: Bonds, Equities, and Loans
(In billions of U.S. dollars)

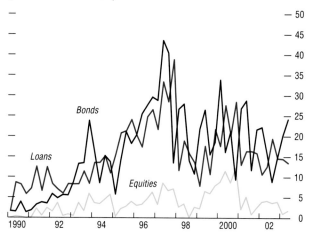

Source: Dealogic.

primary issuance markets for emerging market bonds, equities, and loans were characterized by an "on-off" cycle (see IMF, 2001a, Appendix III; and IMF, 2003). One way to examine the nature of this cycle is to use data on gross issuance of international bonds, equities, and syndicated loans, which are available on a weekly basis (Figure 4.4).[5] As with net private capital flows, gross issuance of international bonds and syndicated lending exhibited a boom-bust cycle, with large increases in issuance before the Asia crises and a secular downturn thereafter. Moreover, the large spikes upward and downward are suggestive of the "on-off" nature of market access. In addition, overall gross issuance was more volatile in the 1990s than in the 1980s (Table 4.4), with bonds and equities less volatile and syndicated loans more volatile.

The pattern of spikes in gross issuance of international bonds and loans also suggests that emerging markets may have experienced periods of high and low volatility. This possibility can be examined using an econometric model that identifies when issuance of international bonds and equities falls into either a high- or a low-volatility regime.[6] The estimations are done for two different sample periods: 1980–2002 and 1991–2002. For the

---

[5]These data capture only syndicated bank loans and do not include other types of short-term credits.

[6]Hamilton (1994) describes a Markov-switching regime econometric model that endogenously identifies recurring regimes of heightened volatility.

Table 4.5. Average Probability of High-Volatility Regime of Gross Issuances to Emerging Markets[1]

(In percent)

	1980–2002		1991–2002	
	1980–1990	1991–2002	1991–1995	1996–2002
Total Gross Issuance				
Asia	0	50	38	53
Western Hemisphere	0	66	22	56
Europe	2	88	0	40
Middle East	13	67	10	11
Africa	5	31	18	30
Bonds	0	85	0	25
Equities	41	75	8	17
Loans	0	86	0	33

Sources: Dealogic; and IMF staff estimates.

[1]For each one of the sample periods (1980–2002 and 1991–2002), the model assumes two states: one of high volatility and one of low volatility. The model estimation delivers monthly probabilities of being in a high-volatility regime. The numbers in this table reflect the frequency of high-volatility months for each subperiod.

period 1980–2002, the model identifies the decade of the 1990s as more volatile than the 1980s (Table 4.5, first two columns). For the 1990s, our estimation results suggest that international issuance of bonds and syndicated loans was much less volatile in the first half of the 1990s than the second half (Table 4.5, last two columns). Moreover, the probability of being in the high-volatility regime for international bonds and syndicated loans peaked with the crises in 1997 and 1998 and the Argentine default in 2001 (Figure 4.5).

The coefficients of variation and regime switching models help characterize the nature of the volatility in the issuance of international issuance of bonds, equities, and syndicated loans by emerging markets, but they do not fully capture the "tail events"—market closures—that have been of most concern to many analysts. To examine this issue, we must first define what constitutes a market closure. Two recent IMF staff studies have used slightly different definitions of a market closure. One study defined a closure as a period of either a single week or two weeks when issuance is less than 20 percent of a 52-week moving average level of issuance (see Appendix III of IMF, 2001a). The other study (IMF, 2003) used the criteria of two weeks or more. Using the two-

Figure 4.5. Probability of Being in a High-Volatility State

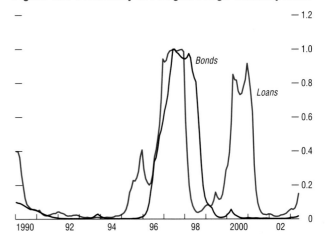

Sources: Dealogic; and IMF staff estimates.

weeks-or-more definition with data from 1994 to 2002, for example, led to the identification of 21 bond market closures with an average length of 22 days (Figure 4.6).

These analyses identified certain common characteristics of market closures. While some closures were associated with developments or anticipated developments in emerging markets, others were a result of extreme uncertainty in international markets. Moreover, the analyses suggested that primary market closures had become more linked to developments in mature markets, especially in the period since 1997.[7] The duration of closures primarily attributable to uncertainty in international markets tended to be shorter than those caused by events in emerging markets. In those cases where the closures did not involve adverse developments in emerging markets, a number of closures were preceded by a rise in the volatility of U.S. equity markets or rising interest spreads on U.S. high-yield ("junk") bonds. While the most severe market closures occurred immediately before and during the Mexican crisis of 1995, many other market closures also coincided with many of the major crises in emerging markets (Figure 4.6) and when yields on emerging market bonds rose sharply.

Determinants of the Pattern and Volatility of Capital Flows

The welfare consequences of the boom-bust pattern and volatility of capital flows have led some analysts to question the desirability of countries' integration into international capital markets. Answering this question requires first a better understanding of the determinants of that pattern. We now review the main studies on the issue, combining them with

Figure 4.6. EMBI+ with Periods of Opening and Closure
(In basis points)

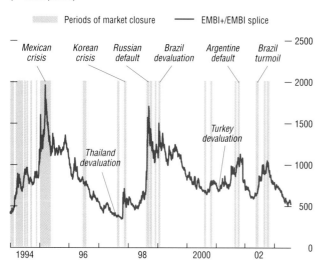

Sources: J.P. Morgan Chase; and IMF staff estimates.

[7]Even if the market closure is primarily driven by a shift in the supply of funds, issuer demand could also vary markedly over such short windows—as good credits choose to postpone issuance when facing very high spreads.

market participants' views on key financial market determinants.

Most studies rely on a standard dichotomy between "push," i.e., external factors, and "pull," or domestic factors, and tend to focus on macroeconomic determinants and consequences of the level and volatility of capital flows.[8] Typical domestic factors are financial liberalization and privatization, while external variables include business cycles and the behavior of asset prices and interest rates in mature markets.[9] Most studies find that both domestic and external variables are important in affecting capital flows, with the more dominant factors changing over time. Some studies have argued, for instance, that external factors are most important in the first half of the decade, while recently domestic factors have become more significant.[10]

The important determinants of the boom-bust pattern and volatility of capital flows, as identified by analysts, are:

• capital account liberalization and financial deregulation in emerging markets;
• large-scale privatization that attracts large FDI inflows;
• a string of crises and contagion effects that propagate financial turbulence across countries and increase the correlation across markets and asset classes;
• international banks' retrenchment in lending to emerging markets in the context of an ongoing shift in business strategy; and
• changes in the composition and broadening of the investor base for emerging market securities.

Financial Deregulation and Capital Account Liberalization

The global trend of deregulation and liberalization of the financial sector in industrial and many developing countries, together with capital account liberalization, catalyzed a vast increase in the volume and speed of capital flows in the boom-phase of the early 1990s. Many developing countries engaged in financial deregulation already in the late 1980s and early 1990s, even before embarking on capital account liberalization (Williamson and Mahar, 1998). Capital account liberalization in the first half of 1990s was closely associated with the surge in capital flows (Figure 4.7).

The surge in capital inflows to Asia, driven by a partial financial liberalization and the supposed implicit guarantees of stable exchange rates, fueled an expansion in banks' balance sheets that led to large increases in lending and asset price bubbles. In Thailand, for example, the establishment of the Bangkok International Banking Facility in 1993 led to a substantial increase in short-term borrowing that was channeled, to a large extent, to finance real estate and stock purchases. In several countries in the region, feedback effects from asset values to domestic lending magnified the expansionary effects of the initial surge in capital inflows.

Stock market liberalization also helped boost portfolio flows during the boom-phase of the first half of the 1990s, as well as increased the transmission of the technology, media, and telecom (TMT) bubble and the increased volatility of the second half of the decade. A recent study (Edison and Warnock, 2003) shows that stock market liberalization has proceeded quite rapidly in many emerging market economies. The authors construct an index of liberalization that demonstrates the depth and persistence of the process, and Figure 4.8 shows how the increased liberalization is associated (albeit weakly) with increased volatility in the emerging equity market.

---

[8]See Calvo, Leiderman, and Reinhart (1996) for an early contribution and Prasad and others (2003) for a more recent summary of the theoretical and empirical evidence of the benefits of capital flows to emerging markets.

[9]These factors are the main underlying determinants of risk-return differentials between emerging and mature market assets, which are the ultimate drivers of cross-border flows.

[10]Montiel and Reinhart (1999) present a good discussion on the literature.

Figure 4.7. Capital Controls and Flows to Emerging Markets

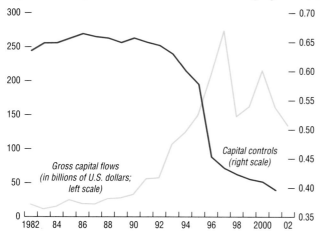

Sources: IMF, *Annual Report on Exchange Arrangements and Exchange Restrictions;* and *World Economic Outlook.*

Figure 4.8. Volatility of Weekly Returns in Emerging Equity Markets and Index of Capital Control[1]

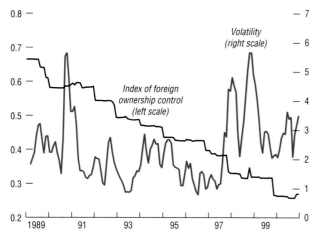

Sources: S&P IFC EMDB; Edison and Warnock (2001); and IMF staff estimates.
[1]Rolling 13-week standard deviation of the S&P IFC Investable Composite Index.

Privatization and Mergers and Acquisitions

The surge in FDI flows to emerging markets in the 1990s mirrored global trends in FDI and was driven to a large extent by the privatization measures undertaken by a number of countries. Most studies find that FDI is most stable among different types of capital flows (Osei, Morrissey, and Lensink, 2002), and this has contributed to the overall stability of flows until recently. Countries in Latin America and Eastern Europe—including Argentina, Brazil, Czech Republic, Hungary, Mexico, and Poland—undertook extensive privatization of state-owned assets during the 1990s, and the FDI flows to both regions accelerated in the second half of the decade (Figure 4.9). In a study that relates the driving forces of FDI to the observed increased integration of capital markets, Albuquerque, Loayza, and Serven (2002) show that the share of FDI variance explained by global ("push") factors has increased notably in the last 15 years, from less than 10 percent to around 50 percent. The authors also show that the development of local financial markets contributes significantly to the growth in FDI, that measures designed to control the level and volatility of international flows act as deterrents to FDI, and that the occurrence of privatization constitutes a strong and statistically significant determinant of FDI. Other studies also suggest that important pull factors appear to be political and economic stability, the size and growth of the domestic market, the proximity of other large markets, predictable rules for investment and a sound legal framework, the ease of profit repatriation, and the availability of skilled labor and infrastructure. Analysts cited three major trends in the recent surge of FDI to emerging markets.

First, FDI has been increasingly directed to the service sector, while it traditionally had concentrated in the natural resources and manufacturing sectors. This shift was led by the progress in privatization of state-owned assets and the large investments needed to keep up with innovations in the information and telecommunication industry. For example, during the second half of 1990s, FDI into the services sector in Brazil accounted for 12 percent of the total FDI into all emerging markets. By the end of the decade, almost 40 percent of the FDI stock in emerging markets was in the services sector (World Bank, 2003).

Second, while traditionally FDI in emerging markets was to a large extent of the "green-field" variety,[11] mergers and acquisitions (M&As)—which used to be the main mode of foreign entry in industrial countries—have played a growing role in developing countries and accounted for a significant part of the privatization programs (Figure 4.10). This was driven not only by investments in the TMT sectors, but also in the financial sectors. The share of investment in the financial industry in the total FDI stock of central and eastern Europe reached 13.6 percent in 1999, the highest sectoral share for that region. The comparable figure for Latin America was 12.3 percent (second only to business activities in the tertiary sector; see Roldos, 2002). Following the Asian crisis, the acquisition of distressed banking and corporate assets in several Asian economies also surged, contributing to an important rise in the value of cross-border M&A in that region during 1998–2000.

Third, FDI has remained relatively resilient during the string of emerging market crises, but a full assessment of the contribution of FDI to the stability of flows would have to consider funding, hedging, and other activities of multinational enterprises. FDI continued to grow steadily after the Mexican crisis and slowed down only marginally after the Asian crises. However, some analysts have noted that hedging activities of multinational enterprises contributed to foreign exchange pressures during the period of financial turbulence leading to the 2002 presidential election in Brazil. Also, some analysts have expressed con-

---

[11]A "green-field" investment involves the setting up of new units or facilities by foreign firms—as opposed to the purchase of existing ones.

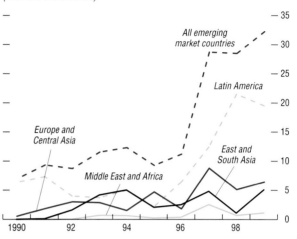

Figure 4.9. Regional Equity Flows Through Privatization
(In billions of U.S. dollars)

Source: World Bank.

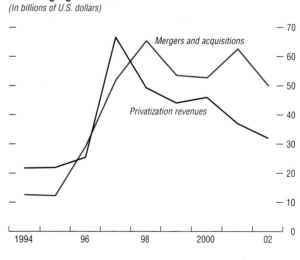

Figure 4.10. Mergers and Acquisitions and Privatization in Emerging Markets
(In billions of U.S. dollars)

Source: World Bank.

cerns that the events in Argentina may have undermined investor sentiment toward the region and that a generalized "sudden stop" in FDI to Latin America could further complicate the region's external financing prospects. However, a number of investors remain committed to FDI in emerging markets notwithstanding slowdowns in Latin America and in global financial conditions. There is little evidence to support worst-case fears of a major pullout from the region or emerging markets as a whole.[12]

Crisis and Contagion

The string of financial crises that first struck Asia in 1997 marked the beginning of the bust phase of capital inflows to emerging markets. The causes of these crises have been widely studied and include, to different degrees, a combination of weak fiscal and financial fundamentals, together with abrupt losses of access to international markets (sometimes referred to as "sudden stops"; see Calvo, 1998). A key feature of these financial crises has also been the fact that, like epidemics, they appear to be contagious. Contagion in financial markets has since been seen as a key source of volatility in capital flows to emerging markets. Recent experience and research in the area have proven, however, that the spillovers across countries are to a large extent due to financial linkages and that these are, in turn, integral to the operation of international financial markets.

The spread of the financial crisis from Thailand to several other countries in Asia

and elsewhere in 1997 and the global financial turmoil triggered by the Russian devaluation and default in 1998 are widely attributed to contagion effects. A broadly accepted definition of contagion is the propagation of shocks in excess of what can be explained by fundamentals. Since there are several ways of quantifying and analyzing fundamentals, however, studies on contagion have been quite controversial.[13] Studies have, nonetheless, shown that trade and financial linkages are important elements in the international propagation of shocks; and, in particular, that financial linkages related to the existence of common creditors in international markets appear to be critical, especially for the immediate volatility that follows the crisis in the source country.[14] Many studies have also found evidence of excess comovement in a variety of asset returns, but correlations are time-varying and there is less consensus on whether this comovement increases during crises.

The recent crises in Brazil (February 1999), Turkey (February 2001), and Argentina (December 2001) have demonstrated a much lower degree of contagion, though financial linkages were clearly at work in these episodes. Analysts attribute the lower incidence of contagion to four factors: the crises were to some extent anticipated; they occurred when capital flows had already subsided; leverage in the system had declined; and investors had increased their ability to differentiate among countries.[15] In the case of Argentina, four main financial linkages transmitted the crisis in the region and globally:

---

[12]This assessment is based on an upcoming report of the Working Group of the Capital Markets Consultative Group (CMCG, forthcoming).

[13]For a detailed discussion on the different mechanisms of contagion and definitions, see Forbes and Rigobon (2000), Moser (2003), and Kaminsky, Reinhart, and Végh (2002).

[14]Countries that share a common lender with another one that suffers a financial crisis could suffer cuts in credit lines as banks reassess exposures in the region and globally (Kaminsky and Reinhart, 2000; Van Rijckeghem and Weder, 2000). Similarly, global investors that suffer losses in one market may hedge by shorting assets that are highly correlated to the affected country (Kodres and Pritsker, 2002; Schinasi and Smith, 2000) or, if they face liquidity pressures, they may sell assets of other less-affected countries.

[15]See, for instance, IMF (2002) and Kaminsky, Reinhart, and Végh (2002).

- Argentina had a 20 percent weight in the EMBI+ and this initiated spillovers to the bond markets of other constituents of the index.
- Some Spanish banks and corporates had large exposures in Argentina and the deterioration in their subsidiaries had a significant impact in the Spanish stock market (Figure 4.11).
- Some of the banks operating in the region saw the spillovers of the crises affecting Brazilian financial assets and, given the difficulty of shorting some of those assets, took short positions in the Chilean peso.[16]
- Uruguayan banks, which had for years been host to Argentine depositors, suffered large deposit runs after those depositors saw their deposits in Argentina frozen by the authorities in December 2001.

A higher degree of investor discrimination, however, helped to offset these linkages and to contain financial spillovers to these and other countries.

One particular feature of investor behavior that could potentially generate excess volatility and comovement across markets is herding behavior. Herding occurs when information is costly and investors follow sporadic and imperfect signals to change their portfolio allocations. Uninformed investors may follow the behavior of informed specialists or may trade blindly to mimic some benchmark or mechanistic trading rule. The empirical evidence concerning investors' herding behavior and momentum trading at the international level is mixed. Although there is some evidence that the correlation among assets increases during crisis periods, it is unclear whether herding behavior is more pronounced during such periods. Froot, O'Connell, and Seasholes (2001) find evidence of momentum trading in portfolio flows. Borensztein and Gelos (2000) find only

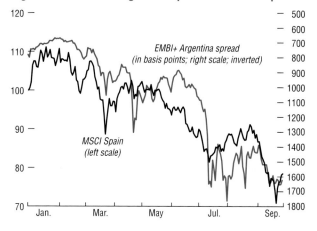

Figure 4.11. EMBI+ Argentina Spread and MSCI Spain

Sources: Bloomberg; and J.P. Morgan Chase.

[16]Proxy hedging was one of the factors behind the depreciation of the peso in 2001.

weak evidence of herding behavior among emerging market mutual funds and report that herding did not seem to worsen during crises. Kaminsky, Lyons, and Schmukler (2001) reported some evidence of momentum trading among U.S. mutual funds investing in emerging markets, which appeared to intensify during crises. In particular, the authors find that funds engaged in contagion trading, which they define as systematic selling of assets from one country when asset prices begin to fall in another.[17] This contagion trading is attributable primarily to (underlying) investor activity, however, and not to the actions of fund managers.

The correlation of returns across markets varies also with the degree of financial integration, and this pattern could make crises more likely when capital flows are at their peak. Goetzmann, Li, and Rouwenhorst (2001) show that long-term correlations of returns in the major world equity markets are highest during periods of economic and financial integration, as in the late nineteenth and twentieth centuries. Although this higher correlation reduces the gains from global portfolio diversification, the authors also find that investors gain from an expansion in the opportunity set—that is, from the availability of additional markets and instruments. A negative implication of the expansion of markets during periods of globalization is that investors may have reduced incentives to pay for fixed country-specific information costs (Calvo and Mendoza, 2000). This might have heightened volatility but could have been countered by the increased availability of information at lower costs during the last decade.

Common lender effects and global portfolio investors are having an increasingly important influence on capital flows to emerging markets. To better understand capital flow volatility, a more thorough study of the structural determinants of the behavior of international banks and the investor base for emerging market asset is required.

Shift in Business Strategy of International Banks

International banks, the main source of external finance for emerging markets during the 1970s and early 1980, saw their role greatly diminished in the 1990s. After a resumption in lending prior to the Asian crises, a massive retrenchment in international lending has been a major cause of the bust phase of capital flows in the past five years. This retrenchment in commercial bank lending can be traced to weak balance sheets and earnings, greater risk awareness, consolidation, and an ongoing shift in business strategies and product lines, among other things. Given that the causes of such changes are likely to have a permanent impact on the banking industry, the role of bank lending in emerging markets may remain diminished going forward.

The string of emerging market crises, spillovers from the bursting of the TMT bubble, and slow growth in the mature markets weakened the balance sheets of many money center banks, leading to a sustained retrenchment in lending activities. Low interest rates in the G-3 countries in the 1990s encouraged banks to seek out higher returns from lending to emerging economies. In Japan, sustained low interest rates gave rise to the attractiveness of the "yen carry" trade. The large interest rate differential and optimism about the growth of Asian economies caused banks to lend aggressively in the region. Subsequent crises quickly reversed the trend and the exodus by Japanese banks from Asia initiated the collapse in international bank lending to emerging markets. The reduction in exposures of European banks to Latin America after Argentina's default and the

---

[17]This kind of contagion trading may also be capturing cross-border hedging activities—that is, financial linkages.

turbulence in Brazil reinforced this trend. As a result, the outstanding loans of international banks to emerging markets have fallen by about 5½ percent a year since the Asian crisis.

These series of shocks have heightened risk awareness in the major banks, which has, in turn, prompted a more cautious approach to lending to emerging markets. Banks are exerting greater scrutiny over the credit quality of their clients and are seeking greater diversification of exposures across sector and countries. They are also increasingly using structured products and credit default swaps (CDS) to shift in part their credit risks off their balance sheets. While these changes may ultimately lead to better-managed balance sheets and hence more ability to take risk, so far they appear to have led to a more cautious lending environment, especially toward emerging markets.

Moreover, the collapse in cross-border bank lending to emerging markets masked other important structural changes in international bank lending: global banks have consolidated, and have increasingly emphasized lending from local subsidiaries and fee-based businesses. Some analysts have argued that the wave of global banks' mergers has reduced the amount of capital dedicated to underwriting and market-making in emerging markets, but the evidence is unclear (see IMF, 2001a, Box 5.1 in particular). Also, the ratio of local currency claims of BIS reporting banks' foreign affiliates with local residents to total foreign claims has been increasing steadily (Figure 4.12), suggesting that banks have redistributed their emerging market portfolios from traditional cross-border lending to in-country lending. The changing business strategy has been one facet of the ongoing consolidation of banking systems in both mature and emerging markets. It has been motivated, among other things, by increasing competition that lowered the margin on lending, a desire for more diversified sources of income, and the incentive to exploit econo-

Figure 4.12. Local Claims and Total Foreign Claims Ratio
(In percent)

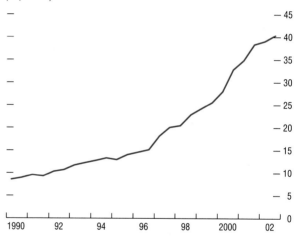

Source: Bank for International Settlement.

mies of scale and scope.[18] Lending in local currency eliminates the inherent currency mismatch in cross-border lending and facilitates penetration in the local retail market. Many emerging market economies have encouraged the entry of foreign banks to improve their domestic banking system by introducing better banking practices and increasing transparency. They also believe that foreign banks' commitment to the local market could help reduce the volatility of capital flows.[19]

The traditional syndicated loan market shrank in the second half of 1990s, owing to low profit margins attributable to intense competition. The role of the "lead bank" has shifted in recent years from that of the agent for the lending group to the "underwriter" of the deal. This means that the lead banks are increasingly motivated by the up-front fee received for syndicating the deal rather than by revenues associated with interest rate spreads. The traditional "buy-and-hold" lenders have seen their spread lending revenue shrink because of competition from new underwriters, many of which sharply reduced the spread on loans to capture market shares. The number of the pro rata investors, the "buy-and-hold" lenders, has dwindled (Figure 4.13). These structural changes have also affected the supply of syndicated loans to emerging markets and contributed to a decline in net private flows.

The response of emerging markets to the string of crises has also contributed to the reduction in bank lending. Prudent liability

Figure 4.13. Most Active Pro Rata Investors
(In numbers)

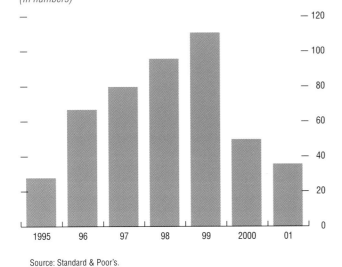

Source: Standard & Poor's.

---

[18]IMF (2000) and Mathieson and Roldos (2001) offer detailed analyses of the reasons for the increased role of foreign banks in emerging markets and its implications for efficiency and financial stability.

[19]Empirical evidence on whether the presence of foreign banks reduces the volatility of capital flows to emerging markets is mixed. Kono and Schuknecht (1998) find supporting evidence, while Beck (2000) finds that penetration of foreign banks tends to increase the volatility of capital flows. Kireyev (2002) finds that liberalization of trade in financial services is conducive to banking sector stability.

management of sovereigns, corporates, and domestic banks has also meant a reduction in short-term external borrowing, especially bank loans, to avoid excessive maturity mismatches. Before 1997, the bank loan market was driven largely by strong demand from emerging markets, as both the interest margin and the loan amount climbed steadily in tandem (Figure 4.14). Immediately after the crisis in 1997, however, the shrinking supply of syndicated loans dominated the market, as higher margins were met with lower loan volumes. Since 1999, falling margins and lower loan volumes suggest that the demand for loans by emerging market borrowers has also decreased in tandem with the bank retrenchment.

Market participants also note that risk management practices and herding behavior by commercial banks have been the main causes of the collapse in trade finance in recent crises. Typically, during a crisis, a bank reduces its overall country exposure following a decision by its management to cap the institution's country limit, including trade finance. Also, since domestic banks intermediate an important share of trade finance in emerging markets, concerns about their credit quality—especially if they are exposed to the sovereign (as happened in Brazil last year)—may increase during crises. Even in more tranquil periods, risk management practices have reportedly changed in the trade finance industry. Indeed, trade finance operations have evolved from being loss-leader operations, established in the context of relationship banking activities, to stand-alone operations. As a result, trade finance has been priced more appropriately and the associated risks are being better managed, with the implication that the stability of relationship lending has been diminished.

Some analysts argue that the combination of consolidation and herding, with the increased use of market-sensitive risk management tools, has led to a decline in market liquidity and to an increase in the volatility of

Figure 4.14. Emerging Markets: Interest Margin and Syndicated Loans

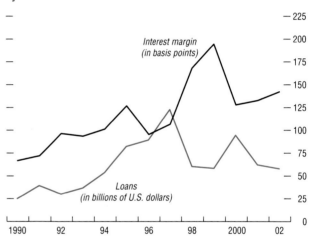

Sources: Dealogic; and IMF staff estimates.

capital flows. Persaud (2000 and 2002) shows that there has been a persistent decline in equity market liquidity (both in mature and emerging markets) since 1998. He attributes the decline to a reduction in the diversity of behavior of market participants, which owes in turn to the decline in information costs, the consolidation of major players, and the wider use of similar market-sensitive risk-management tools—such as Value-at-Risk (VaR) models. Persaud argues that VaR models caused banks to herd and that this herding is not offset by longer-term investors' buying in the wake of "forced" bank selling because investors are increasingly using the same VaR models. While he does not provide evidence on the latter, he then calls for regulators to encourage the adoption of a variety of risk-management models and practices that would allow long-term investors to follow trading strategies that are less sensitive to the short-term risk-management models used by the major banks.

Investor Base Change

The secular withdrawal of international banks from lending to emerging markets is part of a global trend and has contributed to the securitization of international finance. The trend began with the restructuring of bank debts to Brady bonds in the early 1990s, together with the liberalization of investment in equity markets. Emerging market securities have evolved into a more mainstream asset class (Box 4.1). The trend was associated with the boom phase of portfolio flows that reinforced other types of flows in the first half of the 1990s. More important, an active secondary market for emerging market bonds was developed and the behavior of the investor base in this market became crucial for the pricing and volatility of flows. In particular,

the increasing dominance of "mark-to-market" investors has prompted an increased sensitivity to market prices but has also encouraged more transparency and a more diverse investor base. As the market for emerging market securities matures, changes in the investor base for such securities have been, and will continue to be, critical determinants of the volatility of capital flows to emerging markets.

The string of crises and the volatility of capital flows over the last decade were associated with important changes in the investor base for emerging market securities. These changes included a sharp drop in the participation of banks and hedge funds and an increase in the participation of crossover and local investors. The behavior of hedge funds and their impact on volatility and contagion have received a substantial amount of attention in both the academic and official communities, especially after the Asian, Russian, and Long-Term Capital Management (LTCM) crises. An early study (Eichengreen and Mathieson, 1998) finds little evidence linking hedge fund strategies to excess market volatility and only some evidence regarding similar position-taking ("herding") among hedge funds of the same investment style.[20] The study also finds little evidence that hedge funds took short positions against Asian currencies in 1997 earlier than other investors. This study concludes that hedge funds appear to have followed, rather than led, other investors during both the 1994–95 and the 1997 crises in emerging markets. More recent studies in hedge fund performance find mixed results in terms of their risk-adjusted returns.[21] The regulatory response has included strengthening risk-management practices by hedge funds and their counterparties, enhanced regulatory oversight of hedge fund credit providers, enhanced public

[20]Fung, Hsieh, and Tsatsaronis (2000) confirm that evidence.
[21]See, for example, Ackerman, McEnally, and Ravenscraft (1999) and Edwards (1999).

Box 4.1. The Demise of Brady Bonds

Brady bonds were issued by some emerging market countries, particularly in Latin America, as part of a restructuring of defaulted commercial bank loans in the 1980s. The initiative was launched by U.S. Treasury Secretary Nicholas Brady in 1989. It was supported by lending from the IMF, the World Bank, and the Japan Bank for International Cooperation (JBIC), with the goal of reducing the heavy debt burdens faced by these countries. Probably to make the deals more attractive to investors, the bonds were tailor-made in all sizes and carried a mind-boggling array of covenants, conditions, warrants, and other complex features, such as collateral.

Bradys jump started the emerging bond market and facilitated capital market access by the emerging markets. Since the first Brady deal by Mexico in March 1990, the total amount of Brady bonds outstanding rose to $154 billion as of the end of 1994, representing 85 percent of the Latin American debt market—at which point, Mexico accounted for 19 percent of the outstanding amount, second only to Brazil (with 35 percent). Many non-Latin countries, such as Bulgaria, Poland, the Philippines, Nigeria, and Côte d'Ivoire, also issued Brady bonds.

Brady bonds became more expensive to the issuers and less liquid over time, however, because of their exotic structures. As emerging market countries gained more access to capital markets in the 1990s with the surge in capital inflows, their borrowing costs were

lowered and borrowing covenants weakened. In most cases, Bradys became the most expensive liability a country could have.

Since 1995, led by Argentina, many countries that issued Brady bonds started to retire them through exchanges for cheaper Eurobonds, buybacks, calls, and warrant exercises, among other means, exemplifying the concept of sovereign liability management. The stellar performer in this regard is Mexico, which managed to reduce its share of the market from its high of 19 percent in 1994 to almost zero now. The most recent deal, "Adios Bradys," by Mexico wiped its plate clean of dollar-denominated Brady bonds. Many other countries also significantly reduced their Brady bonds, including Brazil, Argentina, the Philippines, Poland, and Vietnam. As a result, the outstanding stock of Brady bonds dropped from $154 billion in 1994 to about $50 billion recently, a decline of 67 percent! Furthermore, many of the exchanges have resulted in net present value savings for the sovereigns, the release of resources that were tied as collateral, and expanded the investor base for the asset class.

Market participants view the retirement by many emerging market issuers of their Brady bonds as a signal that the sovereigns are entering a more mature phase of managing their liabilities. As Brady bonds disappear, mainstream Eurobonds are overtaking them as the liquid bonds. This is gradually leading to a greater institutional and retail acceptance of the asset class and its inclusion in broader global fixed-income portfolios.

disclosure, and guidelines on good practices for foreign exchange trading and a firmer market infrastructure.[22] While some analysts

argue that the withdrawal of hedge funds after 1998 reduced liquidity in emerging market securities,[23] others maintain that their absence

[22]See, for example, the President's Working Group on Financial Markets (United States, 1999), and Financial Stability Forum (FSF) recommendations.
[23]By 2002, the share of emerging market assets accounted for by hedge funds shrunk to about 5 percent from about 20 percent in 1995, while the market share of other crossover investors rose to about 48 percent from about 10 percent in 1995.

has contributed to the easing of contagion and volatility in the more recent crises (see Figure 4.15 for an illustration of the changing investor base for emerging market securities during the past 13 years).

Another important change in the investor base for emerging market securities has been the relative decline in "dedicated" relative to "crossover" investors. A dedicated investor is one whose performance is measured against an emerging market asset benchmark, such as the EMBI or MSCI emerging market index. Crossover investors are the main institutional investors and managers of investment-grade debt and mature market high-yield securities. Crossover investors are usually not measured against any emerging market benchmark; hence they only invest in emerging market assets to improve returns. Their investment decisions thus tend to be more opportunistic and susceptible to developments in competing and complementary asset classes. As a result, fund flows to emerging market assets by crossover investors tend to be more volatile as they go in and out of the asset class, while dedicated investors usually trade within the asset class.

Although the increased importance of crossover investors may have increased volatility in the asset class, it has also led to a broader and more diversified investor base—which could strengthen the asset class. The increased susceptibility of the asset class to developments in competing and complementary asset classes has been demonstrated by the impact of volatility in mature markets in the periods immediately preceding the episodes of closure of emerging bond markets. Some analysts (Bayliss, 2003; and El-Erian, 2003), however, argue that a more diverse investor base contributes to lower volatility, among other things, because it moves investors' focus from narrow benchmarks toward blended benchmarks that combine emerging market securities with more established credit products.

Figure 4.15. Changing Market Share of Emerging Market Investors
(In percent)

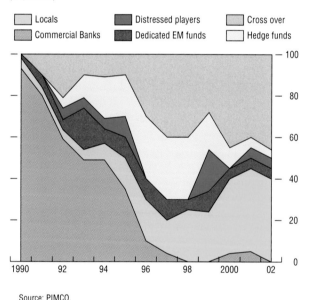

Source: PIMCO.

Toward the end of the last decade, the investor base for emerging market bonds widened with the addition of European institutional investors and local investors in emerging market countries (IMF, 2000). While demand for emerging market bonds in Europe is traditionally retail, institutional demand has grown more recently, fueled by the growth in European high-yield funds. These European investors tend to be more buy-and-hold than their U.S. counterparts, exhibit greater willingness to cross over into emerging market securities, and have fewer holding restrictions based on credit ratings. In addition, emerging market local investors have increasingly invested in foreign-currency-denominated local assets. Market participants cited this trend in some of the largest emerging markets—such as Argentina, Brazil, Mexico, Russia, and Turkey—as well as in smaller countries, such as Kazakhstan and Lebanon. In particular, the growth of pension funds has increased the stability of returns in emerging market bonds, as there is evidence that local investors seem to buy into the asset class when there is a global sell-off (Roldos, 2003). The widening of the investor base for emerging market securities is likely to help reduce volatility in those assets going forward.

The broadening and diversification of the investor base has been reinforced by a broadening and diversification of investment opportunities. Despite the relative stability of the dedicated investor base for emerging market debt, the number of emerging market debt mutual funds has increased from 22 in 1994 to 80 in 2002. Also, the number of countries in the industry's more important benchmark, the EMBIG (a broader version of the EMBI), has increased from 15 in 1993 to 30 in 2002, with an even larger number of new issuers. More important, a number of members of the asset class have graduated to the investment grade. This, combined with an improvement in the credit fundamentals, especially outside South America (Figure 4.16), has provided additional support to,

Figure 4.16. Average Credit Ratings in Emerging Markets[1]

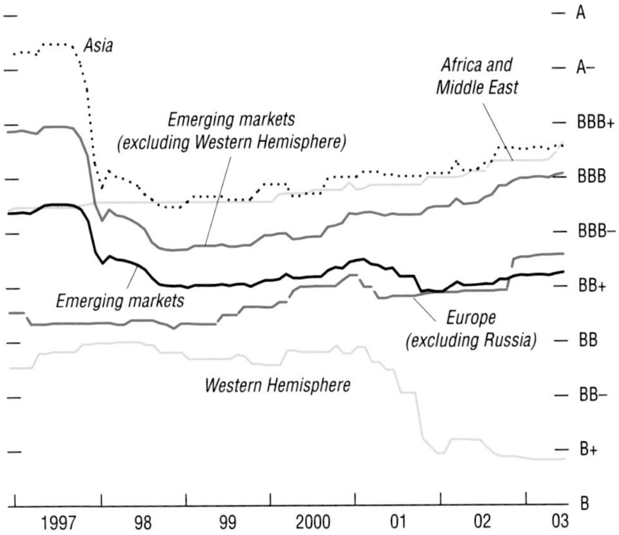

Sources: IMF staff calculations based on data from Moody's, Standard and Poor's, and Capital Data.
[1]Includes all major emerging markets with credit ratings as of December 1996. Weighted average by bond issuance from 1995 to 1999.

and enhanced the attractiveness of, the asset class.

Concluding Remarks and Policy Issues

The pattern and volatility of capital flows to emerging markets in the 1990s does not seem to differ markedly from other historical periods. Indeed, the volatility of these flows—as measured by the coefficient of variation of aggregate net flows—in the last decade has not been as large as that in some earlier periods. However, data limitations suggest some degree of caution in the conclusions derived from a comparison of very distant historical periods.

The most stable capital flow has been foreign direct investment. Much of the volatility in capital flows in the 1990s can be attributed to a sudden loss of access by many emerging markets to the primary issuance markets for international bonds, equities, and syndicated loans. While this loss of access was at times associated with political and economic developments in individual emerging markets, developments in mature markets sometimes restricted the access of many emerging markets.

The boom-bust pattern and the volatility of capital flows to emerging markets was the result of several factors, many of which are likely to continue to affect flows going forward. The winding down of the process of liberalization and privatization in emerging markets means that these "pull" factors are likely to be less important in the near future, with the exception perhaps of some countries—for example, FDI to China. FDI will be supported, however, by the long-term strategies of major corporations operating on a global scale and prospects will be linked to host country factors with likely regional variations. The retrenchment in bank lending to

emerging markets is likely to persist, reflecting a deep structural change in the way the industry operates. It is not possible to rule out, however, some recovery of bank lending to emerging markets once the structural changes run their full course.

The securitization of international finance means that portfolio flows are going to continue to be an increasingly important part of emerging market financing, and a certain degree of volatility will inevitably persist. Equity flows are likely to remain subdued, especially in those countries where the increase in volatility is related to global trends toward a concentration of issuance and trading in major regional financial centers.[24] The pattern of volatility of issuance for bond flows will be determined by the interaction of two opposing forces. On the one hand, changes in the investor base—the relative importance of crossover investors and, perhaps, a return of hedge funds—are likely to continue to impart some volatility to issuance and prices. On the other hand, a broadening of the investor base and the investable universe—including countries and instruments—together with a strengthening of the asset class is likely to increase the stability of flows somewhat. Among the factors contributing to a strengthening of the asset class, as analysts have noted, is that most of the major emerging markets have already suffered severe financial crises and are now improving their fundamentals and adopting a series of "self-insurance" policy measures.

The experience with the volatility of capital flows during the 1990s appears to have convinced the authorities in many emerging markets that such volatility is likely to be a feature of the increasingly integrated international financial system. As a result, most emerging markets have adopted measures—or "self-insurance policies"—to reduce their depend-

---

[24]IMF (2001a) and Mathieson and Roldos (forthcoming) discuss the drying up of liquidity in the major emerging market stock exchanges and its implications for international investors.

ence on international borrowing.[25] Although some of these measures could lead to increased capital flows and lower volatility for the countries adopting them over the medium term, they have contributed to a general fall in the demand for flows—and hence to the fall in capital inflows toward the end of the 1990s—that is likely to persist for a while. While establishing sound macroeconomic policies has been one obvious element in strengthening perceived creditworthiness and helping to sustain access to international capital markets, many emerging markets have taken additional measures designed to "self-insure" against volatile capital flows and asset prices. These measures have centered on:

- changes in external asset and liability management practices;
- adapting exchange rate arrangements to the degree of capital account openness;
- strengthening domestic financial institutions and enhancing prudential supervision and regulation in order to increase resilience to volatility; and
- developing local securities and derivatives markets to provide an alternative source of funding for the public and corporate sectors and to facilitate the management of the financial risks associated with periods of high asset price volatility.

After the Asian crisis of 1997, a number of commentators suggested that emerging markets increase their holdings of international reserves to provide a degree of self-insurance against a sudden reversal of capital flows.[26] Indeed, holdings of foreign exchange reserves by emerging markets more than doubled between the end of 1995 and the end of 2002.[27] Reserve accumulation was particularly notable for some countries that experienced "sudden stops" (or reversals) of capital flows (such as Korea, Taiwan Province of China, and Mexico).

Emerging market borrowers have also adapted to the volatile nature of market access. In part, this has involved greater transparency in data and policies (as demonstrated by the increasing number of countries subscribing to the IMF's Special Data Dissemination Standards, or SDDS, and undertaking Financial Stability Assessment Programs, or FSAPs), as well as other initiatives such as the adoption of Reviews of Standards and Codes (ROSCs), to help reduce the volatility of capital flows by reducing the scope for herding behavior and increasing differentiation of credit quality. In addition, they have attempted to develop access to the retail and institutional bond markets denominated in euros and yen when the U.S. dollar bond market has been closed.[28] They have also employed staff in debt management agencies with extensive investment banking and trading experience, and have exploited "windows of opportunity" to prefund their yearly financing requirement. Moreover, they have engaged in debt exchanges to extend the maturity of their external debt and avoid a bunching of maturities, established benchmark external bond issues both to improve secondary market liquidity and to facilitate the pricing of external corporate debt issues, and made greater use of local debt markets.

While changes in public sector external asset and liability practices have been key elements of the self-insurance response to the

---

[25]See IMF (2003) for a more detailed description of these policies, with emphasis on the development of local securities markets.

[26]See Feldstein (1999) and Greenspan (1999). The IMF's approach to international reserves adequacy, which is now focused on the role of potential capital account pressures, can be found at http://www.imf.org/external/np/pdr/resad/2001/reserve.htm, http://www.imf.org/external/np/pdr/debtres/index.htm, or IMF (2001b).

[27]Moreover, the ratio of emerging markets foreign exchange reserves to nominal GDP at the end of 2002 was at the highest levels since 1990. Similar results hold for the ratios of reserves to imports and reserves to broad money (M2).

[28]In the period since the Argentine default, accessing these alternative markets has proved difficult.

volatility of capital flows, the authorities in many countries have continued to use capital controls in part to affect the private sector's external asset and liability position. Indeed, the evidence for the period 1998–2001 shows that there was also a slowdown in the removal of capital controls by countries that have had restricted capital accounts (Figure 4.7).[29] These de jure capital controls do not necessarily provide a measure of possible changes in the de facto level of capital market integration. But they do provide a measure of the relative unwillingness of the authorities to undertake further capital account liberalization in an environment of volatile capital flows and global asset prices.

Although external asset and liability management techniques can provide a buffer against volatile capital flows and asset prices, emerging markets have also been adapting policies and the strength of their financial institutions to the degree of openness of their capital account. These adaptations have been most noticeable in the nature of exchange rate arrangements and in efforts to strengthen the ability of banking systems to withstand volatile capital flows and asset prices.

While the accumulation of larger foreign exchange reserves could create more scope for the authorities to fix the exchange rate, countries have generally moved away from pegged but adjustable exchange rate arrangements since the mid-1990s, especially those with access to international capital markets. For countries with access to international capital markets, the move to either a flexible exchange rate or a hard peg represents an alternative solution to the well-known problem of trying to maintain a fixed exchange

rate and an independent monetary policy with a high degree of capital mobility. Moreover, it reflects the difficulties that a number of emerging markets experienced in attempting to defend a fixed exchange rate during periods of sudden stops or reversals of capital flows.

While the changes in exchange rate arrangements removed some of the incentives for banks to borrow abroad—a major cause of the emerging market crises in the second half of the 1990s—country authorities still faced the difficulties of restructuring and recapitalizing the banks (and heavily indebted corporates), as well as ensuring that banks improve their risk management techniques amid volatile capital flows and asset prices (IMF, 2003). In short, in the period since 1997, the results have been mixed. Asia, for example, has shown a slow but steady improvement in its soundness indicators. In contrast, Latin America presents a more differentiated picture—with countries such as Mexico and Chile continuing to improve while Argentina and Uruguay deteriorated until recently. Central Europe has achieved the sharpest improvement in bank soundness.

Finally, the efforts to develop local securities and derivatives markets have been motivated in large part by the desire to provide an alternative source of funding for both the sovereign and corporate sectors in order to self-insure against a reversal in capital flows. In addition, it has been argued that the development of local markets will help improve the intermediation of domestic savings and attract foreign investors.[30] This has become particularly important as a greater number of emerging markets have privatized their pension systems. In central Europe, foreign investors

[29]Habermeier and Ishii (2003) report, for example, that during 1998–2000, the number of countries maintaining controls on both current and capital account transactions remained relatively unchanged (falling from 74 percent to 70 percent of all IMF members). Moreover, although the overall use of capital controls did not change, a growing number of countries began to regulate selected transactions. In particular, the number of countries maintaining controls on institutional investors rose sharply.

[30]In Asia, this has also involved efforts to develop a regional market through the establishment of the Asian Bond Fund (in June 2003).

have provided a steady source of demand for local currency sovereign bonds. Moreover, local derivatives markets have been seen as providing a vehicle for managing financial risks, especially those related to exchange rates and interest rates. Despite the rapid expansion of local securities markets, it remains unclear whether they will be able to offset future losses of access to international markets. Continued efforts to develop markets will nevertheless buffer "sudden-stops" and contribute to reduced volatility in capital flows.

References

Ackerman, Carl, Richard McEnally, and David Ravenscraft, 1999, "The Performance of Hedge Funds: Risk, Return, and Incentives," *The Journal of Finance*, Vol. 54 (June).

Albuquerque, R., N. Loayza, and L. Serven, 2002, "World Market Integration Through the Lens of Foreign Direct Investors," paper presented at the conference, "The FDI Race: Who gets the Prize? Is it Worth the Effort?" organized by the Inter-American Development Bank and the World Bank (Washington, October).

Bayliss, Jonathan, 2003, "Emerging Market as an Asset Class," J.P. Morgan.

Beck, Roland, 2000, "The Volatility of Capital Flows to Emerging Markets and Financial Services to Trade," CFS Working Paper No. 2000/11 (Frankfurt: Center for Financial Studies).

Bloomfield, Arthur, 1968, "Patterns of Fluctuation in International Investment Before 1914," *Princeton Studies in International Finance*, No. 21 (Princeton, New Jersey: Princeton University Press).

Borensztein, Eduardo, and Gaston Gelos, 2000, "A Panic-Prone Pack? The Behavior of Emerging Market Mutual Funds," IMF Working Paper No. 00/198 (Washington: International Monetary Fund).

Calvo, Guillermo A., 1998, "Understanding the Russian Virus—with special reference to Latin America," paper presented at the Deutsche Bank's conference "Emerging Markets: Can They Be Crisis Free?" (Washington, October).

———, Leonardo Leiderman, and Carmen Reinhart, 1996, "Inflows of Capital to Developing Countries in the 1990s," *Journal of Economic Perspectives*, Vol. 10 (Spring), pp. 123–39.

Calvo, Guillermo, and Enrique Mendoza, 2000, "Rational Contagion and the Globalization of Securities Markets," *Journal of International Economics*, Vol. 51 (June), pp. 79–113.

Capital Markets Consultative Group, forthcoming, "Foreign Direct Investment in Emerging Market Countries" (Washington).

Edison, Hali, and Francis Warnock, 2003, "A Simple Measure of the Intensity of Capital Controls," *Journal of Empirical Finance*, Vol. 10 (February), pp. 81–103.

Edwards, Franklin R., 1999, "Hedge Funds and the Collapse of Long-Term Capital Management," *Journal of Economic Perspectives*, Vol. 13 (Spring), pp. 189–210.

Eichengreen, Barry, and Donald Mathieson, 1998, "Hedge Funds: What Do We Really Know?" Economic Issues No. 19 (Washington: International Monetary Fund).

El-Erian, Mohamed, 2003, "The Capital Flows Transition," *Emerging Market Watch* (May).

Feldstein, Martin, 1999, "Self-Protection for Emerging Market Economies," NBER Working Paper No. 6907 (Cambridge, Mass.: National Bureau of Economic Research).

Forbes, Kristin, and Roberto Rigobon, 2000, "Contagion in Latin America: Definitions, Measurement, and Policy Implications," NBER Working Paper No. 7885 (Cambridge, Mass.: National Bureau of Economic Research).

Froot, Kenneth A., Paul G. J. O'Connell, and Mark S. Seasholes, 2001, "The Portfolio Flows of International Investors," *Journal of Financial Economics* (Netherlands), Vol. 59, No. 2 (February), pp. 151–93.

Fung, William, David A. Hsieh, and Konstantinos Tsatsaronis, 2000, "Do Hedge Funds Disrupt Emerging Markets?" *Brookings-Wharton Papers on Financial Services*, Brookings Institution, pp. 377–401.

Goetzmann, William N., Lingfeng Li, and K. Geert Rouwenhorst, 2001, "Long-Term Global Market Correlations," NBER Working Paper No. 8612 (Cambridge, Mass.: National Bureau of Economic Research).

Greenspan, Alan, 1999, "Lessons from the Global Crises," remarks before the World Bank Group and the International Monetary Fund, Annual Meetings Program of Seminars (Washington, September 27). Available on the Internet at

http://www.federalreserve.gov/Boarddocs/Speeches/
1999/199909272.htm.

Habermeier, Karl, and Shogo Ishii, 2003,
"Exchange Arrangements and Foreign Exchange
Markets: Developments and Issues," World
Economic and Financial Surveys (Washington:
International Monetary Fund).

Hamilton, James, 1994, *Time Series Analysis* (Princeton, New Jersey: Princeton University Press).

IMF, 2000, *International Capital Markets:*
Developments, Prospects, and Key Policy Issues, World
Economic and Financial Surveys (Washington).

————, 2001a, *International Capital Markets:*
Developments, Prospects, and Key Policy Issues, World
Economic and Financial Surveys (Washington).

————, 2001b, "Reserves Should Be Adequate to
Reflect Increase in Capital Account Flows, Need
for Crisis Prevention," *IMF Survey,* February 19.

————, 2002, *Global Financial Stability Report,* World
Economic and Financial Surveys (Washington,
March).

————, 2003, *Global Financial Stability Report,* World
Economic and Financial Surveys (Washington,
March).

Kaminsky, Graciela, R. Lyons, and S. Schmukler,
2001, "Mutual Fund Investment in Emerging
Markets: An Overview," The World Bank
Economic Review, Vol. 15, No. 2, pp. 315–340.

Kaminsky, Graciela, and Carmen Reinhart, 2000,
"On Crises, Contagion, and Confusion," *Journal*
of International Economics, Vol. 51 (June), pp.
145–68.

————, and Carlos, Végh, 2002, "Two Hundred
Years of Contagion" (unpublished; Washington:
International Monetary Fund, Research
Department).

Kireyev, Alexei, 2002, "Liberalization of Trade in
Financial Services and Financial Sector Stability,"
IMF Working Paper No. 02/139 (Washington:
International Monetary Fund).

Kodres, Laura, and Matthew Pritsker, 2002, "A
Rational Expectation Model of Financial
Contagion," *Journal of Finance,* Vol. 57 (April),
pp. 769–99.

Kono, Masamichi, and Ludger Schuknecht, 1998,
"Financial Services Trade, Capital Flows, and
Financial Stability," Staff Working Paper No.
ERAD-98-12 (Geneva: World Trade Organization,
Economic Research and Analysis Division).

Mathieson, Donald, and Jorge Roldos, 2001,
"Foreign Banks in Emerging Markets," in *Open*

Doors: Financial Participation in Financial Systems in
Developing Countries, ed. by Robert E. Litan, Paul
Masson, and Michael Pomerleano, (Washington:
Brookings Institution Press), pp. 15–55.

————, forthcoming, "Local Emerging Securities
Markets," IMF Occasional Paper (Washington:
International Monetary Fund).

Montiel, Peter, and Carmen Reinhart, 1999, "Short-
Term Capital Movements and Balance of
Payments Crises," in *The Dynamics of Capital*
Movements to Emerging Economies During the 1990s,"
ed. by Griffith-Jones, Montes (Oxford: Oxford
University Press).

Moser, Thomas, 2003, "What Is International
Contagion?" *International Finance,* Vol. 6, No.2,
pp. 157–78.

Obstfeld, Maurice, and A. Taylor, 1998, "The Great
Depression as a Watershed: International Capital
Mobility over the Long-Run," in *The Defining*
Moment: The Great Depression and the American
Economy in the Twentieth Century, edited by
Michael Bordo, C. Goldin, and E. White
(Chicago: University of Chicago Press),
pp. 353–402.

O'Rourke, K., and J. Williamson, 1999, *Globalization*
and History: The Evolution of a Nineteenth Century
Atlantic Economy (Cambridge: MIT Press).

Osei, Robert, Oliver Morrissey, and Robert Lensink,
2002, "The Volatility of Capital Inflows: Measures
and Trends for Developing Countries," CREDIT
Research Paper 02/20 (University of
Nottingham: Centre for Research in Economic
Development and International Trade).

Persaud, Avinash, 2000, "The Liquidity Puzzle,"
Risk (June).

————, 2002, "Liquidity Black Holes: And Why
Modern Financial Regulation in Developed
Countries Is Making Short-Term Capital Flows to
Developing Countries Even More Volatile,"
WIDER Discussion Paper No. 2002/31 (United
Nations University, World Institute for
Development Economics Research).

Prasad, Eswar, Kenneth Rogoff, Shang-Jin Wei, and
M. Kose, 2003, "Effects of Financial Globalization
on Developing Countries: Some Empirical
Evidence," paper discussed at an informal ses-
sion of the IMF Executive Board and available
on the Internet at http://www.imf.org/external/
np/res/docs/2003/031703.htm.

Roldos, Jorge, 2002, "FDI in Emerging Markets
Banking Systems," in *New Horizons for Foreign*

Direct Investment (OECD Global Forum on International Investment).

———, 2003, "Pension Reform and Capital Markets," paper presented at the conference on "Results and Challenges of Pension Reform," organized by the International Federation of Pension Fund Administrators (FIAP), Cancun, Mexico, May 15–16.

Schinasi, Garry, and R. Smith, 2000, "Portfolio Diversification, Leverage, and Financial Contagion," *IMF Staff Papers,* International Monetary Fund, Vol. 47.

United States, 1999, *Hedge Funds, Leverage, and the Lessons of Long-Term Capital Management,* President's Working Group on Financial Markets (Washington, April). Available via the Internet at http://www.treas.gov/press/releases/99report.htm.

Van Rijckeghem, Caroline, and Beatrice Weder, 2000, "Spillovers Through Banking Centers: A Panel Data Analysis," IMF Working Paper No. 00/88 (Washington: International Monetary Fund).

World Bank, 2003, *Global Development Finance* (Washington).

Williamson, John, and Molly Mahar, 1998, "A Survey of Financial Liberalization," *Essays in International Finance,* No. 211, Princeton University.

GLOSSARY

Balance sheet mismatch	A balance sheet is a financial statement showing a company's assets, liabilities, and equity on a given date. Typically, a mismatch in a balance sheet implies that the maturities of the liabilities differ (are typically shorter) from those of the assets and/or that some liabilities are denominated in a foreign currency while the assets are not.
Banking soundness	The financial health of a single bank or of a country's banking system.
Benchmark issues	High-quality debt securities, typically bonds. Investors use their yield for comparison purposes and to price other bond issues.
Brady Bonds	Bonds issued by emerging market countries as part of a restructuring of defaulted commercial bank loans. These bonds are named after former U.S. Treasury Secretary Nicholas Brady and the first bonds were issued in March of 1990.
Capital account liberalization	Removal of statutory restrictions on cross-border private capital flows, an important part of financial liberalization. In particular, the relaxation of controls or prohibitions on transactions in the capital and financial accounts of the balance of payments, including the removal of foreign exchange convertability restrictions.
Carry trade	A leveraged transaction in which borrowed funds are used to buy a security whose yield is expected to exceed the cost of the borrowed funds.
Collective action clause	A clause in bond contracts that includes provisions allowing a qualified majority of lenders to amend key financial terms of the debt contract and bind a minority to accept these new terms.
Common lender effect	Describes how contagion can occur across several emerging bond markets that are exposed to a common (to all these markets) group of investors.
Contagion	The transmission or spillover of financial shocks or crises across countries and/or across asset classes, characterized by an apparent increase in the comovement of asset prices.
Convergence fund	A fund that invests in Eastern European countries' debt securities on the assumption that interest rates in these countries will converge to those in the European Union.
Convexity	A measure of the relationship between bond prices and bond yields. The more positive a bond's convexity, the *less* sensitive is the price of the bond to interest rate changes, other things being equal. Negative convexity implies the bond's price is *more* sensitive to interest rate changes, other things being equal.

Corporate governance	The governing relationships between all the stakeholders in a company—including the shareholders, directors, and management—as defined by the corporate charter, bylaws, formal policy, and rule of law.
Credit default swap	A financial contract under which an agent buys protection against credit risk for a periodic fee in return for a payment by the protection seller contingent on the occurrence of a credit/default event.
Credit spreads	The spread between sovereign benchmark securities and other debt securities that are comparable in all respects except for credit quality, (e.g., the difference between yields on U.S. treasuries and those on single A-rated corporate bonds of a certain term to maturity).
Defined benefit pensions	A retirement pension plan where the benefits that retirees receive are determined by such factors as salary history and the duration of employment. The company is typically responsible for the investment risk and portfolio management.
Derivatives	Financial contracts whose value derives from underlying securities prices, interest rates, foreign exchange rates, market indexes, or commodity prices.
Dollarization	The widespread domestic use of another country's currency (typically the U.S. dollar) to perform the standard functions of money—that of a unit of account, medium of exchange, and store of value.
Double gearing	Situations where multiple companies use shared capital to protect against risk occurring in separate entities. For example, an insurance company may purchase shares in a bank as a reciprocal arrangement for loans. In these cases, both institutions are leveraging their exposure to risk.
Dynamic hedging	A dynamic-hedging scheme involves the periodic re-balancing of a portfolio of hedging instruments (the buying or selling of securities) in order to maintain a specific hedging level.
EMBI	The acronym for the J.P. Morgan *Emerging Market Bond Index* that tracks the total returns for traded external debt instruments in the emerging markets.
Emerging markets	Developing countries' financial markets that are less than fully developed, but are nonetheless broadly accessible to foreign investors.
Foreign direct investment	The acquisition abroad (i.e., outside the home country) of physical assets, such as plant and equipment, or of a controlling stake (usually greater than 10 percent of shareholdings).
Forward price-earnings ratio	The multiple of future expected earnings at which a stock sells. It is ratio calculated by dividing the current stock price (adjusted for stock splits) by the estimated earnings per share for a future period (typically the next 12 months).

Hedge funds	Investment pools, typically organized as private partnerships and often resident offshore for tax and regulatory purposes. These funds face few restrictions on their portfolios and transactions. Consequently, they are free to use a variety of investment techniques—including short positions, transactions in derivatives, and leverage—to raise returns and cushion risk.
Hedging	Offsetting an existing risk exposure by taking an opposite position in the same or a similar risk, for example, by buying derivatives contracts.
Interest rate swaps	An agreement between counterparties to exchange periodic interest payments on some predetermined dollar principal, which is called the notional principal amount. For example, one party will make fixed-rate and receive variable-rate interest payments.
Intermediation	The process of transferring funds from the ultimate source to the ultimate user. A financial institution, such as a bank, intermediates credit when it obtains money from depositors and relends it to borrowers.
Investment-grade issues (Sub-investment-grade issues)	A bond that is assigned a rating in the top four categories by commercial credit rating agencies. S&P classifies investment-grade bonds as BBB or higher, and Moody's classifies investment grade bonds as Baa or higher. (Sub-investment-grade bond issues are rated bonds that are below investment-grade.)
Leverage	The magnification of the rate of return (positive and negative) on a position or investment beyond the rate obtained by direct investment of own funds in the cash market. It is often measured as the ratio of on- and off-balance-sheet exposures to capital. Leverage can be built up by borrowing (on-balance-sheet leverage, commonly measured by debt-to-equity ratios) or by using off-balance-sheet transactions.
Mark-to-market	The valuation of a position or portfolio by reference to the most recent price at which a financial instrument can be bought or sold in normal volumes. The mark-to-market value might equal the current market value—as opposed to historic accounting or book value—or the present value of expected future cash flows.
Nonperforming loans	Loans that are in default or close to being in default (i.e., typically past due for 90 days or more).
Offshore instruments	Securities issued outside of national boundaries.
(Pair-wise) correlations	A statistical measure of the degree to which the movements of two variables (for example asset returns) are related.
Pension funding gaps	The difference between the discounted value of accumulating future pension obligations and the present value of investment assets.

Primary market	The market where a newly issued security is first offered/sold to the public.
Put (call) option	A financial contract that gives the buyer the right, but not the obligation, to sell (buy) a financial instrument at a set price on or before a given date.
Retrenchment from risk	A reduction in the purchases or holdings of risky securities.
Risk aversion	Describes an investor's preference to avoid uncertain outcomes or payoffs. A risk averse investor will demand a risk premium when considering holding a risky asset or portfolio.
Secondary markets	Markets in which securities are traded after they are initially offered/sold in the primary market.
Spread	See "credit spread" above (the word credit is sometimes omitted). Other definitions include: (1) the gap between bid and ask prices of a financial instrument; (2) the difference between the price at which an underwriter buys an issue from the issuer and the price at which the underwriter sells it to the public.
Swaptions	Options on interest rate swaps.
Syndicated loans	Large loans made jointly by a group of banks to one borrower. Usually, one lead bank takes a small percentage of the loan and partitions (syndicates) the rest to other banks.
Tail events	The occurrence of large or extreme security price movements, that, in terms of their probability of occurring, lie within the tail region of the distribution of possible price movements.
Yield curve	A chart that plots the yield to maturity at a specific point in time for debt securities having equal credit risk but different maturity dates.

CONCLUDING REMARKS BY THE CHAIRMAN

The following remarks by the Chairman were made at the conclusion of the Executive Board's discussion of the Global Financial Stability Report *on August 22, 2003.*

Executive Directors welcomed the opportunity to discuss the global financial situation and prospects. They broadly agreed with the staff's assessment that financial markets had remained resilient during 2003, notwithstanding continued lackluster economic growth, geopolitical uncertainties, and high market volatility. However, they noted that some concerns remain, associated with risks related to the macroeconomic outlook, rising long-term bond yields, the potential for weak corporate earnings, and the vulnerability of emerging bond markets to a correction.

Recent Developments and Risks

Directors noted that further progress continued to be made by different sectors of the mature market economies in addressing the effects of the bursting of the equity price bubble. Household and corporate balance sheets continued to improve, as these sectors built up liquidity further and locked in fixed-rate borrowing at longer maturities. In addition, banks' balance sheets generally strengthened as corporate defaults declined and earnings began to recover. Many Directors also observed that the improved balance sheet positions of corporations placed them in a better position to contribute to the global economic recovery by increasing investment spending.

Directors agreed that historically low policy interest rates in the major financial centers had helped improve financial soundness. At the same time, low interest rates had

prompted a search for yield in early 2003 that had led investors to be increasingly willing to take on credit risk and market risk, which had left those investors vulnerable to an upturn in longer-term yields. Flows had also been attracted to higher-yielding emerging markets, allowing many borrowers from these markets to complete their borrowing programs for 2003. In addition, international equity markets had recovered since March.

Directors agreed that the rebound in bond yields in major markets since mid-June had been accentuated by the unwinding of carry trades and other technical factors, including a large volume of hedging of exposures in the U.S. mortgage market. Many Directors noted that there were signs that credit spreads on corporate and emerging market bonds might have become compressed, making them vulnerable to further increases in government bond yields, and that a rotation of funds away from fixed-income instruments and toward equities could make financing more difficult for emerging market borrowers.

Directors noted that, ultimately, a further steepening of government bond yield curves could, on balance, be positive for financial markets, including the emerging markets, if it were driven by prospects of faster economic growth. Stronger growth would allow further improvements in the balance sheets of firms and households, while higher yields would benefit financial institutions. Meanwhile, low short-term rates could contribute to further balance sheet repair and underpin investors' risk appetite. Directors cautioned, however, that there were risks in the transition to higher long-term yields, including capital losses for some investors and rising bond market volatility, even though they noted that to date the market reaction to increasing yields had been relatively orderly. Some Directors also warned that a key source of concern could arise if higher yields were prompted by worries about the magnitude of fiscal deficits in systemically important countries.

Directors observed that in the household sector a further sharp increase in bond yields would prompt steep falls in mortgage refinancing in the United States. This would reduce households' ability to further access home equity values and the saving on mortgage payments, which have provided important support to consumer spending of late. Furthermore, concern was expressed by some Directors that, in this scenario, the liquidity of cash and derivatives markets might be tested given the unprecedented size of hedging needs arising from the U.S. mortgage markets. As had been demonstrated in recent weeks, a rise in bond yields could be amplified by the need to sell fixed-rate assets to hedge the increasing duration of mortgages and mortgage-backed securities. Some Directors encouraged regulators to assess whether the capital bases of the U.S. and other mortgage agencies are adequate to absorb the risks that would arise in volatile market conditions.

Directors noted that additional risks could emerge if corporate earnings disappointed expectations. Such an outturn could undermine progress made earlier this year in strengthening balance sheets. However, many Directors observed that equity valuations were in general more sustainable than they had been for several years. Overall, most corporations and financial institutions were better prepared to cope with slower economic growth than they were last fall.

Directors welcomed the increased inflows into emerging markets in early 2003, which had reduced borrowing costs and improved access for many countries. Local markets as well as international markets for emerging

debt had benefited. More recently, the yield increase in mature markets had caused some consolidation in emerging bond markets. Nevertheless, most Directors noted that yield spreads in many cases remained well below historical averages, and there were signs that the search for yield had led recently to reduced investor discrimination among issuers. They cautioned that the recent increased correlation between mature and emerging bond markets raised the risk of a generalized weakness in emerging markets should yields in the major financial centers rise further.

Directors noted that, for several Eastern European countries, strong expectations of EMU entry appeared to be embedded in their secondary bond yields, thus keeping borrowing costs down. Nevertheless, they warned that increased reliance on foreign portfolio inflows had increased the risk for market volatility, and this underscored the need to persevere with sound economic policies, including further fiscal consolidation.

Directors expressed disappointment with the continued decline in foreign direct investment. They noted that, although the downturn largely reflected cyclical factors such as the weaker investment climate in mature markets and diminished growth prospects in some emerging market regions, there also appeared to be some indications of an increase in investors' perceptions of contractual risks in some recipient countries. Directors stressed the importance of predictable inward investment regimes and sound legal frameworks.

Directors welcomed the indicators of improved stability of banking systems in a number of emerging markets, particularly in Latin America, Asia, and Eastern Europe. They noted that the risk of contagion in Latin America had subsided, although vulnerabilities remain, including those relating to dollarization. Improvements in Asia have been more robust, while some financial institutions in the Middle East and Africa continue to exhibit structural weaknesses. Directors stressed the importance of continued efforts to strengthen regulation and governance in the financial sector in all regions.

Policy Implications of Recent Mature Market Developments

Directors urged authorities in major market financial centers to persist in reforms to strengthen market foundations.

Directors stressed that corporate governance must be strengthened further to restore investor confidence. They urged full implementation of recent measures to enhance the independence of corporate boards from management and dominant shareholder influence and to encourage more active participation by institutional investors in corporate decision making.

Directors emphasized the need for further improvements in the regulation and supervision of insurance companies. They noted that increased participation by insurers in financial markets had heightened their importance for systemic stability and that, although the recent rises in equity markets and long-term interest rates had likely strengthened their financial position, they remained vulnerable. Directors urged the strengthening of regulations for the valuation of financial assets and liabilities, and greater cooperation between supervisors, both cross-border and cross-sector.

Directors called for improvements in the accounting practices and regulation of defined-benefit pension funds. They acknowledged that the policy choices were not always easy, and that the magnitude of fund shortfalls meant that they could only be eliminated gradually. Nevertheless, it was important to improve transparency and risk management. Directors also urged that firms be encouraged to build up prudent pension fund surpluses over time to guard against future financial risks, and a few Directors observed that pay-as-you-go systems faced particular long-term funding risks owing to demographic developments.

Policy Lessons from Past Episodes of High Volatility

Directors agreed that price volatility in markets should not necessarily be of concern to policymakers, unless it is amplified to a point where it triggers financial instability. They noted that past episodes of extreme volatility offered lessons about the amplifying mechanisms that could lead to instability, for example, by forcing or creating incentives for sales into falling markets.

Directors noted that amplifying factors could take a number of forms. Weak corporate governance, lack of transparency by market participants, benchmarking, and index tracking can also increase herd behavior during both a boom and a subsequent crisis. It was suggested that the staff should conduct further work on the effect of volatility on financial stability and ways to achieve the appropriate balance between market discipline and regulation.

Policy Implications for Emerging Market Countries

Although the external financing climate for emerging market countries had improved somewhat this year, Directors cautioned that the public sector debt in these countries remains high and that there was no room for complacency by borrowers. They urged countries to take advantage of enhanced access to press ahead with the implementation of sound policies, and improve the structure of their liabilities, including extending maturities and reducing the dependence on dollar-linked debt. Directors noted that several countries had undertaken successful liability management operations. They also welcomed the use of collective action clauses in recent debt contracts.

Directors welcomed the discussion in the *Global Financial Stability Report* (GFSR) of the volatility of capital flows to emerging markets, and agreed that foreign direct investment should be encouraged. They noted that changes in the composition of the investor base for emerging market assets had increased the volatility of overall capital flows and expressed concerns about the persistence of boom-bust cycles for investment. Directors recommended that the staff continue to work on analyzing the sources of volatility in the supply of funds to emerging markets.

Directors pointed out that, while volatility of capital flows seemed somewhat inevitable, sound economic policies and transparency could help to make flows more stable. There was also much that emerging countries could do to "self-insure" themselves against the effects of volatility, including through asset and liability management; adapting exchange rate arrangements to the degree of capital account openness; strengthening domestic financial institutions; enhancing supervision and regulation; and developing local securi-

ties markets. Some Directors also felt that self-insurance efforts might also be complemented by increased holdings of international reserves. Directors noted that developing efficient and stable local sources of finance had become all the more relevant now that emerging markets as a group had become net exporters of capital in recent years.

Looking ahead, Directors saw merit in future staff work in the next GFSR on a number of issues raised in the discussion, including on the factors behind and the implications of the shift in the status of emerging markets as a group to be net exporters of capital, including through the accumulation of external reserves. It would also be important to assess the recent slowdown in foreign direct investment and the rise in international reserves in emerging markets, in the context of floating exchange rates.

STATISTICAL APPENDIX

This statistical appendix presents data on financial developments in key financial centers and emerging markets. It is designed to complement the analysis in the text by providing additional data that describe key aspects of financial market developments. These data are derived from a number of sources external to the IMF, including banks, commercial data providers, and official sources, and are presented for information purposes only; the IMF does not, however, guarantee the accuracy of the data from external sources.

Presenting financial market data in one location and in a fixed set of tables and charts, in this and future issues of the GFSR, is intended to give the reader an overview of developments in global financial markets. Unless otherwise noted, the statistical appendix reflects information available up to July 16, 2003.

Mirroring the structure of the chapters of the report, the appendix presents data sepa-rately for key financial centers and emerging market countries. Specifically, it is organized into three sections:

- Figures 1–14 and Tables 1–9 contain information on market developments in key financial centers. This includes data on global capital flows, and on markets for foreign exchange, bonds, equities, and derivatives as well as sectoral balance sheet data for the United States, Japan, and Europe.
- Figures 15 and 16, and Tables 10–21 present information on financial developments in emerging markets, including data on equity, foreign exchange, and bond markets, as well as data on emerging market financing flows.
- Tables 22–25 report key financial soundness indicators for selected countries, including bank profitability, asset quality, and capital adequacy.

STATISTICAL APPENDIX

List of Tables and Figures

Key Financial Centers

Figures

Tables

Emerging Markets

Figures

Tables

Financial Soundness Indicators

Figure 1. Global Capital Flows: Sources and Uses of Global Capital in 2002

Countries That Export Capital[1]

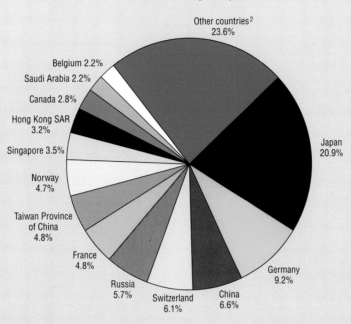

Other countries[2]
23.6%

Belgium 2.2%
Saudi Arabia 2.2%
Canada 2.8%
Hong Kong SAR
3.2%
Singapore 3.5%
Norway
4.7%
Taiwan Province
of China
4.8%
France
4.8%
Russia
5.7%
Switzerland
6.1%
China
6.6%
Germany
9.2%
Japan
20.9%

Countries That Import Capital[3]

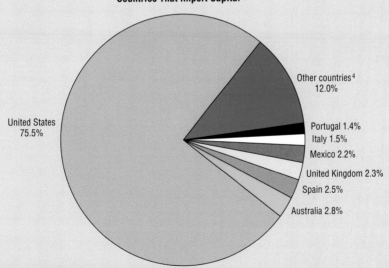

United States
75.5%

Other countries[4]
12.0%

Portugal 1.4%
Italy 1.5%
Mexico 2.2%
United Kingdom 2.3%
Spain 2.5%
Australia 2.8%

Source: International Monetary Fund, World Economic Outlook database as of August 21, 2003.
[1]As measured by countries' current (capital) account surplus (deficit).
[2]Other countries include all countries with shares of total surplus less than 2.2 percent.
[3]As measured by countries' current (capital) account deficit (surplus).
[4]Other countries include all countries with shares of total deficit less than 1.4 percent.

Figure 2. Exchange Rates: Selected Major Industrial Countries

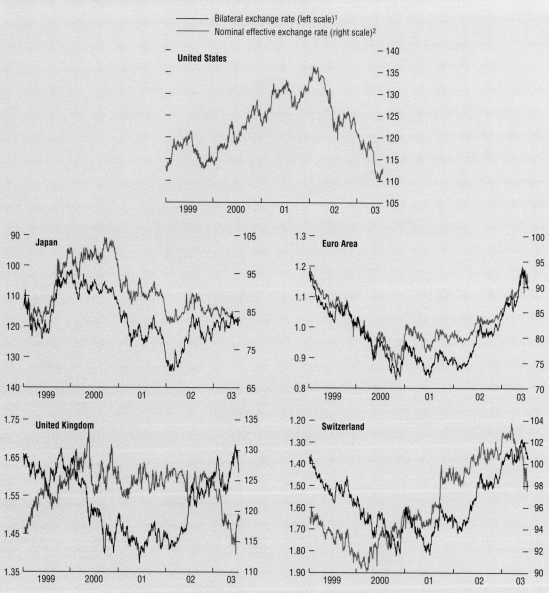

Sources: Bloomberg L.P.; and the IMF Competitive Indicators System.

Note: In each panel, the effective and bilateral exchange rates are scaled so that an upward movement implies an appreciation of the respective local currency.

[1]Local currency units per U.S. dollar except for the euro area and the United Kingdom, for which data are shown as U.S. dollars per local currency.

[2]1995 = 100; constructed using 1989–91 trade weights.

Figure 3. United States: Yields on Corporate and Treasury Bonds
(Weekly data)

Sources: Bloomberg L.P.; and Merrill Lynch.

Figure 4. Selected Spreads
(In basis points)

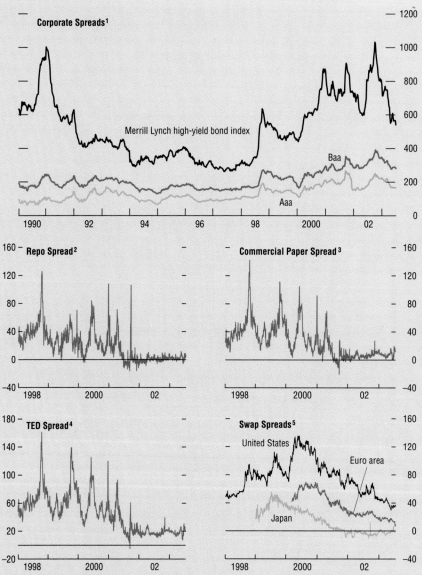

Corporate Spreads[1]

Merrill Lynch high-yield bond index

Baa

Aaa

Repo Spread[2]

Commercial Paper Spread[3]

TED Spread[4]

Swap Spreads[5]

United States

Euro area

Japan

Sources: Bloomberg L.P.; and Merrill Lynch.
[1]Spreads over 10-year U.S. treasury bond; weekly data.
[2]Spread between yields on three-month U.S. treasury repo and on three-month U.S. treasury bill.
[3]Spread between yields on 90-day investment-grade commercial paper and on three-month U.S. treasury bill.
[4]Spread between three-month U.S. dollar LIBOR and yield on three-month U.S. treasury bill.
[5]Spread over 10-year government bond.

Figure 5. Nonfinancial Corporate Credit Spreads
(In basis points)

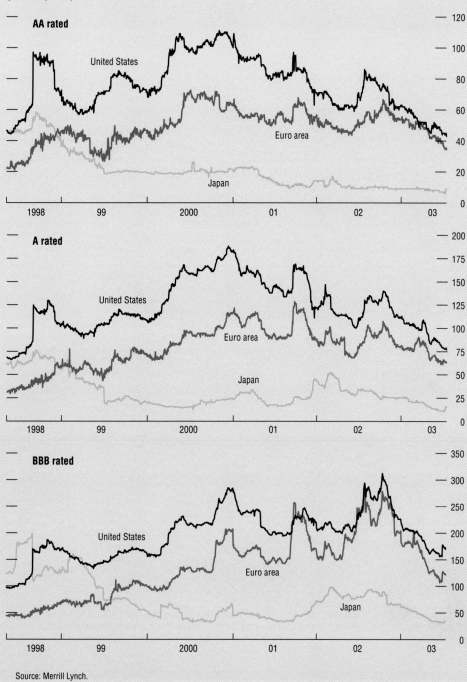

Source: Merrill Lynch.

Figure 6. Equity Markets: Price Indexes
(January 1, 1990 = 100; weekly data)

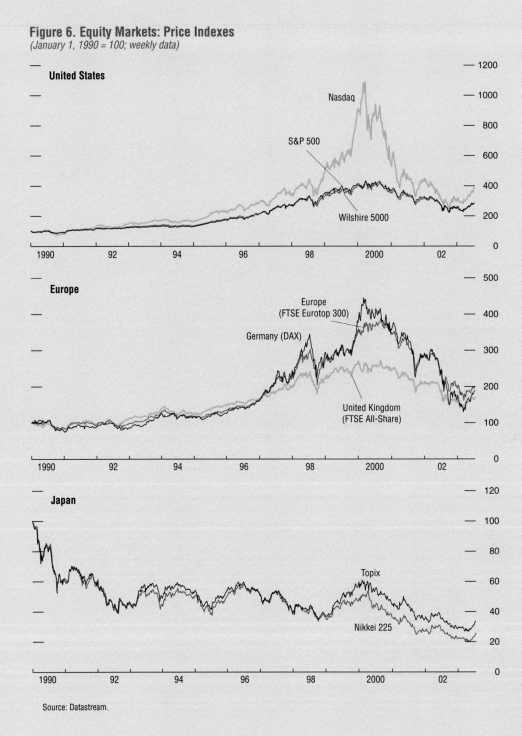

Source: Datastream.

Figure 7. Implied and Historical Volatility in Equity Markets

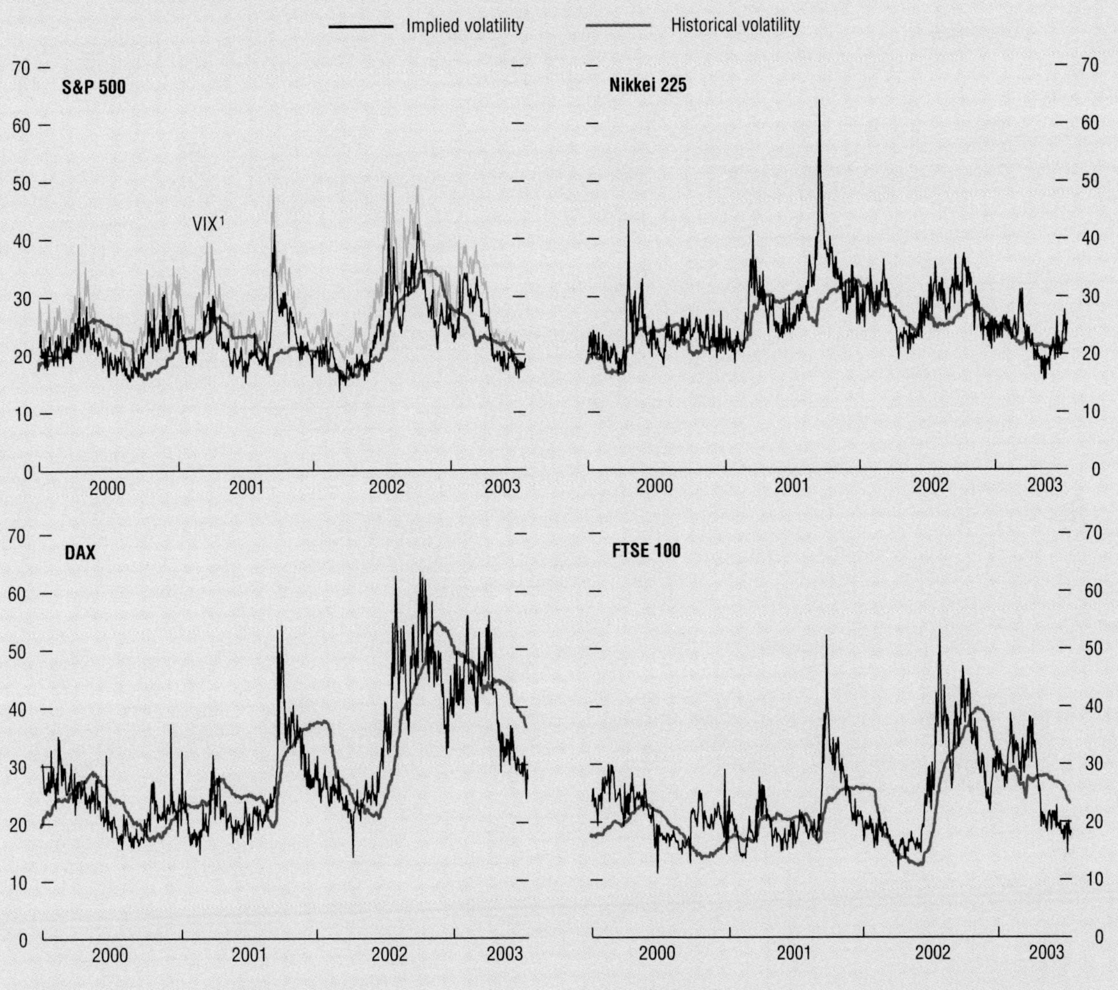

Sources: Bloomberg L.P.; and IMF staff estimates.
Note: Implied volatility is a measure of the equity price variability implied by the market prices of call options on equity futures. Historical volatility is calculated as a rolling 100-day annualized standard deviation of equity price changes. Volatilities are expressed in percent rate of change.
[1]VIX is the Chicago Board Options Exchange volatility index. This index is calculated by taking a weighted average of implied volatility for the eight S&P 100 calls and puts.

Figure 8. Historical Volatility of Government Bond Yields and Bond Returns for Selected Countries[1]

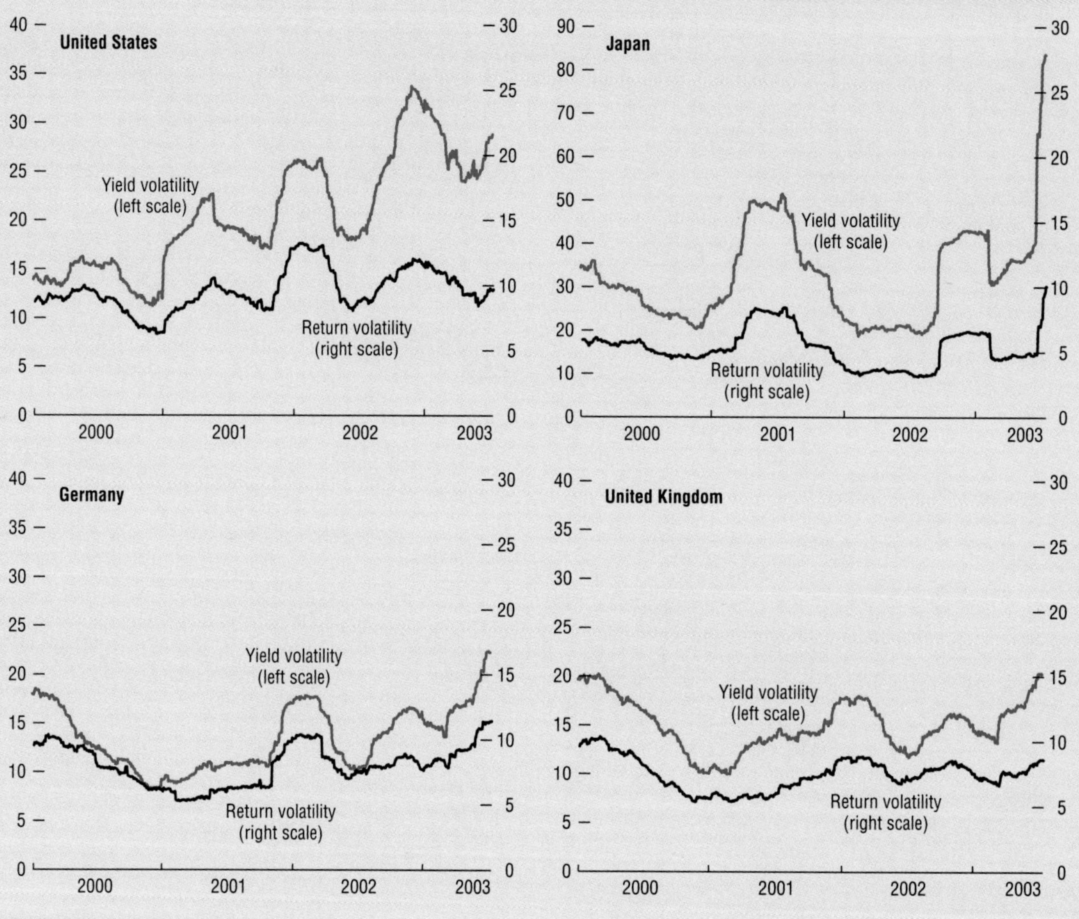

Sources: Bloomberg L.P.; and Datastream.
[1]Volatility calculated as a rolling 100-day annualized standard deviation of changes in yield and returns on 10-year government bonds. Returns are based on 10-plus year government bond indexes.

Figure 9. Twelve-Month Forward Price/Earnings Ratios

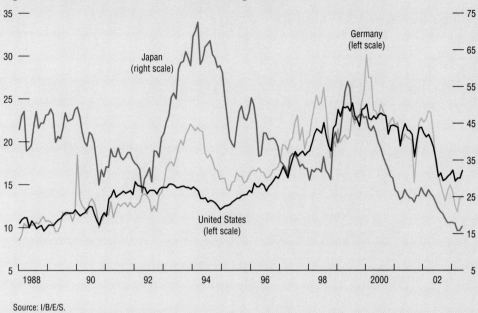

Source: I/B/E/S.

Figure 10. Flows into U.S.-Based Equity Funds

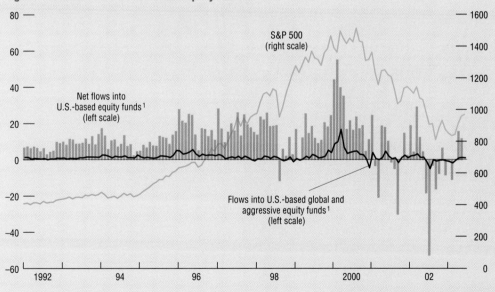

Sources: AMG Data Services; and Investment Company Institute.
[1]In billions of U.S. dollars.

Figure 11. United States: Corporate Bond Market

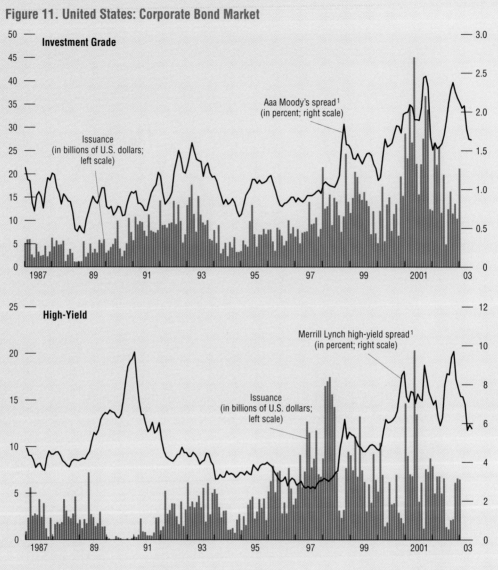

Sources: Board of Governors of the Federal Reserve System; and Bloomberg L.P.
[1]Spread against yield on 10-year U.S. government bonds.

Figure 12. Europe: Corporate Bond Market[1]

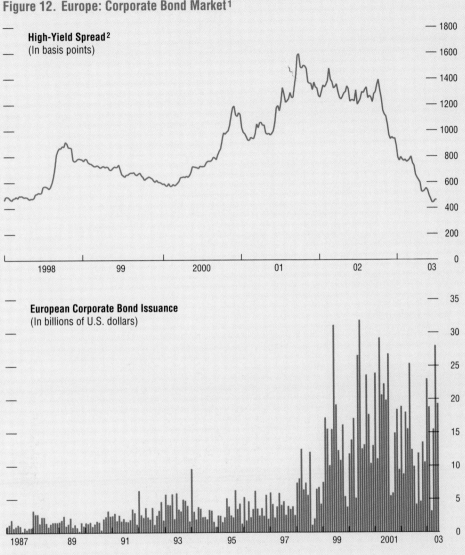

High-Yield Spread[2]
(In basis points)

European Corporate Bond Issuance
(In billions of U.S. dollars)

Sources: Bondware; and Datastream.
[1]Nonfinancial corporate bonds.
[2]Spread between yields on a Merrill Lynch High Yield European Issuers Index bond and a 10-year German government benchmark bond.

Figure 13. United States: Commercial Paper Market[1]

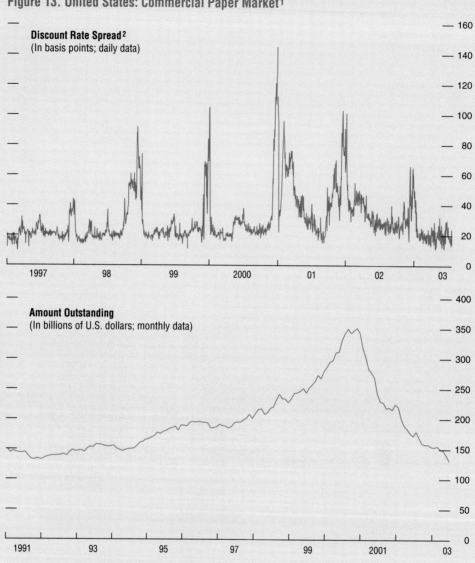

Discount Rate Spread[2]
(In basis points; daily data)

Amount Outstanding
(In billions of U.S. dollars; monthly data)

Source: Board of Governors of the Federal Reserve System.
[1]Nonfinancial commercial paper.
[2]Difference between 30-day A2/P2 and AA commercial paper.

Figure 14. United States: Asset-Backed Securities

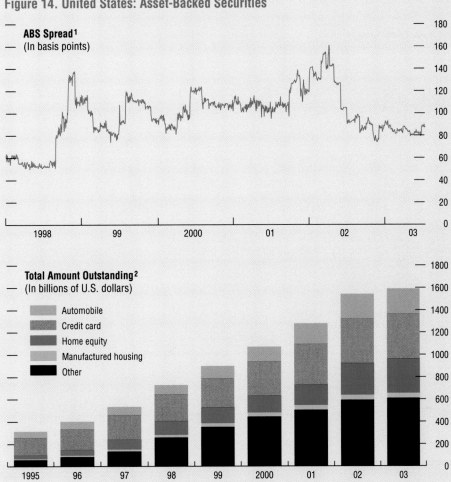

ABS Spread[1]
(In basis points)

Total Amount Outstanding[2]
(In billions of U.S. dollars)

- Automobile
- Credit card
- Home equity
- Manufactured housing
- Other

Sources: Merrill Lynch; Datastream; and the Bond Market Association.
[1]Merrill Lynch AAA Asset-Backed Master Index (fixed rate) option-adjusted spread.
[2]Data for 2003 refer to 2003:Q1.

Table 1. Global Capital Flows: Inflows and Outflows[1]

(In billions of U.S. dollars)

	Inflows										
	1992	1993	1994	1995	1996	1997	1998	1999	2000	2001	2002
United States											
Direct investment	19.8	51.4	46.1	57.8	86.5	105.6	179.0	289.4	321.3	151.6	39.6
Portfolio investment	72.0	111.0	139.4	210.4	332.8	333.1	187.6	285.6	420.0	425.1	421.4
Other investment	78.9	119.7	120.5	170.4	131.8	268.1	57.0	165.2	284.9	188.9	245.9
Reserve assets	n.a.	n.a.	n.a.	n.a.	n.a.	n.a.	n.a.	n.a.	n.a.	n.a.	n.a.
Total capital flows	170.7	282.1	306.0	438.6	551.1	706.8	423.6	740.2	1,026.1	765.5	707.0
Canada											
Direct investment	4.8	4.7	8.2	9.3	9.6	11.5	22.7	24.8	66.1	28.8	20.5
Portfolio investment	20.5	41.4	17.2	18.4	13.7	11.7	16.6	2.7	10.1	22.2	13.5
Other investment	−2.2	−6.7	16.0	−3.9	15.7	28.0	5.4	−10.8	0.6	7.4	6.0
Reserve assets	n.a.	n.a.	n.a.	n.a.	n.a.	n.a.	n.a.	n.a.	n.a.	n.a.	n.a.
Total capital flows	23.1	39.4	41.4	23.9	39.1	51.2	44.8	16.6	76.8	58.4	39.9
Japan											
Direct investment	2.8	0.1	0.9	—	0.2	3.2	3.3	12.3	8.2	6.2	9.1
Portfolio investment	9.6	−6.1	64.5	59.8	66.8	79.2	56.1	126.9	47.4	60.5	−20.0
Other investment	−105.2	−32.7	−5.6	97.3	31.1	68.0	−93.3	−265.1	−10.2	−17.6	26.6
Reserve assets	n.a.	n.a.	n.a.	n.a.	n.a.	n.a.	n.a.	n.a.	n.a.	n.a.	n.a.
Total capital flows	−92.9	−38.7	59.8	157.1	98.1	150.4	−34.0	−125.9	45.4	49.1	15.7
United Kingdom											
Direct investment	16.6	16.5	10.7	21.7	27.4	37.4	74.7	89.5	119.9	62.0	28.2
Portfolio investment	16.2	43.6	47.0	58.8	68.0	43.5	35.3	185.5	255.1	58.5	92.1
Other investment	96.4	191.4	−10.8	106.2	254.4	328.4	97.2	79.7	423.2	332.2	81.4
Reserve assets	n.a.	n.a.	n.a.	n.a.	n.a.	n.a.	n.a.	n.a.	n.a.	n.a.	n.a.
Total capital flows	129.1	251.6	46.9	186.7	349.7	409.2	207.2	354.8	798.3	452.7	201.7
Euro area											
Direct investment	...	...	...	...	...	...	...	212.1	402.5	139.8	120.6
Portfolio investment	...	...	...	...	...	...	...	283.4	264.7	316.7	267.0
Other investment	...	...	...	...	...	...	...	208.3	337.2	229.8	35.3
Reserve assets	n.a.	n.a.	n.a.	n.a.	n.a.	n.a.	n.a.	n.a.	n.a.	n.a.	n.a.
Total capital flows	...	...	...	...	...	...	...	703.8	1,004.4	686.3	422.9
Emerging markets[2]											
Direct investment	48.7	71.7	97.5	127.8	147.5	183.3	178.4	205.1	196.2	202.3	165.5
Portfolio investment	51.7	89.5	93.2	35.2	104.6	82.9	41.0	52.6	31.0	−5.4	−23.3
Other investment	78.0	39.7	15.2	128.1	74.0	45.3	47.9	−23.0	−15.1	−35.7	42.1
Reserve assets	n.a.	n.a.	n.a.	n.a.	n.a.	n.a.	n.a.	n.a.	n.a.	n.a.	n.a.
Total capital flows	178.3	200.9	206.0	291.1	326.1	311.4	267.3	234.6	212.0	161.2	184.4

Sources: IMF, World Economic Outlook database as of August 21, 2003; and *International Financial Statistics*.

[1]The total net capital flows are the sum of direct investment, portfolio investment, other investment flows, and reserve assets. "Other investment" includes bank loans and deposits.

[2]Excludes Hong Kong SAR.

					Outflows					
1992	1993	1994	1995	1996	1997	1998	1999	2000	2001	2002
−48.3	−84.0	−80.2	−98.8	−91.9	−104.8	−142.6	−224.9	−159.2	−120.0	−137.8
−49.2	−146.2	−60.3	−122.5	−149.8	−119.0	−124.2	−116.2	−121.9	−84.6	15.8
19.1	31.0	−40.9	−121.4	−178.9	−262.8	−74.2	−171.2	−288.4	−140.4	−53.3
3.9	−1.4	5.3	−9.7	6.7	−1.0	−6.7	8.7	−0.3	−4.9	−3.7
−74.4	−200.6	−176.1	−352.4	−413.9	−487.6	−347.8	−503.7	−569.8	−350.0	−179.0
−3.5	−5.7	−9.3	−11.5	−13.1	−23.1	−34.1	−17.3	−46.4	−36.8	−28.9
−9.8	−13.8	−6.6	−5.3	−14.2	−8.6	−15.1	−15.6	−42.9	−24.4	−15.8
−3.5	−0.4	−20.4	−8.3	−21.1	−16.2	9.4	10.2	−4.2	−10.2	−6.9
4.8	−0.9	0.4	−2.7	−5.5	2.4	−5.0	−5.9	−3.7	−2.2	0.2
−12.1	−20.8	−35.9	−27.9	−53.9	−45.4	−44.8	−28.5	−97.3	−73.5	−51.4
−17.4	−13.8	−18.1	−22.5	−23.4	−26.1	−24.6	−22.3	−31.5	−38.5	−32.0
−34.0	−63.7	−92.0	−86.0	−100.6	−47.1	−95.2	−154.4	−83.4	−106.8	−85.9
46.6	15.1	−35.1	−102.2	5.2	−192.0	37.9	266.3	−4.1	46.6	36.4
−0.6	−27.5	−25.3	−58.6	−35.1	−6.6	6.2	−76.3	−49.0	−40.5	−46.1
−5.4	−90.0	−170.4	−269.4	−154.0	−271.6	−75.8	13.4	−168.0	−139.2	−127.7
−19.7	−27.3	−34.9	−45.3	−34.8	−62.4	−122.1	−201.6	−266.2	−68.2	−7.5
−49.3	−133.6	31.5	−61.7	−93.1	−85.0	−53.0	−34.2	−97.7	−124.2	2.5
−60.5	−68.5	−42.4	−74.9	−215.3	−275.9	−26.8	−94.1	−411.5	−255.1	−202.9
2.4	−1.3	−1.5	0.9	0.7	3.9	0.3	1.0	−5.3	4.5	0.6
−127.0	−230.5	−47.4	−181.0	−342.6	−419.4	−201.6	−328.8	−780.8	−443.0	−207.3
...	...	...	...	...	...	...	−338.5	−405.0	−231.7	−163.1
...	...	...	...	...	...	...	−331.1	−382.2	−261.1	−158.7
...	...	...	...	...	...	...	−34.5	−166.2	−227.5	−219.1
...	...	...	...	...	...	...	11.6	16.2	16.9	−2.6
...	...	...	...	...	...	...	−692.5	−937.3	−703.4	−543.4
−10.0	−17.9	−17.1	−26.2	−31.3	−39.4	−22.4	−29.7	−30.4	−21.4	−22.3
−1.7	−2.8	−1.3	−12.9	−25.0	−29.2	−32.5	−39.8	−50.2	−55.9	−31.9
−19.2	−2.7	−38.1	−12.9	−47.9	−77.6	−83.2	−71.1	−97.7	−18.8	−43.7
−58.9	−66.2	−70.2	−117.9	−104.6	−71.1	−49.7	−88.3	−117.1	−122.4	−211.7
−89.7	−89.7	−126.7	−169.9	−208.8	−217.4	−187.9	−229.0	−295.4	−218.5	−309.6

Table 2. Global Capital Flows: Amounts Outstanding and Net Issues of International Debt Securities by Currency of Issue and Announced International Syndicated Credit Facilities by Nationality of Borrower
(In billions of U.S. dollars)

	1995	1996	1997	1998	1999	2000	2001	2002	2003 Q1
Amounts outstanding of international debt securities by currency of issue									
U.S. dollar	875.6	1,114.5	1,434.8	1,834.2	2,358.5	2,908.9	3,613.8	4,051.6	4,130.8
Japanese yen	437.8	464.7	446.1	464.5	499.5	454.3	413.2	436.8	438.3
Pound sterling	175.6	225.7	266.7	322.4	391.1	453.1	506.4	619.3	622.1
Canadian dollar	83.2	76.5	67.2	55.5	56.4	51.7	47.6	51.5	55.3
Swedish krona	5.1	5.1	4.1	7.5	7.2	7.7	8.2	11.1	11.6
Swiss franc	178.8	151.2	138.5	153.5	135.5	132.0	123.6	159.2	164.5
Euro[1]	742.9	832.7	848.9	1,133.9	1,452.9	1,775.0	2,290.2	3,285.0	3,609.9
Other	53.0	68.7	78.6	84.1	98.4	92.7	110.8	151.9	165.6
Total	2,552.0	2,939.1	3,284.9	4,055.6	4,999.5	5,875.4	7,112.8	8,766.4	9,198.1
Net issues of international debt securities by currency of issue									
U.S. dollar	65.9	238.8	320.3	399.4	524.3	550.3	704.1	438.7	79.2
Japanese yen	76.8	81.7	34.0	−33.0	−23.5	10.9	18.6	−15.8	−3.5
Pound sterling	6.7	30.8	46.4	53.9	77.8	92.4	65.4	52.5	15.4
Canadian dollar	−2.2	−6.5	−6.2	−7.5	−2.3	−2.7	−1.1	3.5	0.1
Swedish krona	−0.1	0.2	−0.4	3.6	0.1	1.2	1.4	1.1	0.2
Swiss franc	−0.3	−1.3	−1.6	6.3	4.0	−0.2	−5.2	8.0	1.5
Euro	72.3	140.0	130.2	214.6	508.4	423.9	624.0	495.0	193.9
Other	13.8	13.5	23.5	8.6	14.9	9.3	19.6	30.4	10.3
Total	232.9	497.2	546.2	645.9	1,103.7	1,085.1	1,426.8	1,013.4	297.1
Announced international syndicated credit facilities by nationality of borrower									
All countries	703.3	839.3	1,080.6	905.3	1,025.8	1,464.9	1,388.8	1,299.7	215.7
Industrial countries	610.6	732.2	904.8	820.1	960.6	1,328.5	1,280.1	1,202.4	199.1
Of which:									
United States	393.1	490.8	616.5	577.3	624.9	805.9	855.9	743.2	125.9
Japan	4.7	9.5	9.0	12.9	15.4	21.7	26.0	19.5	5.0
Germany	13.3	8.6	13.8	13.4	47.4	42.4	35.8	85.4	5.9
France	20.5	23.3	39.1	19.5	33.7	74.1	50.0	65.6	20.4
Italy	15.5	5.8	10.0	6.2	15.9	35.2	35.9	22.7	1.7
United Kingdom	55.4	66.3	97.7	78.2	92.9	125.3	100.5	105.1	16.6
Canada	22.4	25.7	38.3	41.6	23.3	38.4	40.6	35.3	3.6

Source: Bank for International Settlements.
[1]For 1995–98, the euro includes euro area currencies.

Table 3. Selected Indicators on the Size of the Capital Markets, 2002

(In billions of U.S. dollars unless noted otherwise)

	GDP	Total Reserves Minus Gold[1]	Stock Market Capitalization	Debt Securities Public	Debt Securities Private	Debt Securities Total	Bank Assets[2]	Bonds, Equities, and Bank Assets[3]	Bonds, Equities, and Bank Assets[3] (In percent of GDP)
World	32,163.7	2,513.9	22,077.4	16,531.2	26,826.4	43,357.6	85,002.5	150,437.5	467.7
European Union	8,652.8	289.1	5,524.0	4,941.3	7,662.0	12,603.3	34,712.8	52,840.1	610.7
Euro area	6,672.9	207.9	3,467.5	4,235.3	5,836.2	10,071.5	25,899.2	39,438.2	591.0
North America	11,182.4	104.9	11,625.8	5,043.6	14,786.0	19,829.6	24,329.1	55,784.5	498.9
Canada	736.1	37.0	570.2	499.1	315.8	814.9	1,200.0	2,585.1	351.2
United States	10,446.3	68.0	11,055.6	4,544.5	14,470.2	19,014.7	23,129.1	53,199.4	509.3
Japan	3,992.9	461.2	2,069.3	4,841.9	2,163.2	7,005.1	15,348.6	24,423.0	611.7
Memorandum items:									
EU countries									
Austria	204.8	9.7	33.6	156.3	152.5	308.8	564.1	906.5	442.7
Belgium	246.2	11.9	127.5	303.3	252.6	555.9	2,352.9	3,036.3	1,233.0
Denmark	172.6	27.0	76.7	99.8	234.6	334.4	646.3	1,057.4	612.7
Finland	131.2	9.3	138.8	82.1	48.3	130.4	360.9	630.1	480.2
France	1,438.0	28.4	905.0	790.8	998.5	1,789.3	6,420.9	9,115.2	633.9
Germany	1,991.0	51.2	686.0	860.0	2,344.6	3,204.6	8,391.6	12,282.2	616.9
Greece	133.3	8.1	66.0	161.2	11.8	173.0	181.4	420.4	315.4
Ireland	122.5	5.4	59.9	30.7	76.3	107.0	422.1	589.0	480.9
Italy	1,188.4	28.6	477.1	1,208.3	818.3	2,026.6	2,538.7	5,042.4	424.3
Luxembourg	20.6	0.2	24.6	—	29.4	29.4	592.2	646.2	3,137.2
Netherlands	419.3	9.6	442.6	198.4	672.5	870.9	2,350.6	3,664.1	873.8
Portugal	122.1	11.2	44.8	79.7	79.7	159.4	340.5	544.7	446.1
Spain	655.4	34.5	461.6	364.5	351.7	716.2	1,383.3	2,561.1	390.8
Sweden	241.1	14.9	179.1	132.1	206.9	339.0	769.3	1,287.4	534.1
United Kingdom	1,566.3	39.4	1,800.7	474.1	1,384.3	1,858.4	7,398.0	11,057.1	706.0
Emerging market countries	7,297.8	1,415.8	1,806.1	1,467.0	1,057.1	2,524.1	10,612.0	14,942.2	204.7
of which:									
Asia	3,447.5	902.1	1,259.8	657.8	814.9	1,472.7	6,997.8	9,730.3	282.2
Latin America	1,640.2	148.7	308.5	472.5	179.6	652.1	1,667.0	2,627.6	160.2
Middle East	810.3	122.9	52.5	5.4	13.5	18.9	840.8	912.2	112.6
Africa	448.0	67.4	116.5	47.7	20.8	68.5	589.1	774.1	172.8
Europe	951.7	174.7	68.6	283.6	28.3	311.9	517.3	897.8	94.3

Sources: World Federation of Exchanges; Bank for International Settlements; International Monetary Fund, *International Financial Statistics* (IFS) and World Economic Outlook database as of August 5, 2003; and (c)2003 Bureau van Dijk Electronic Publishing-Bankscope.

[1]Data are from IFS. For United Kingdom, excludes the assets of the Bank of England.
[2]Data are for 2001.
[3]Sum of the stock market capitalization, debt securities, and bank assets.

Table 4. Global Over-the-Counter Derivatives Markets: Notional Amounts and Gross Market Values of Outstanding Contracts[1]

(In billions of U.S. dollars)

	Notional Amounts					Gross Market Values				
	End-Dec. 2000	End-June 2001	End-Dec. 2001	End-June 2002	End-Dec. 2002	End-Dec. 2000	End-June 2001	End-Dec. 2001	End-June 2002	End-Dec. 2002
Total	**95,199**	**99,755**	**111,178**	**127,564**	**141,737**	**3,183**	**3,045**	**3,788**	**4,450**	**6,361**
Foreign exchange	**15,666**	**16,910**	**16,748**	**18,075**	**18,469**	**849**	**773**	**779**	**1,052**	**881**
Outright forwards and forex swaps	10,134	10,582	10,336	10,427	10,723	469	395	374	615	468
Currency swaps	3,194	3,832	3,942	4,220	4,509	313	314	335	340	337
Options	2,338	2,496	2,470	3,427	3,238	67	63	70	97	76
Interest rate[2]	**64,668**	**67,465**	**77,568**	**89,995**	**101,699**	**1,426**	**1,573**	**2,210**	**2,468**	**4,267**
Forward rate agreements	6,423	6,537	7,737	9,146	8,792	12	15	19	19	22
Swaps	48,768	51,407	58,897	68,274	79,161	1,260	1,404	1,969	2,214	3,864
Options	9,476	9,521	10,933	12,575	13,746	154	154	222	235	381
Equity-linked	**1,891**	**1,884**	**1,881**	**2,214**	**2,309**	**289**	**199**	**205**	**243**	**255**
Forwards and swaps	335	329	320	386	364	61	49	58	62	61
Options	1,555	1,556	1,561	1,828	1,944	229	150	147	181	194
Commodity[3]	**662**	**590**	**598**	**777**	**923**	**133**	**83**	**75**	**78**	**85**
Gold	218	203	231	279	315	17	21	20	28	28
Other	445	387	367	498	608	116	62	55	51	57
Forwards and swaps	248	229	217	290	402	...	...	...	...	...
Options	196	158	150	208	206	...	...	...	...	...
Other	**12,313**	**12,906**	**14,384**	**16,503**	**18,337**	**485**	**417**	**519**	**609**	**871**
Memorandum items:										
Gross credit exposure[4]	n.a.	n.a.	n.a.	n.a.	n.a.	1,080	1,019	1,171	1,316	1,511
Exchange-traded derivatives	15,666	16,910	16,748	18,075	18,469	...	...	...	...	...

Source: Bank for International Settlements.

[1]All figures are adjusted for double-counting. Notional amounts outstanding have been adjusted by halving positions vis-à-vis other reporting dealers. Gross market values have been calculated as the sum of the total gross positive market value of contracts and the absolute value of the gross negative market value of contracts with non-reporting counterparties.

[2]Single-currency contracts only.

[3]Adjustments for double-counting are estimated.

[4]Gross market values after taking into account legally enforceable bilateral netting agreements.

Table 5. Global Over-the-Counter Derivatives Markets: Notional Amounts and Gross Market Values of Outstanding Contracts by Counterparty, Remaining Maturity, and Currency[1]
(In billions of U.S. dollars)

	Notional Amounts					Gross Market Values				
	End-Dec. 2000	End-June 2001	End-Dec. 2001	End-June 2002	End-Dec. 2002	End-Dec. 2000	End-June 2001	End-Dec. 2001	End-June 2002	End-Dec. 2002
Total	**95,199**	**99,755**	**111,178**	**127,564**	**141,737**	**3,183**	**3,045**	**3,788**	**4,450**	**6,361**
Foreign exchange	**15,666**	**16,910**	**16,748**	**18,075**	**18,469**	**849**	**773**	**779**	**1,052**	**881**
By counterparty										
With other reporting dealers	5,729	5,907	5,912	6,595	6,836	271	229	237	371	284
With other financial institutions	6,597	7,287	6,755	7,210	7,602	357	334	319	421	377
With non-financial customers	3,340	3,716	4,081	4,270	4,031	222	210	224	260	221
By remaining maturity										
Up to one year[2]	12,888	13,012	13,427	14,403	14,536	...	...	...	...	...
One to five years[2]	1,902	2,833	2,340	2,541	2,725	...	...	...	...	...
Over five years[2]	876	1,065	981	1,131	1,208	...	...	...	...	...
By major currency										
U.S. dollar[3]	14,073	15,141	15,410	15,979	16,509	771	679	704	948	813
Euro[3]	5,981	6,425	6,368	7,298	7,819	361	322	266	445	429
Japanese yen[3]	4,254	4,254	4,178	4,461	4,800	274	217	313	254	189
Pound sterling[3]	2,391	2,472	2,315	2,522	2,462	82	78	69	112	98
Other[3]	4,633	5,528	5,225	5,890	5,348	210	250	206	345	233
Interest rate[4]	**64,668**	**67,465**	**77,568**	**89,995**	**101,699**	**1,426**	**1,573**	**2,210**	**2,468**	**4,267**
By counterparty										
With other reporting dealers	31,494	32,319	35,472	43,300	46,681	638	703	912	1,081	1,847
With other financial institutions	27,048	28,653	32,510	36,310	43,607	610	683	945	1,025	1,845
With non-financial customers	6,126	6,494	9,586	10,385	11,411	179	187	353	362	575
By remaining maturity										
Up to one year[2]	24,107	25,605	27,886	33,688	36,950	...	...	...	...	...
One to five years[2]	25,923	26,308	30,566	34,458	40,161	...	...	...	...	...
Over five years[2]	14,638	15,553	19,115	21,849	24,588	...	...	...	...	...
By major currency										
U.S. dollar	19,421	23,083	27,427	32,178	34,400	486	581	952	1,127	1,917
Euro	21,311	22,405	26,230	30,671	38,429	477	461	677	710	1,499
Japanese yen	13,107	11,278	11,799	13,473	14,691	232	313	304	327	379
Pound sterling	4,852	5,178	6,216	6,978	7,442	113	99	148	151	252
Other	5,977	5,521	5,896	6,695	6,737	118	119	129	153	220
Equity-linked	**1,891**	**1,884**	**1,881**	**2,214**	**2,309**	**289**	**199**	**205**	**243**	**255**
Commodity[5]	**662**	**590**	**598**	**777**	**923**	**133**	**83**	**75**	**78**	**85**
Other	**12,313**	**12,906**	**14,384**	**16,503**	**18,337**	**485**	**417**	**519**	**609**	**871**

Source: Bank for International Settlements.

[1]All figures are adjusted for double-counting. Notional amounts outstanding have been adjusted by halving positions vis-à-vis other reporting dealers. Gross market values have been calculated as the sum of the total gross positive market value of contracts and the absolute value of the gross negative market value of contracts with non-reporting counterparties.

[2]Residual maturity.

[3]Counting both currency sides of each foreign exchange transaction means that the currency breakdown sums to twice the aggregate.

[4]Single-currency contracts only.

[5]Adjustments for double-counting are estimated.

Table 6. Exchange-Traded Derivative Financial Instruments: Notional Principal Amounts Outstanding and Annual Turnover

	1986	1987	1988	1989	1990	1991	1992	1993
	(In billions of U.S. dollars)							
Notional principal amounts outstanding								
Interest rate futures	370.0	487.7	895.4	1,201.0	1,454.8	2,157.4	2,913.1	4,960.4
Interest rate options	144.0	122.6	279.0	386.0	595.4	1,069.6	1,383.8	2,361.4
Currency futures	10.2	14.6	12.1	16.0	17.0	18.3	26.5	34.7
Currency options	39.2	59.5	48.0	50.2	56.5	62.9	71.6	75.9
Stock market index futures	14.5	17.8	27.1	41.3	69.1	76.0	79.8	110.0
Stock market index options	37.8	27.7	42.7	70.5	93.6	136.9	163.7	232.4
Total	615.7	729.8	1,304.3	1,765.0	2,286.4	3,521.2	4,638.5	7,774.9
North America	515.6	578.0	951.5	1,154.0	1,264.4	2,153.0	2,698.7	4,360.7
Europe	13.1	13.3	177.4	250.9	461.4	710.7	1,114.4	1,777.9
Asia-Pacific	87.0	138.5	175.5	360.1	560.5	657.0	823.5	1,606.0
Other	0.0	0.0	0.0	0.0	0.1	0.5	1.9	30.3
	(In millions of contracts traded)							
Annual turnover								
Interest rate futures	91.0	145.7	156.4	201.0	219.1	230.9	330.1	112.7
Interest rate options	22.2	29.3	30.5	39.5	52.0	50.8	64.8	22.7
Currency futures	19.9	21.2	22.5	28.2	29.7	30.0	31.3	10.0
Currency options	13.0	18.3	18.2	20.7	18.9	22.9	23.4	5.5
Stock market index futures	28.4	36.1	29.6	30.1	39.4	54.6	52.0	21.6
Stock market index options	140.0	130.9	71.8	75.3	90.4	85.2	85.8	22.3
Total	314.9	389.6	336.3	421.2	478.2	510.4	635.6	210.9
North America	288.7	318.3	252.3	288.0	312.3	302.6	341.4	96.0
Europe	10.3	35.9	40.8	64.3	83.0	110.5	185.1	75.4
Asia-Pacific	14.3	30.0	34.3	63.6	79.1	85.8	82.9	27.2
Other	1.6	5.4	8.9	5.3	3.8	11.5	26.2	12.3

Source: Bank for International Settlements.

	1994	1995	1996	1997	1998	1999	2000	2001	2002	2003 Q1
					(In billions of U.S. dollars)					
	5,807.6	5,876.2	5,979.0	7,586.7	8,031.4	7,924.8	7,907.8	9,265.3	9,950.7	10,952.3
	2,623.2	2,741.8	3,277.8	3,639.9	4,623.5	3,755.5	4,734.2	12,492.8	11,759.5	17,622.4
	40.4	33.8	37.7	42.3	31.7	36.7	74.4	65.6	47.2	65.2
	55.7	120.4	133.4	118.6	49.2	22.4	21.4	27.4	27.4	29.5
	127.7	172.2	195.7	211.3	292.1	344.3	377.3	341.7	334.2	378.3
	242.8	337.7	394.5	809.5	907.9	1,522.1	1,162.9	1,605.2	1,754.7	1,894.2
	8,897.3	9,282.0	10,017.9	12,408.3	13,935.7	13,605.7	14,278.0	23,798.0	23,873.7	30,941.9
	4,823.6	4,852.4	4,841.0	6,349.1	7,355.1	6,930.6	8,167.9	16,198.9	13,689.1	16,812.4
	1,831.8	2,241.3	2,828.1	3,587.4	4,398.1	4,024.2	4,217.7	6,179.5	8,863.6	12,857.9
	2,171.8	1,990.2	2,154.0	2,235.7	1,882.5	2,401.3	1,606.2	1,308.4	1,191.7	1,124.5
	70.1	198.1	194.8	236.1	300.0	249.6	286.2	111.2	129.3	147.1
					(In millions of contracts traded)					
	137.5	121.5	146.9	182.0	162.1	147.9	179.0	290.8	273.6	327.8
	26.5	51.1	26.3	29.9	32.2	25.7	26.2	62.8	62.9	75.5
	22.9	23.8	19.4	14.6	9.5	8.8	11.3	14.9	10.2	12.9
	4.1	7.2	5.5	5.0	2.1	1.7	1.8	3.1	3.4	3.5
	27.9	27.6	23.5	33.4	50.6	49.9	63.3	98.2	160.0	173.1
	34.9	25.7	20.6	22.5	18.2	16.7	15.5	15.5	20.2	20.5
	270.3	275.2	263.1	310.6	313.5	329.5	431.1	906.0	1,231.3	1,343.8
	126.2	97.9	96.1	124.6	126.3	100.5	115.1	189.8	238.5	247.5
	80.5	86.3	105.1	121.4	118.7	152.0	164.9	257.4	276.7	350.5
	30.8	23.5	27.6	37.5	49.8	52.5	113.2	391.4	682.5	711.0
	32.8	67.5	34.3	27.1	18.7	24.5	37.9	67.4	33.6	34.8

Table 7. United States: Sectoral Balance Sheets
(In percent)

	1996	1997	1998	1999	2000	2001	2002
Corporate sector							
Debt/equity	40.5	34.6	32.7	27.7	36.2	44.8	62.1
Short-term debt/total debt	41.0	40.5	40.1	39.0	39.7	34.5	31.7
Interest burden[1]	10.2	10.6	12.1	13.0	15.2	17.8	17.1
Household sector							
Net worth/assets	84.7	85.3	85.5	86.0	84.8	83.6	81.8
Equity/total assets	25.8	29.8	31.5	35.1	31.0	26.7	20.7
Equity/financial assets	38.2	42.9	45.0	49.3	45.3	40.4	33.1
Home mortgage debt/total assets	10.1	9.6	9.5	9.2	10.0	11.0	12.6
Consumer credit/total assets	3.4	3.2	3.1	2.9	3.2	3.5	3.7
Total debt/financial assets	22.7	21.2	20.7	19.7	22.1	24.9	29.2
Debt service burden[2]	13.3	13.4	13.4	13.7	13.9	14.4	14.0
Banking sector[3]							
Credit quality							
Nonperforming loans[4]/total loans	1.0	1.0	1.0	1.0	1.1	1.4	1.5
Net loan losses/average total loans	0.6	0.6	0.6	0.6	0.6	0.7	0.7
Loan-loss reserve/total loans	2.0	1.8	1.8	1.7	1.7	1.9	1.9
Net charge-offs/total loans	0.6	0.6	0.7	0.6	0.7	0.9	1.1
Capital ratios							
Total risk-based capital	12.5	12.2	12.2	12.2	12.1	12.7	12.8
Tier 1 risk-based capital	10.0	9.6	9.5	9.5	9.4	9.9	10.0
Equity capital/total assets	8.2	8.3	8.5	8.4	8.5	9.1	9.2
Core capital (leverage ratio)	7.6	7.6	7.5	7.8	7.7	7.8	7.8
Profitability measures							
Return on assets (ROA)	1.2	1.2	1.2	1.3	1.2	1.2	1.3
Return on equity (ROE)	14.5	14.7	13.9	15.3	14.0	13.1	14.5
Net interest margin	4.3	4.2	4.1	4.1	4.0	3.9	4.1
Efficiency ratio[5]	60.8	59.2	61.0	58.7	58.4	57.7	55.7

Sources: Board of Governors of the Federal Reserve System, *Flow of Funds;* Department of Commerce, Bureau of Economic Analysis; Federal Deposit Insurance Corporation; and Federal Reserve Bank of St. Louis.

[1]Ratio of net interest payments to pre-tax income.

[2]Ratio of debt payments to disposable personal income.

[3]All FDIC-insured.

[4]Noncurrent loans and leases.

[5]Noninterest expense less amortization of intangible assets as a percent of net interest income plus noninterest income.

Table 8. Japan: Sectoral Balance Sheets[1]
(In percent)

	FY1996	FY1997	FY1998	FY1999	FY2000	FY2001	FY2002
Corporate sector							
Debt/shareholders' equity (book value)	206.3	207.9	189.3	182.5	156.8	156.0	146.1
Short-term debt/total debt	40.5	41.8	39.0	39.4	37.7	36.8	39.0
Interest burden[2]	38.2	39.1	46.5	36.3	28.4	32.3	27.8
Debt/operating profits	1,344.7	1,498.5	1,813.8	1,472.1	1,229.3	1,480.0	1,370.0
Memorandum items:							
Total debt/GDP	105.5	106.6	106.5	107.8	101.6	100.1	99.0
Household sector							
Net worth/assets	85.5	85.3	85.1	85.5	85.4	85.1	...
Equity	4.7	4.3	3.1	5.6	4.9	3.7	...
Real estate	40.7	40.0	39.5	37.6	36.7	35.8	...
Interest burden[3]	5.4	5.3	5.1	4.9	4.9	5.0	...
Memorandum items:							
Debt/equity	307.6	345.1	477.6	259.4	297.3	408.6	...
Debt/real estate	35.6	36.7	37.8	38.6	39.9	41.8	...
Debt/net disposable income	125.4	126.3	126.7	126.1	127.8	129.8	...
Debt/net worth	16.9	17.2	17.6	17.0	17.1	17.6	...
Equity/net worth	5.5	5.0	3.7	6.5	5.8	4.3	...
Real estate/net worth	47.7	46.4	46.7	43.9	42.6	42.0	...
Total debt/GDP	74.7	75.8	77.1	77.3	75.9	76.7	...
Banking sector							
Credit quality							
Nonperforming loans[4]/total loans	3.9	5.5	6.6	6.4	6.9	9.3	7.9
Capital ratio							
Stockholders' equity/assets	3.3	2.7	4.2	4.5	4.5	4.0	3.4
Profitability measures							
Return on equity (ROE)	−0.7	−27.6	−18.0	−0.6	−1.2	−16.3	−19.3

Sources: Ministry of Finance, *Financial Statements of Corporations by Industries;* Cabinet Office, Economic and Social Research Institute, *Annual Report on National Accounts;* Bank of Japan, *Financial Statements of Japanese Banks;* and Financial Services Agency, *The Status of Nonperforming Loans.*

[1]Data are fiscal year beginning April 1.

[2]Interest payments as a percent of operating profits.

[3]Interest payments as a percent of income.

[4]From 1999 onwards, nonperforming loans are based on figures reported under the Financial Reconstruction Law. Up to 1998, they are based on loans reported by banks for risk management purposes.

Table 9. Europe: Sectoral Balance Sheets[1]
(In percent)

	1996	1997	1998	1999	2000	2001	2002
Corporate sector							
Debt/equity[2]	90.8	90.1	88.0	90.7	90.4	91.0	...
Short-term debt/total debt	36.5	38.1	37.3	37.9	40.0	39.1	...
Interest burden[3]	17.9	17.1	16.7	17.1	18.8	20.1	...
Debt/operating profits	262.1	262.9	258.0	288.8	314.8	328.3	...
Memorandum items:							
Financial assets/equity	1.6	1.7	1.8	2.1	2.0	1.9	...
Liquid assets/short-term debt	100.3	94.5	92.9	88.8	84.5	89.0	...
Household sector							
Net worth/assets	85.7	86.0	86.0	86.4	86.0	...	...
Equity/net worth	12.5	14.4	15.2	17.9	17.1	...	...
Equity/net financial assets	35.3	37.8	39.3	44.0	43.3	42.7	...
Interest burden[4]	6.4	6.3	6.7	6.4	6.6	6.4	...
Memorandum items:							
Nonfinancial assets/net worth	64.3	61.4	60.7	58.6	59.8	...	...
Debt/net financial assets	50.3	45.9	44.7	41.7	43.2	46.1	...
Debt/income	87.1	88.6	90.9	94.0	95.6	95.8	...
Banking sector[5]							
Credit quality							
Nonperforming loans/total loans	...	5.0	6.1	5.6	5.0	4.6	...
Loan-loss reserve/nonperforming loans	...	74.3	65.9	66.3	70.9	75.7	...
Loan-loss reserve/total loans	...	3.7	4.0	3.7	3.5	3.5	...
Loan-loss provisions/total operating income[6]	...	13.2	11.7	9.1	7.6	11.5	...
Capital ratios							
Total risk-based capital	...	10.7	10.6	10.5	10.4	10.4	...
Tier 1 risk-based capital	...	7.2	7.0	7.2	7.2	7.1	...
Equity capital/total assets	...	4.1	4.0	4.0	4.0	3.9	3.9
Capital funds/liabilities	...	6.2	6.2	6.1	6.2	6.1	6.2
Profitability measures	...						
Return on assets, or ROA (after tax)	...	0.6	0.5	0.5	0.7	0.4	0.3
Return on equity, or ROE (after tax)	...	15.2	12.7	11.9	17.7	11.3	8.2
Net interest margin	...	1.9	1.6	1.3	1.3	1.2	1.3
Efficiency ratio[7]	...	65.0	67.9	67.7	67.4	69.8	71.7

Sources: ©2003 Bureau van Dijk Electronic Publishing-Bankscope; ECB *Monthly Bulletin,* August 2002; and IMF staff estimates.
[1]GDP-weighted average for France, Germany, and the United Kingdom, unless otherwise noted.
[2]Corporate equity adjusted for changes in asset valuation.
[3]Interest payments as a percent of gross operating profits.
[4]Interest payments as percent of disposable income.
[5]Fifty largest European banks. Data availability may restrict coverage to less than 50 banks for specific indicators.
[6]Includes the write-off of goodwill in foreign subsidiaries by banks with exposure to Argentina.
[7]Cost to income ratio.

Figure 15. Emerging and Mature Market Volatilities

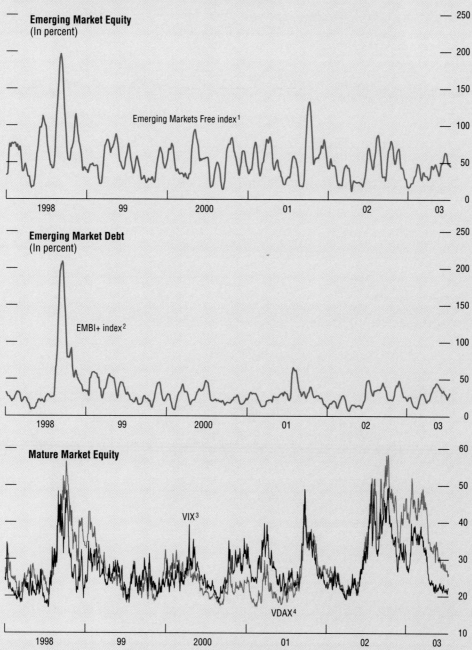

Sources: For "Emerging Market Equity," Morgan Stanley Capital International; and IMF staff estimates. For "Emerging Market Debt," J.P. Morgan Chase; and IMF staff estimates. For "Mature Market Equity," Bloomberg L.P.

[1]Data utilize the Emerging Markets Free index in U.S. dollars to calculate 30-day rolling volatilities.

[2]Data utilize the EMBI+ total return index in U.S. dollars to calculate 30-day rolling volatilities.

[3]The VIX is a market estimate of future stock market volatility, and is based on the weighted average of the implied volatilities of 8 Chicago Board Options Exchange calls and puts (the nearest in- and out-of-the-money call and put options from the first and second month expirations).

[4]The VDAX represents the implied volatility of the German DAX assuming a constant 45 days remaining until expiration of DAX index contracts.

Figure 16. Emerging Market Debt Cross-Correlations

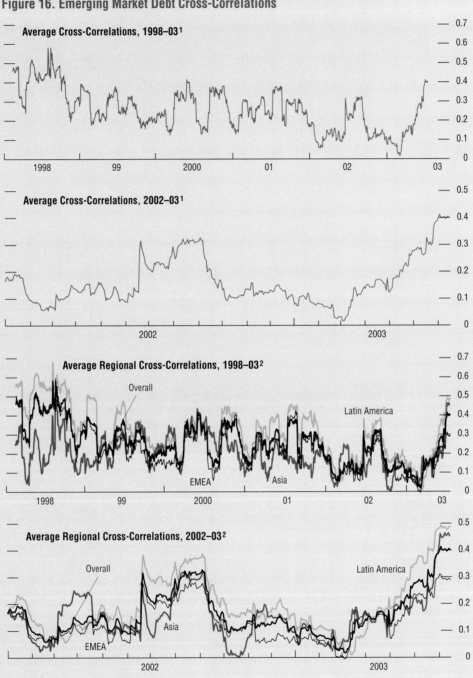

Average Cross-Correlations, 1998–03[1]

Average Cross-Correlations, 2002–03[1]

Average Regional Cross-Correlations, 1998–03[2]

Overall

Latin America

EMEA   Asia

Average Regional Cross-Correlations, 2002–03[2]

Overall

Latin America

Asia

EMEA

Sources: J.P. Morgan Chase; and IMF staff estimates.
[1]Thirty-day moving simple average across all pair-wise return correlations of 20 constituents included in the EMBI Global.
[2]Simple average of all pair-wise correlations of all markets in a given region with all other emerging bond markets, regardless of region.

Table 10. Emerging Market Equity Indices

	End of Period 2003		End of Period 2002				1999	2000	2001	2002	12-Month High	12-Month Low	All Time High[1]	All Time Low[1]
	Q1	Q2	Q1	Q2	Q3	Q4								
World	**748.6**	**871.1**	**1,003.6**	**907.8**	**738.2**	**792.2**	**1,420.9**	**1,221.3**	**1,003.5**	**792.2**	**907.3**	**703.7**	**1,448.8**	**423.1**
Emerging Markets														
Emerging Markets Free	272.3	332.7	351.4	319.8	266.1	292.1	489.4	333.8	317.4	292.1	353.4	254.8	587.1	175.3
EMF Latin America	**652.9**	**800.2**	**938.8**	**731.9**	**551.0**	**658.9**	**1,121.9**	**915.6**	**876.2**	**658.9**	**—**	**—**	**1,352.5**	**185.6**
Argentina	559.9	700.1	511.5	338.4	361.7	470.3	1,667.6	1,232.7	959.6	470.3	745.7	352.1	2,052.2	152.6
Brazil	410.1	503.1	627.1	464.7	281.8	395.4	889.5	763.2	597.1	395.4	533.8	278.8	1,306.4	84.1
Chile	446.0	560.4	561.6	471.2	392.6	445.5	728.4	604.7	568.7	445.5	586.6	378.9	1,119.6	180.2
Colombia	65.9	84.1	57.2	61.9	57.6	68.3	71.6	42.1	57.7	68.3	91.5	54.3	183.8	41.2
Mexico	1,350.9	1,637.3	1,988.2	1,597.7	1,353.8	1,442.8	1,866.4	1,464.9	1,698.2	1,442.8	1,688.1	1,302.2	2,193.1	306.7
Peru	187.1	207.8	171.8	160.3	150.0	182.7	170.6	125.0	144.1	182.7	216.2	144.1	311.6	73.5
Venezuela	67.4	125.2	91.1	77.1	65.4	77.7	105.3	106.1	95.4	77.7	136.8	56.1	278.4	56.1
EMF Asia	**127.2**	**154.4**	**172.0**	**161.2**	**133.8**	**140.4**	**250.0**	**143.6**	**149.7**	**140.4**	**—**	**—**	**433.0**	**104.1**
China	13.9	16.3	16.2	16.4	14.0	14.1	33.5	22.8	16.8	14.1	18.2	13.1	136.9	12.9
India	132.4	151.9	152.7	141.0	129.5	148.8	209.5	173.4	141.2	148.8	157.3	124.3	323.9	77.7
Indonesia	474.9	633.5	572.5	604.4	508.7	519.6	899.7	456.4	437.2	519.6	656.0	372.1	1,077.7	280.0
Korea	158.0	196.7	247.0	215.8	184.6	184.7	226.5	125.6	190.4	184.7	223.3	153.8	266.0	59.5
Malaysia	240.6	262.8	280.5	270.6	238.9	244.0	296.3	245.2	250.7	244.0	278.9	232.7	465.7	88.3
Pakistan	140.7	158.9	100.8	89.9	104.6	146.0	103.5	99.1	67.4	146.0	171.0	91.7	228.9	54.4
Philippines	210.6	257.0	348.1	259.1	254.3	210.1	519.4	352.6	292.2	210.1	276.9	202.2	917.3	132.6
Taiwan Province of China	184.1	210.9	277.8	227.3	178.9	189.5	385.2	222.2	255.6	189.5	236.8	162.8	483.5	103.9
Thailand	138.1	170.7	134.9	135.6	116.8	130.2	205.0	102.5	107.5	130.2	185.3	113.4	669.4	72.0
EMF Europe, Middle East, & Africa	**102.6**	**126.9**	**108.2**	**105.7**	**94.6**	**108.4**	**. . .**	**. . .**	**103.5**	**108.4**	**—**	**—**	**130.1**	**85.2**
Czech Republic	123.1	126.7	106.0	99.6	110.9	116.2	102.0	107.6	97.5	116.2	141.0	98.1	150.3	62.8
Egypt	114.4	158.5	107.5	97.3	97.8	97.4	251.4	154.9	101.9	97.4	170.9	89.9	287.3	89.9
Hungary	524.3	538.3	573.3	494.4	493.7	535.5	724.9	582.9	507.9	535.5	591.1	451.3	941.4	77.1
Israel	97.2	135.8	110.9	91.9	87.5	90.8	157.1	196.0	132.7	90.8	138.4	83.7	236.2	67.6
Jordan	157.6	182.3	156.8	167.8	153.9	153.5	154.0	116.1	149.5	153.5	193.8	145.7	247.4	103.1
Morocco	142.5	163.7	168.8	148.5	137.0	138.5	249.2	198.9	180.1	138.5	167.4	127.1	302.1	99.6
Poland	797.4	914.0	959.8	861.0	766.6	861.0	1,373.3	1,307.9	891.9	861.0	1,013.1	746.1	1,792.9	99.6
Russia	264.6	388.6	281.1	276.6	255.2	270.7	223.0	155.2	237.8	270.7	402.1	240.1	538.4	30.6
South Africa	227.6	244.3	324.5	315.7	278.1	272.7	247.7	244.8	309.3	272.7	306.0	216.1	350.5	99.7
Turkey	154,021.6	179,224.6	202,643.8	155,689.5	144,758.0	169,900.4	245,019.7	163,011.9	234,490.3	169,900.4	232,454.8	144,094.0	329,685.0	425.8
EMF Sectors														
Energy	161.7	205.8	185.1	170.3	149.6	163.1	197.3	148.5	162.1	163.1	212.5	147.0	240.0	81.7
Materials	163.5	178.1	206.8	199.3	173.7	182.8	178.2	140.8	173.9	182.8	199.7	155.0	214.1	98.5
Industrials	60.9	71.3	72.0	67.9	56.9	61.8	125.9	73.4	63.8	61.8	74.6	54.2	276.8	52.6
Consumer discretionary	130.8	166.8	163.9	157.9	128.5	138.8	215.9	126.0	130.6	138.8	178.6	123.2	236.8	74.1
Consumer staple	82.8	101.1	102.3	94.7	81.9	88.2	129.2	103.1	94.6	88.2	102.9	80.4	148.6	80.4
Healthcare	183.8	243.9	148.9	157.9	152.7	169.8	172.6	173.9	146.5	169.8	253.2	143.8	253.2	83.3
Financials	89.5	106.8	115.0	109.1	88.8	98.6	148.7	112.6	107.7	98.6	114.1	84.7	185.0	74.6
Information technology	93.5	117.2	151.3	124.6	100.4	103.9	237.7	130.9	134.2	103.9	137.5	89.4	300.0	73.1
Telecommunications	64.6	80.0	92.3	79.1	66.6	72.7	165.2	113.8	91.9	72.7	83.4	62.9	211.5	62.9
Utilities	72.7	92.8	95.4	80.7	65.6	72.4	127.6	95.7	91.5	72.4	97.7	63.1	247.8	63.1

Table 10 *(continued)*

	2003 Q1	2003 Q2	2002 Q1	2002 Q2	2002 Q3	2002 Q4	1999	2000	2001	2002	12-Month High	12-Month Low	All Time High[1]	All Time Low[1]
World	**−5.5**	**16.4**	**0.0**	**−9.5**	**−18.7**	**7.3**	**23.6**	**−14.1**	**−17.8**	**−21.1**	...	...	...	...
Emerging Markets											...	...	...	
Emerging Markets Free	**−6.8**	**22.2**	**10.7**	**−9.0**	**−16.8**	**9.8**	**63.7**	**−31.8**	**−4.9**	**−8.0**	...	...	...	...
EMF Latin America	**−0.9**	**22.6**	**7.1**	**−22.0**	**−24.7**	**19.6**	**55.5**	**−18.4**	**−4.3**	**−24.8**	...	...	...	...
Argentina	19.1	25.0	−46.7	−33.8	6.9	30.0	30.0	−26.1	−22.2	−51.0	...	...	...	...
Brazil	3.7	22.7	5.0	−25.9	−39.4	40.3	61.6	−14.2	−21.8	−33.8	...	...	...	...
Chile	0.1	25.7	−1.2	−16.1	−16.7	13.5	36.4	−17.0	−6.0	−21.7	...	...	...	...
Colombia	−3.5	27.6	−1.0	8.1	−6.9	18.6	−19.8	−41.2	37.1	18.3	...	...	...	...
Mexico	−6.4	21.2	17.1	−19.6	−15.3	6.6	78.5	−21.5	15.9	−15.0	...	...	...	...
Peru	2.4	11.1	19.2	−6.6	−6.4	21.8	16.3	−26.7	15.3	26.8	...	...	...	...
Venezuela	−13.3	85.8	−4.5	−15.4	−15.2	18.9	1.7	0.8	−10.0	−18.6	...	...	...	...
EMF Asia	**−9.3**	**21.4**	**14.9**	**−6.3**	**−17.0**	**4.9**	**67.7**	**−42.5**	**4.2**	**−6.2**	...	...	...	...
China	−1.5	17.1	−3.6	1.1	−14.5	0.8	10.2	−32.0	−26.0	−16.0	...	...	...	...
India	−11.0	14.7	8.1	−7.6	−8.2	14.8	89.1	−17.2	−18.6	5.3	...	...	...	...
Indonesia	−8.6	33.4	30.9	5.6	−15.8	2.1	70.3	−49.3	−4.2	18.9	...	...	...	...
Korea	−14.4	24.5	29.7	−12.6	−14.4	0.0	79.2	−44.6	51.6	−3.0	...	...	...	...
Malaysia	−1.4	9.2	11.9	−3.5	−11.7	2.1	48.1	−17.3	2.3	−2.7	...	...	...	...
Pakistan	−3.6	12.9	49.7	−10.8	16.3	39.6	50.5	−4.3	−32.0	116.7	...	...	...	...
Philippines	0.2	22.0	19.1	−25.6	−1.8	−17.4	6.0	−32.1	−17.1	−28.1	...	...	...	...
Taiwan Province of China	−2.9	14.6	8.7	−18.2	−21.3	6.0	47.4	−42.3	15.0	−25.8	...	...	...	...
Thailand	6.0	23.6	25.5	0.5	−13.9	11.5	51.8	−50.0	4.9	21.1	...	...	...	...
EMF Europe, Middle East, & Africa	**−5.3**	**23.7**	**4.6**	**−2.4**	**−10.5**	**14.6**	**...**	**...**	**...**	**4.7**	...	...	...	...
Czech Republic	6.0	2.9	8.7	−6.0	11.3	4.8	24.3	5.5	−9.4	19.2	...	...	...	...
Egypt	17.5	38.6	5.6	−9.5	0.6	−0.4	80.7	−38.4	−34.2	−4.4	...	...	...	...
Hungary	−2.1	2.7	12.9	−13.8	−0.1	8.5	30.7	−19.6	−12.9	5.4	...	...	...	...
Israel	7.0	39.7	−16.5	−17.1	−4.8	3.8	56.3	24.7	−32.3	−31.6	...	...	...	...
Jordan	2.7	15.6	4.9	7.0	−8.3	−0.3	1.7	−24.7	28.8	2.6	...	...	...	...
Morocco	2.9	14.9	−6.2	−12.1	−7.7	1.1	−6.4	−20.2	−9.5	−23.1	...	...	...	...
Poland	−7.4	14.6	7.6	−10.3	−11.0	12.3	53.9	−4.8	−31.8	−3.5	...	...	...	...
Russia	−2.3	46.9	18.2	−1.6	−7.7	6.1	246.2	−30.4	53.2	13.9	...	...	...	...
South Africa	−16.6	7.4	4.9	−2.7	−11.9	−1.9	60.6	−1.2	26.3	−11.8	...	...	...	...
Turkey	−9.3	16.4	−13.6	−23.2	−7.0	17.4	492.2	−33.5	43.8	−27.5	...	...	...	...
EMF Sectors														
Energy	−0.9	27.2	14.2	−8.0	−12.2	9.1	97.3	−24.7	9.2	0.6	...	...	...	...
Materials	−10.6	8.9	19.0	−3.6	−12.8	5.2	78.2	−21.0	23.5	5.2	...	...	...	...
Industrials	−1.5	17.2	12.8	−5.7	−16.1	8.6	25.9	−41.7	−13.1	−3.2	...	...	...	...
Consumer discretionary	−5.8	27.5	25.5	−3.7	−18.6	8.0	115.9	−41.6	3.6	6.3	...	...	...	...
Consumer staple	−6.1	27.2	8.2	−7.4	−13.5	7.6	29.2	−20.2	−8.2	−6.7	...	...	...	...
Healthcare	−10.6	32.7	1.7	6.0	−3.3	11.2	72.6	0.7	−15.8	15.9	...	...	...	...
Financials	−9.3	19.4	6.8	−5.2	−18.5	11.0	48.7	−24.3	−4.3	−8.4	...	...	...	...
Information technology	−10.0	25.3	12.7	−17.6	−19.4	3.5	137.7	−44.9	2.6	−22.6	...	...	...	...
Telecommunications	−11.1	23.8	0.5	−14.4	−15.8	9.2	65.2	−31.1	−19.2	−20.9	...	...	...	...
Utilities	0.5	27.6	4.2	−15.4	−18.7	10.4	27.6	−25.0	−4.4	−20.9	...	...	...	...

Period on Period Percent Change

Table 10 *(concluded)*

	End of Period 2003		End of Period 2002				1999	2000	2001	2002	12-Month High	12-Month Low	All Time High[1]	All Time Low[1]
	Q1	Q2	Q1	Q2	Q3	Q4								
Developed Markets														
Australia	580.4	601.6	686.6	647.6	593.7	604.4	617.3	640.1	690.8	604.4	639.6	539.9	712.9	250.2
Austria	92.8	101.6	106.5	101.3	86.0	91.8	104.9	96.9	94.6	91.8	105.4	79.7	105.4	96.2
Belgium	44.0	52.3	76.9	69.7	50.5	55.3	98.7	85.8	78.6	55.3	65.0	38.1	53.9	51.2
Canada	796.3	868.0	978.5	888.6	762.6	818.3	1,070.1	1,156.4	965.8	818.3	886.4	705.8	1,511.4	338.3
Denmark	1,370.1	1,554.7	2,099.2	1,840.6	1,432.8	1,448.8	2,122.6	2,333.3	2,060.1	1,448.8	1,752.8	1,245.8	2,776.6	556.5
Finland	84.0	94.4	152.4	104.8	89.6	100.3	293.7	267.5	171.8	100.3	126.0	78.8	383.1	78.8
France	69.2	81.2	125.0	104.7	75.4	81.3	150.0	152.0	123.1	81.3	95.3	63.4	178.6	63.4
Germany	46.9	60.4	103.7	84.4	53.5	56.0	139.1	124.0	100.1	56.0	78.4	42.9	163.6	41.4
Greece	38.2	50.7	66.4	63.6	50.6	46.8	172.9	106.1	76.8	46.8	61.9	38.2	197.2	38.2
Hong Kong SAR	4,501.2	4,838.9	6,033.7	5,667.0	4,758.2	4,808.4	9,231.5	7,690.1	6,058.0	4,808.4	5,553.6	4,305.4	10,165.3	1,995.5
Ireland	56.8	60.7	79.2	70.2	55.4	56.8	100.7	92.1	93.1	56.8	67.1	51.9	107.3	51.9
Italy	62.6	72.2	95.2	81.3	63.8	69.6	115.4	119.9	91.2	69.6	78.4	58.7	132.1	58.7
Japan	480.4	542.9	664.9	640.6	570.5	524.3	1,013.7	808.2	650.3	524.3	628.7	462.1	1,655.3	462.1
Netherlands	53.4	60.3	107.3	90.9	61.9	66.0	123.3	124.5	100.4	66.0	80.9	47.4	134.9	47.4
New Zealand	88.8	101.4	93.7	93.2	92.2	90.0	111.8	83.9	94.2	90.0	101.4	86.6	141.0	56.7
Norway	804.4	994.1	1,361.5	1,137.4	863.5	898.3	1,361.5	1,458.0	1,278.4	898.3	1,116.3	762.2	1,599.1	455.9
Portugal	51.3	55.9	78.0	68.0	48.1	57.0	104.4	97.9	79.5	57.0	64.6	48.1	123.1	48.1
Singapore	725.6	831.9	1,058.4	897.5	776.0	764.9	1,580.0	1,173.4	936.8	764.9	922.1	687.3	1,624.2	508.2
Spain	67.8	79.3	96.2	79.4	61.7	69.9	121.3	107.7	99.0	69.9	81.9	61.1	133.7	27.4
Sweden	3,271.7	3,827.3	5,853.4	4,434.7	3,156.9	3,517.4	8,971.5	7,735.0	6,178.8	3,517.4	4,173.8	2,914.9	12,250.4	787.2
Switzerland	534.3	626.6	849.9	766.2	622.6	603.2	957.8	1,017.0	813.4	603.2	716.9	481.4	1,032.8	158.1
United Kingdom	1,082.4	1,215.4	1,600.9	1,405.5	1,116.3	1,179.2	1,974.2	1,841.4	1,586.2	1,179.2	1,336.7	986.4	1,974.2	585.4
United States	796.1	916.1	1,083.7	925.7	762.6	824.6	1,445.9	1,249.9	1,084.5	824.6	950.4	726.5	1,493.0	273.7
Period on Period Percent Change														
Developed Markets														
Australia	−4.0	3.7	−0.6	−5.7	−8.3	1.8	8.0	3.7	7.9	−12.5	...	...	...	...
Austria	1.1	9.5	12.6	−4.9	−15.1	6.8	...	−7.6	−2.4	−3.0	...	...	...	...
Belgium	−20.4	18.9	−2.2	−9.4	−27.5	9.5	...	−13.1	−8.3	−29.7	...	...	...	...
Canada	−2.7	9.0	1.3	−9.2	−14.2	7.3	43.4	8.1	−16.5	−15.3	...	...	...	...
Denmark	−5.4	13.5	1.9	−12.3	−22.2	1.1	29.3	9.9	−11.7	−29.7	...	...	...	...
Finland	−16.2	12.4	−11.3	−31.2	−14.5	11.9	...	−8.9	−35.8	−41.6	...	...	...	...
France	−14.9	17.3	1.5	−16.2	−28.0	7.8	...	1.4	−19.0	−34.0	...	...	...	...
Germany	−16.2	28.7	3.6	−18.6	−36.6	4.7	39.1	−10.8	−19.3	−44.0	...	...	...	...
Greece	−18.4	32.8	−13.6	−4.1	−20.4	−7.5	72.9	−38.6	−27.6	−39.1	...	...	...	...
Hong Kong SAR	−6.4	7.5	−0.4	−6.1	−16.0	1.1	55.4	−16.7	−21.2	−20.6	...	...	...	...
Ireland	−0.1	7.0	−15.0	−11.3	−21.1	2.6	...	−8.5	1.1	−39.0	...	...	...	...
Italy	−10.0	15.3	4.5	−14.7	−21.5	9.1	...	3.9	−24.0	−23.6	...	...	...	...
Japan	−8.4	13.0	2.2	−3.7	−10.9	−8.1	45.7	−20.3	−19.5	−19.4	...	...	...	...
Netherlands	−19.1	12.9	6.9	−15.3	−31.9	6.6	...	1.0	−19.4	−34.3	...	...	...	...
New Zealand	−1.4	14.2	−0.6	−0.5	−1.1	−2.4	11.1	−24.9	12.2	−4.4	...	...	...	...
Norway	−10.5	23.6	6.5	−16.5	−24.1	4.0	36.6	7.1	−12.3	−29.7	...	...	...	...
Portugal	−10.1	9.1	−1.9	−12.8	−29.3	18.6	...	−6.2	−18.8	−28.3	...	...	...	...
Singapore	−5.1	14.6	13.0	−15.2	−13.5	−1.4	99.0	−25.7	−20.2	−18.4	...	...	...	...
Spain	−2.9	16.8	−2.9	−17.4	−22.3	13.2	21.3	−11.2	−8.0	−29.5	...	...	...	...
Sweden	−7.0	17.0	−5.3	−24.2	−28.8	11.4	87.4	−13.8	−20.1	−43.1	...	...	...	...
Switzerland	−11.4	17.3	4.5	−9.8	−18.7	−3.1	7.4	6.2	−20.0	−25.8	...	...	...	...
United Kingdom	−8.2	12.3	0.9	−12.2	−20.6	5.6	13.3	−6.7	−13.9	−25.7	...	...	...	...
United States	−3.5	15.1	−0.1	−14.6	−17.6	8.1	20.9	−13.6	−13.2	−24.0	...	...	...	...

Data are provided by Morgan Stanley Capital International and are for local currency indices. Regional and sectoral compositions conform to Morgan Stanley Capital International definitions.

[1]From 1990 or initiation of the index.

Table 11. Foreign Exchange Rates
(Units per U.S. dollar)

	End of Period 2002		End of Period 2003				1999	2000	2001	2002	12-Month Low	12-Month High	All Time Low[1]	All Time High[1]
	Q1	Q2	Q1	Q2	Q3	Q4								
Emerging Markets														
Latin America														
Argentina	2.97	2.81	2.94	3.81	3.74	3.36	1.00	1.00	1.00	3.36	3.76	2.75	3.86	0.98
Brazil	3.35	2.84	2.33	2.82	3.74	3.54	1.80	1.95	2.31	3.54	3.95	2.84	3.95	0.0004
Chile	733.25	700.90	656.50	686.15	749.25	720.25	529.30	573.85	661.25	720.25	759.75	690.85	759.75	295.18
Colombia	2,958.00	2,817.00	2,273.00	2,404.25	2,870.00	2,867.00	1,872.50	2,236.00	2,277.50	2,867.00	2,980.00	2,517.55	2,980.00	689.21
Mexico	10.77	10.46	9.04	9.95	10.21	10.37	9.51	9.62	9.16	10.37	11.23	9.65	11.23	2.68
Peru	3.47	3.47	3.44	3.51	3.63	3.51	3.51	3.53	3.44	3.51	3.65	3.46	3.65	1.28
Venezuela	1,598.00	1,598.00	906.00	1,380.50	1,462.75	1,388.80	648.75	699.51	757.50	1,388.80	1,921.80	1,254.50	1,921.80	45.00
Asia														
China	8.28	8.28	8.28	8.28	8.28	8.28	8.28	8.28	8.28	8.28	8.28	8.28	8.92	5.96
India	47.47	46.49	48.82	48.89	48.38	47.98	43.55	46.68	48.25	47.98	48.78	46.40	49.05	16.92
Indonesia	8,902	8,275	9,825	8,713	9,000	8,950	7,100	9,675	10,400	8,950	9,345	8,175	16,650	1,977
Korea	1,254.45	1,193.05	1,327.00	1,201.25	1,222.50	1,185.70	1,140.00	1,265.00	1,313.50	1,185.70	1,265.50	1,165.40	1,962.50	681.40
Malaysia	3.80	3.80	3.80	3.80	3.80	3.80	3.80	3.80	3.80	3.80	3.80	3.80	4.71	2.44
Pakistan	58.00	57.85	60.05	60.05	58.95	58.25	51.80	57.60	59.90	58.25	60.05	57.27	64.35	21.18
Philippines	53.53	53.48	51.00	50.40	52.40	53.60	40.25	50.00	51.60	53.60	55.10	50.35	55.10	23.10
Taiwan Province of China	34.75	34.64	34.95	33.54	34.86	34.64	31.40	33.08	34.95	34.64	35.19	32.85	35.19	24.48
Thailand	42.84	42.00	43.50	41.51	43.26	43.11	37.49	43.38	44.21	43.11	44.17	40.43	55.50	23.15
Europe, Middle East, & Africa														
Czech Republic	29.37	27.51	35.46	29.67	30.73	30.07	35.84	37.28	35.60	30.07	32.08	26.44	42.17	25.39
Egypt	5.76	6.08	4.63	4.66	4.65	4.62	3.44	3.89	4.58	4.62	6.08	4.58	6.08	3.29
Hungary	227.19	231.27	279.31	246.77	246.72	224.48	252.51	282.34	274.81	224.48	253.30	207.23	317.56	90.20
Israel	4.70	4.32	4.75	4.75	4.88	4.74	4.15	4.04	4.40	4.74	4.93	4.32	5.01	1.96
Jordan	0.71	0.71	0.71	0.71	0.71	0.71	0.71	0.71	0.71	0.71	0.72	0.70	0.72	0.64
Morocco	9.85	9.45	11.69	10.61	10.64	10.18	10.08	10.56	11.59	10.18	10.85	9.20	12.06	7.75
Poland	4.10	3.90	4.11	4.05	4.15	3.83	4.15	4.13	3.96	3.83	4.21	3.67	4.71	1.72
Russia	31.39	30.37	31.21	31.48	31.69	31.96	27.55	28.16	30.51	31.96	31.96	30.32	31.96	0.98
South Africa	7.87	7.47	11.33	10.30	10.54	8.57	6.15	7.58	11.96	8.57	10.88	7.10	12.45	2.50
Turkey	1,714,000	1,418,500	1,349,100	1,587,500	1,664,100	1,655,100	544,300	668,500	1,450,100	1,655,100	1,769,000	1,415,000	1,769,000	5,036
Developed Markets														
Australia[2]	0.60	0.67	0.53	0.56	0.54	0.56	0.66	0.56	0.51	0.56	0.53	0.67	0.48	0.84
Canada	1.47	1.35	1.59	1.52	1.59	1.57	1.45	1.50	1.59	1.57	1.60	1.33	1.61	1.12
Denmark	6.80	6.45	8.53	7.49	7.53	7.08	7.39	7.92	8.35	7.08	7.69	6.23	9.00	5.34
Euro[2]	1.09	1.15	0.87	0.99	0.99	1.05	1.01	0.94	0.89	1.05	0.97	1.19	0.83	1.19
Hong Kong SAR	7.80	7.80	7.80	7.80	7.80	7.80	7.77	7.80	7.80	7.80	7.80	7.80	7.82	7.70
Japan	118.09	119.80	132.73	119.47	121.81	118.79	102.51	114.41	131.66	118.79	125.51	115.88	159.90	80.63
New Zealand[2]	0.56	0.59	0.44	0.49	0.47	0.52	0.52	0.44	0.42	0.52	0.45	0.59	0.39	0.72
Norway	7.27	7.20	8.84	7.50	7.41	6.94	8.02	8.80	8.96	6.94	7.81	6.62	9.58	5.51
Singapore	1.76	1.76	1.84	1.77	1.78	1.73	1.67	1.73	1.85	1.73	1.80	1.72	1.91	1.39
Sweden	8.45	7.99	10.36	9.16	9.26	8.69	8.52	9.42	10.48	8.69	9.68	7.65	11.03	5.09
Switzerland	1.35	1.35	1.68	1.48	1.48	1.38	1.59	1.61	1.66	1.38	1.52	1.28	1.82	1.12
United Kingdom[2]	1.58	1.65	1.43	1.53	1.57	1.61	1.62	1.49	1.45	1.61	1.52	1.69	1.37	2.01

Table 11 *(concluded)*

| | Period on Period Percent Change | | | | | | | | | | 12-Month Low | 12-Month High | All Time Low[1] | All Time High[1] |
| | 2003 | | 2002 | | | | | | | | | | | |
	Q1	Q2	Q1	Q2	Q3	Q4	1999	2000	2001	2002				
Emerging Markets														
Latin America														
Argentina	13.0	5.7	−65.9	−23.0	2.0	11.2	0.0	0.2	−0.2	−70.2	...	...	...	...
Brazil	5.6	17.9	−0.6	−17.5	−24.7	5.6	−32.8	−7.7	−15.6	−34.7	...	...	...	...
Chile	−1.8	4.6	0.7	−4.3	−8.4	4.0	−10.6	−7.8	−13.2	−8.2	...	...	...	...
Colombia	−3.1	5.0	0.2	−5.5	−16.2	0.1	−17.2	−16.3	−1.8	−20.6	...	...	...	...
Mexico	−3.7	3.0	1.4	−9.2	−2.5	−1.6	4.1	−1.2	5.1	−11.7	...	...	...	...
Peru	1.2	0.2	0.0	−1.9	−3.4	3.3	−10.0	−0.5	2.4	−2.0	...	...	...	...
Venezuela	−13.1	0.0	−16.4	−34.4	−5.6	5.3	−13.0	−7.3	−7.7	−45.5	...	...	...	...
Asia														
China	0.0	0.0	0.0	0.0	0.0	0.0	0.0	0.0	0.0	0.0	...	...	...	...
India	1.1	2.1	−1.2	−0.1	1.1	0.8	−2.4	−6.7	−3.3	0.6	...	...	...	...
Indonesia	0.5	7.6	5.9	12.8	−3.2	0.6	12.7	−26.6	−7.0	16.2	...	...	...	...
Korea	−5.5	5.1	−1.0	10.5	−1.7	3.1	5.6	−9.9	−3.7	10.8	...	...	...	...
Malaysia	0.0	0.0	0.0	0.0	0.0	0.0	0.0	0.0	0.0	0.0	...	...	...	...
Pakistan	0.4	0.3	−0.2	0.0	1.9	1.2	−4.1	−10.1	−3.8	2.8	...	...	...	...
Philippines	0.1	0.1	1.2	1.2	−3.8	−2.2	−3.6	−19.5	−3.1	−3.7	...	...	...	...
Taiwan Province of China	−0.3	0.3	0.0	4.2	−3.8	0.6	2.6	−5.1	−5.3	0.9	...	...	...	...
Thailand	0.6	2.0	1.6	4.8	−4.0	0.3	−2.2	−13.6	−1.9	2.6	...	...	...	...
Europe, Middle East, & Africa														
Czech Republic	2.4	6.8	0.4	19.5	−3.5	2.2	−15.8	−3.9	4.7	18.4	...	...	...	...
Egypt	−19.8	−5.1	−1.1	−0.6	0.3	0.5	−0.9	−11.5	−15.1	−0.9	...	...	...	...
Hungary	−1.2	−1.8	−1.6	13.2	0.0	9.9	−14.3	−10.6	2.7	22.4	...	...	...	...
Israel	1.0	8.7	−7.4	0.0	−2.7	2.9	0.2	2.7	−8.1	−7.3	...	...	...	...
Jordan	0.0	0.1	0.0	0.6	−0.6	−0.1	0.0	−0.3	0.2	−0.1	...	...	...	...
Morocco	3.3	4.2	−0.9	10.2	−0.2	4.5	−7.7	−4.6	−8.9	13.9	...	...	...	...
Poland	−6.6	5.0	−3.6	1.6	−2.5	8.4	−15.4	0.4	4.2	3.5	...	...	...	...
Russia	1.8	3.4	−2.3	−0.8	−0.7	−0.8	−25.2	−2.2	−7.7	−4.5	...	...	...	...
South Africa	9.0	5.3	5.6	10.1	−2.3	23.0	−4.7	−18.8	−36.6	39.6	...	...	...	...
Turkey	−3.4	20.8	7.5	−15.0	−4.6	0.5	−42.0	−18.6	−53.9	−12.4	...	...	...	...
Developed Markets														
Australia[2]	7.6	11.4	4.6	5.7	−3.7	3.5	7.6	−14.9	−8.8	10.2	...	...	...	...
Canada	...	8.9	−0.1	5.1	−4.4	1.0	6.4	−3.5	−5.9	1.3	...	...	...	...
Denmark	4.1	5.4	−2.2	13.9	−0.5	6.3	−14.0	−6.7	−5.1	17.9	...	...	...	...
Euro[2]	4.0	5.5	−2.0	13.7	−0.5	6.3	−13.8	−6.3	−5.6	18.0	...	...	...	...
Hong Kong SAR	0.0	0.0	0.0	0.0	0.0	0.0	−0.4	−0.3	0.0	0.0	...	...	...	...
Japan	0.6	−1.4	−0.8	11.1	−1.9	2.5	10.8	−10.4	−13.1	10.8	...	...	...	...
New Zealand[2]	5.8	5.9	5.7	10.6	−3.8	11.9	−1.5	−14.9	−6.1	25.9	...	...	...	...
Norway	−4.6	1.0	1.4	17.9	1.3	6.7	−5.8	−8.9	−1.8	29.2	...	...	...	...
Singapore	−1.7	0.2	0.1	4.3	−0.7	2.6	−1.0	−4.0	−6.0	6.4	...	...	...	...
Sweden	2.8	5.8	1.2	13.1	−1.1	6.6	−4.9	−9.5	−10.2	20.6	...	...	...	...
Switzerland	2.4	0.0	−1.2	13.5	0.4	6.6	−13.5	−1.3	−3.0	20.0	...	...	...	...
United Kingdom[2]	−1.7	4.5	−2.0	7.5	2.3	2.7	−2.5	−7.7	−2.6	10.7	...	...	...	...

Source: Bloomberg L.P.
[1]From 1990 or initiation of the index.
[2]U.S. dollars per unit.

Table 12. Emerging Market Bond Index: EMBI+ Total Returns Index

	End of Period 2003		End of Period 2002				End of Period				12-Month High	12-Month Low	All Time High	All Time Low
	Q1	Q2	Q1	Q2	Q3	Q4	1999	2000	2001	2002				
Composite	**246.2**	**273.4**	**213.5**	**202.0**	**199.8**	**228.9**	**174.6**	**201.9**	**200.3**	**228.9**	**284.4**	**189.4**	**284.4**	**62.1**
Latin America														
Argentina	60.5	78.9	58.0	47.6	54.8	57.7	171.2	184.3	61.1	57.7	81.8	49.2	195.6	47.6
Brazil	276.8	322.1	257.3	194.3	163.9	229.8	196.4	221.8	237.7	229.8	344.7	153.3	344.7	67.3
Colombia	183.7	205.4	157.0	159.1	139.9	176.0	116.7	119.2	155.9	176.0	208.5	137.7	208.5	96.5
Ecuador	301.8	352.7	276.3	258.4	198.8	230.1	115.2	177.3	241.3	230.1	388.3	184.8	388.3	60.9
Mexico	261.2	277.2	222.8	226.0	233.0	252.0	160.8	189.6	216.5	252.0	286.8	222.1	286.8	58.5
Panama	414.5	437.0	367.4	350.5	359.1	395.2	276.9	299.9	353.7	395.2	445.5	340.1	445.5	55.6
Peru	377.6	385.3	330.6	302.4	284.6	340.2	243.1	243.6	307.4	340.2	404.3	272.3	404.3	52.3
Poland	313.2	334.7	278.1	285.1	296.9	308.3	212.4	246.2	272.2	308.3	344.3	286.5	344.3	60.4
Venezuela	259.6	312.3	259.2	251.6	265.9	276.5	191.9	220.6	232.9	276.5	324.7	242.2	324.7	58.6
Asia														
Korea	167.7	167.7	157.0	164.1	167.7	167.7	122.4	135.3	154.9	167.7	170.8	167.0	170.8	75.9
Malaysia	119.0	126.2	100.9	105.6	115.5	116.3	...	...	...	116.3	129.0	106.9	129.0	99.5
Europe, Middle East, & Africa														
Bulgaria	510.8	526.4	452.2	459.1	463.4	494.1	338.3	355.7	447.1	494.1	535.2	451.4	535.2	76.4
Egypt	123.0	132.8	...	99.7	103.3	116.6				116.6	135.2	101.0	135.2	98.7
Morocco	243.8	253.7	233.4	226.6	227.1	238.6	189.8	200.3	222.6	238.6	254.7	224.5	254.7	72.6
Nigeria	324.9	369.3	275.9	264.6	238.2	281.4	180.8	209.0	255.9	281.4	373.4	224.3	373.4	60.5
Philippine	144.8	161.5	134.1	137.1	140.9	143.5	102.9	98.3	125.4	143.5	168.3	136.0	168.3	78.0
Qatar	141.5	141.5	128.7	137.3	141.5	141.5	...	103.6	125.8	141.5	141.8	139.6	141.8	100.0
Russia	303.3	334.8	227.3	239.3	247.3	275.5	84.0	130.2	202.8	275.5	346.6	232.4	346.6	24.4
South Africa	118.6	122.3	...	102.3	108.4	113.2	...	...	...	113.2	125.8	103.2	125.8	99.9
Turkey	137.5	160.3	137.3	123.2	128.5	153.8	106.5	104.7	127.5	153.8	166.8	119.6	166.8	93.2
Ukraine	164.8	169.6	138.8	142.2	149.8	152.4	...	...	126.0	152.4	172.4	141.3	172.4	105.9
Latin	204.4	229.0	184.3	164.8	157.4	186.7	179.3	201.9	174.2	186.7	239.7	148.9	239.7	62.2
Non-Latin	361.9	397.0	295.9	303.9	315.0	344.3	159.5	202.6	274.2	344.3	409.2	299.3	409.2	62.8

	Period on Period Percent Change													
EMBI+	**7.6**	**11.0**	**6.6**	**−5.4**	**−1.1**	**14.6**	**26.0**	**15.7**	**−0.8**	**14.2**	...	...	...	...
Latin America														
Argentina	4.8	30.4	−5.0	−18.0	15.2	5.3	13.0	7.7	−66.8	−5.6	...	...	...	...
Brazil	20.5	16.4	8.2	−24.5	−15.7	40.2	40.7	12.9	7.2	−3.3	...	...	...	...
Colombia	4.4	11.8	0.7	1.3	−12.1	25.8	...	2.2	30.8	12.8	...	...	...	...
Ecuador	31.2	16.9	14.5	−6.5	−23.1	15.7	−28.4	53.9	36.1	−4.7	...	...	...	...
Mexico	3.7	6.1	2.9	1.4	3.1	8.1	15.3	17.9	14.2	16.4	...	...	...	...
Panama	11.0	2.0	7.5	−8.5	−5.9	19.5	17.2	0.2	26.2	10.7	...	...	...	...
Peru	1.6	6.8	2.1	2.5	4.2	3.8	0.9	15.9	10.6	13.3	...	...	...	...
Venezuela	−6.1	20.3	11.3	−2.9	5.7	4.0	29.9	15.0	5.5	18.7	...	...	...	...
Asia														
Korea	0.0	0.0	1.3	4.6	2.2	0.0	11.0	10.5	14.5	8.3	...	...	...	...
Malaysia	2.3	6.1	...	4.8	9.3	0.7	...	...	...	...	...	...	...	...
Philippines	4.9	5.4	3.9	−4.6	2.5	10.0	8.1	8.3	17.9	11.7	...	...	...	...
Europe, Middle East, & Africa														
Bulgaria	3.4	3.0	1.1	1.5	0.9	6.6	27.3	5.1	25.7	10.5	...	...	...	...
Egypt	5.5	8.0	...		3.7	12.8	...	...	...	...	...	...	...	...
Morocco	2.2	4.0	4.8	−2.9	0.2	5.1	27.0	5.5	11.1	7.2	...	...	...	...
Nigeria	15.5	13.7	7.8	−4.1	−10.0	18.1	1.4	15.6	22.4	9.9	...	...	...	...
Poland	0.9	11.6	6.9	2.3	2.7	1.8	−14.1	−4.4	27.6	14.4	...	...	...	...
Qatar	0.0	0.0	2.3	6.7	3.0	0.0	...	...	21.4	12.4	...	...	...	...
Russia	10.1	10.4	12.1	5.3	3.3	11.4	165.7	54.9	55.8	35.9	...	...	...	...
South Africa	4.8	3.1	...	...	6.0	4.4	...	...	...	...	...	...	...	...
Turkey	−10.6	16.6	7.7	−10.3	4.3	19.7	...	−1.7	21.7	20.7	...	...	...	...
Ukraine	8.1	2.9	10.2	2.4	5.4	1.8	...	...	...	21.0	...	...	...	...
Latin	9.4	12.0	5.8	−10.6	−4.5	18.6	20.9	12.6	−13.7	7.2	...	...	...	...
Non-Latin	5.1	9.7	7.9	2.7	3.6	9.3	50.0	27.0	35.4	25.6	...	...	...	...

Source: J.P. Morgan Chase.

Table 13. Emerging Market Bond Index: EMBI+ Yield Spreads

(In basis points)

	End of Period 2003		End of Period 2002				End of Period				12-Month High	12-Month Low	All Time High	All Time Low
	Q1	Q2	Q1	Q2	Q3	Q4	1999	2000	2001	2002				
EMBI+	**676**	**539**	**596**	**798**	**1,040**	**759**	**824**	**756**	**799**	**759**	**1,040**	**499**	**1,483**	**499**
Latin America														
Argentina	6,167	4,570	5,013	6,791	6,629	6,358	533	773	4,404	6,358	7,163	4,354	7,199	515
Brazil	1,059	788	717	1,527	2,396	1,439	636	749	870	1,439	2,443	684	2,443	626
Colombia	608	448	532	614	1,067	640	423	755	516	640	1,096	408	1,096	402
Ecuador	1,371	1,159	1,037	1,253	1,980	1,794	3,353	1,415	1,254	1,794	2,200	1,025	4,712	960
Mexico	294	232	250	321	434	324	363	392	308	324	441	207	979	207
Panama	402	370	348	447	553	439	410	501	411	439	557	346	592	337
Peru	480	487	418	622	874	606	443	687	520	606	897	359	897	359
Venezuela	1,419	973	886	1,115	1,156	1,118	844	958	1,128	1,118	1,491	921	1,668	701
Asia														
Korea	74	74	87	82	74	74	142	218	124	74	98	64	449	64
Malaysia	156	99	...	173	171	166	...	...	...	166	330	88	330	88
Philippines	546	435	376	424	529	524	324	644	470	524	572	397	743	315
Europe, Middle East, & Africa														
Bulgaria	255	230	415	357	390	288	626	772	449	288	425	220	1,000	220
Egypt	311	222	...	...	572	383	...	...	...	383	572	185	572	185
Morocco	373	252	365	498	545	390	380	584	545	390	732	−78	891	−78
Nigeria	1,440	1,094	1,105	1,584	3,931	2,212	1,338	2,037	1,488	2,212	3,931	982	3,931	982
Poland	192	59	154	200	303	178	212	241	196	178	305	5	307	5
Qatar	222	222	233	211	222	222	...	...	270	222	269	220	371	202
Russia	370	278	495	511	615	472	2,432	1,172	670	472	615	260	6,357	260
South Africa	179	178	...	241	305	233	...	...	...	233	425	131	425	131
Turkey	979	740	599	890	1,024	687	420	800	720	687	1,103	610	1,197	370
Ukraine	405	367	622	651	663	668	...	...	941	668	894	239	1,677	239
Excluding Argentina	582	461	642	642	920	664	...	...	642	664	920	423	920	423
			Period on Period Spread Change											
EMBI+	**−83**	**−137**	**−203**	**202**	**242**	**−281**	**−320**	**−68**	**43**	**−40**	...	...	...	...
Latin America														
Argentina	−191	−1,597	609	1,778	−162	−271	−167	240	3,631	1,954	...	...	...	...
Brazil	−380	−271	−153	810	869	−957	−567	113	121	569	...	...	...	...
Colombia	−32	−160	16	82	453	−427	...	332	−239	124	...	...	...	...
Ecuador	−423	−212	−217	216	727	−186	1,743	−1,938	−161	540	...	...	...	...
Mexico	−30	−62	−58	71	113	−110	−379	29	−84	16	...	...	...	...
Panama	−37	−32	−63	99	106	−114	−43	91	−90	28	...	...	...	...
Peru	−126	7	−102	204	252	−268	−169	244	−167	86	...	...	...	...
Venezuela	301	−446	−242	229	41	−38	−432	114	170	−10	...	...	...	...
Asia														
Korea	...	...	−30	−6	−10	...	−60	54	−43	−40	...	...	...	...
Malaysia	−10	−57	...	...	−2	−5	...	...	...	...	...	...	...	...
Philippines	22	−111	−94	48	105	−5	...	320	−174	54	...	...	...	...
Europe, Middle East, & Africa														
Bulgaria	−33	−25	−34	−58	33	−102	−223	146	−323	−161	...	...	...	...
Egypt	−72	−89	...	...	...	−189	...	...	...	...	...	...	...	...
Morocco	−17	−121	−180	133	47	−155	−296	204	−39	−155	...	...	...	...
Nigeria	−772	−346	−383	479	2,347	−1,719	−182	699	−549	724	...	...	...	...
Poland	14	−133	−42	46	103	−125	−53	29	−45	−18	...	...	...	...
Qatar	...	...	−37	−22	11	0	...	...	...	−48	...	...	...	...
Russia	−102	−92	−175	16	104	−143	−2,908	−1,260	−502	−198	...	...	...	...
South Africa	−54	−1	...	...	64	−72	...	...	...	...	...	...	...	...
Turkey	292	−239	−121	291	134	−337	...	380	−80	−33	...	...	...	...
Ukraine	−263	−38	−319	29	12	5	...	...	...	−273	...	...	...	...
Excluding Argentina	−82	−121	...	...	278	−256	...	...	...	22	...	...	...	...

Source: J.P. Morgan Chase.

Table 14. Total Emerging Market Financing
(In millions of U.S. dollars)

	1998	1999	2000	2001	2002	2002 Q1	Q2	Q3	Q4	2003 Q1	Q2
Total	**148,977**	**163,572**	**216,406**	**162,138**	**135,644**	**37,044**	**32,887**	**32,134**	**33,578**	**35,952**	**42,456**
Africa	**3,892**	**4,707**	**9,383**	**6,992**	**7,170**	**1,330**	**1,910**	**2,220**	**1,709**	**2,354**	**3,236**
Algeria	...	...	...	50	150	...	...	150	...	75	...
Angola	310	...	...	455	350	...	...	350	...	...	117
Botswana	...	...	...	22	...	...	...	...	...	...	...
Cameroon	...	...	...	54	...	...	...	...	...	...	...
Chad	...	...	...	400	...	...	...	...	...	...	...
Côte d'Ivoire	...	179	...	15	...	...	...	...	...	...	...
Ghana	509	30	320	300	420	...	...	420	...	...	...
Guinea	130	...	...	...	...	...	...	...	...	...	...
Kenya	...	...	8	80	...	...	...	...	...	134	...
Mali	24	...	...	...	150	...	...	...	150	...	...
Mauritius	...	160	...	...	...	...	...	...	...	...	...
Morocco	280	323	56	136	...	...	...	...	...	...	465
Mozambique	...	...	...	200	...	...	...	...	...	36	...
Nigeria	...	90	...	100	1,000	...	...	...	1,000	460	169
Senegal	...	...	...	...	40	40	...	...	...	...	...
Seychelles	...	...	50	...	150	...	...	150	...	...	...
South Africa	2,569	3,423	8,699	4,647	4,160	1,290	1,260	1,100	509	1,292	2,485
Tanzania	...	...	135	...	...	...	...	50	50	...	...
Tunisia	40	352	94	533	750	...	650	...	...	357	...
Zaire	...	...	21	...	...	...	...	...	...	...	...
Zambia	30	...	...	...	...	...	...	...	...	...	...
Zimbabwe	...	150	...	...	...	...	...	...	...	...	...
Asia	**34,211**	**55,959**	**85,883**	**67,484**	**53,901**	**13,311**	**11,875**	**14,092**	**14,623**	**12,956**	**15,927**
Brunei	...	...	...	...	129	...	129	...	...	...	...
China	6,975	3,461	23,063	5,567	5,051	723	1,133	1,088	2,108	1,239	1,374
Hong Kong SAR	1,655	8,119	17,958	18,011	4,158	2,118	736	559	744	538	262
India	1,433	2,376	2,225	2,382	1,560	412	289	173	686	382	419
Indonesia	374	1,465	1,283	965	756	100	256	250	150	2,928	651
Korea	6,260	13,542	14,231	17,021	14,546	1,340	2,231	4,956	6,019	2,385	6,238
Lao P.D.R.	...	...	...	...	30	...	30	...	...	...	...
Macao	...	...	29	...	...	...	...	...	...	...	...
Malaysia	2,527	5,177	4,507	4,432	5,109	1,808	2,171	838	292	1,826	735
Marshall Islands	...	...	...	...	35	...	...	35	...	...	...
Nepal	57	...	...	...	...	...	...	...	...	...	...
Pakistan	323	...	...	182	85	...	...	...	85	...	9
Papua New Guinea	...	...	...	...	...	...	...	...	...	...	...
Philippines	4,113	7,182	5,022	3,658	5,797	2,400	650	1,240	1,507	1,700	248
Singapore	2,467	4,339	6,080	10,383	3,084	1,209	104	1,054	716	421	2,566
Sri Lanka	65	23	100	105	...	...	...	...	...	...	...
Taiwan Province of China	2,439	4,019	6,704	3,794	9,309	3,102	3,844	656	1,707	1,409	2,035
Thailand	5,047	2,552	1,573	685	1,003	18	266	226	493	128	1,258
Vietnam	37	100	20	...	392	...	...	293	100	...	45
Europe	**35,584**	**26,193**	**37,021**	**22,788**	**30,330**	**7,225**	**7,281**	**6,871**	**8,955**	**10,517**	**9,434**
Azerbaijan	...	77	...	16	...	...	...	...	...	...	...
Bulgaria	10	54	9	242	1,261	1,261	...	...	...	...	...
Croatia	529	1,505	1,499	1,766	1,400	561	307	325	207	768	524
Cyprus	556	289	86	632	548	480	68	...	...	...	...
Czech Republic	1,664	541	127	565	463	...	428	10	25	188	...
Estonia	382	289	413	202	440	...	242	198	...	411	35
Gibraltar	...	65	80	...	...	...	...	...	...	...	...
Hungary	3,053	3,472	1,309	1,365	1,057	266	96	424	270	1,081	887
Kazakhstan	185	417	430	574	773	135	130	304	205	30	20
Kyrgyz Republic	...	...	...	...	95	...	95	...	...	...	...
Latvia	114	289	23	212	75	...	75	...	...	...	...
Lithuania	35	960	684	247	375	19	356	...	...	432	...
Macedonia, FYR of	15	...	...	...	...	...	...	...	...	...	...
Malta	503	57	...	85	...	...	...	...	...	...	...
Moldova	...	40	...	...	...	...	...	...	...	...	...

Table 14 *(concluded)*

	1998	1999	2000	2001	2002	2002 Q1	Q2	Q3	Q4	2003 Q1	Q2
Europe *(continued)*											
Poland	4,162	3,781	5,252	4,837	6,002	877	1,000	3,210	915	2,171	1,606
Romania	338	176	595	1,348	1,742	150	702	450	440	202	976
Russia	13,156	167	3,951	3,200	8,684	1,710	2,108	1,064	3,802	3,366	1,358
Slovak Republic	1,501	995	1,466	220	143	. . .	143	. . .	. . .	79	574
Slovenia	647	688	673	827	309	9	56	86	159	. . .	239
Tajikistan	75	. . .	. . .	. . .	. . .	. . .	. . .	. . .	. . .	. . .	. . .
Turkey	6,948	11,900	20,386	6,405	6,385	1,742	1,475	754	2,414	1,725	2,404
Turkmenistan	612	. . .	. . .	. . .	. . .	. . .	. . .	. . .	. . .	. . .	. . .
Ukraine	1,100	291	. . .	15	514	15	. . .	. . .	499	60	800
Uzbekistan	. . .	142	40	30	46	. . .	. . .	46	. . .	4	. . .
Yugoslavia	. . .	. . .	. . .	. . .	19	. . .	. . .	. . .	19	. . .	11
Middle East	**9,567**	**15,388**	**15,000**	**11,021**	**10,831**	**3,310**	**3,512**	**2,856**	**1,152**	**1,831**	**2,600**
Bahrain	650	152	1,202	207	340	. . .	. . .	340	. . .	. . .	1,050
Egypt	646	1,533	919	2,545	670	. . .	485	. . .	185	. . .	. . .
Iran, I.R. of	. . .	692	758	887	2,671	500	1,185	608	378	. . .	250
Israel	1,147	3,719	2,908	1,603	344	344	. . .	. . .	. . .	. . .	750
Jordan	. . .	. . .	60	. . .	81	81	. . .	. . .	. . .	. . .	. . .
Kuwait	365	148	250	770	750	450	300	. . .	. . .	. . .	. . .
Lebanon	1,770	1,421	1,752	3,300	990	. . .	100	890	. . .	. . .	. . .
Libya	. . .	. . .	50	. . .	. . .	. . .	. . .	. . .	. . .	. . .	. . .
Oman	100	357	685	. . .	2,417	1,300	210	438	469	. . .	. . .
Qatar	902	2,000	1,980	913	1,572	545	607	300	120	771	. . .
Saudi Arabia	3,837	4,375	2,201	275	300	. . .	300	. . .	. . .	400	. . .
United Arab Emirates	150	781	2,045	521	370	90	. . .	280	. . .	160	300
Latin America	**65,723**	**61,325**	**69,119**	**53,854**	**33,412**	**11,868**	**8,309**	**6,094**	**7,139**	**8,294**	**11,259**
Argentina	23,162	17,844	16,649	3,424	824	56	82	86	599	87	61
Bolivia	. . .	. . .	. . .	20	90	. . .	. . .	90	. . .	. . .	. . .
Brazil	14,214	12,952	23,239	19,533	11,032	7,032	2,900	425	675	348	3,873
Chile	5,226	8,032	5,783	3,935	3,012	170	1,030	406	1,405	1,150	435
Colombia	1,947	3,556	3,093	4,895	2,221	485	500	616	620	500	250
Costa Rica	274	300	250	400	250	250	. . .	. . .	. . .	450	. . .
Dominican Republic	74	. . .	74	531	333	188	. . .	. . .	145	600	24
Ecuador	. . .	73	. . .	910	10	. . .	. . .	10	. . .	. . .	. . .
El Salvador	60	316	160	489	1,252	. . .	500	300	452	349	. . .
Grenada	. . .	. . .	. . .	. . .	100	. . .	100	. . .	. . .	. . .	. . .
Guadeloupe	. . .	. . .	. . .	. . .	17	. . .	. . .	. . .	. . .	. . .	. . .
Guatemala	120	222	505	325	44	44	. . .	. . .	. . .	. . .	. . .
Jamaica	250	. . .	421	727	345	. . .	345	. . .	. . .	. . .	. . .
Mexico	13,514	14,100	15,314	13,824	10,172	1,930	2,113	3,646	2,483	4,014	6,615
Paraguay	. . .	55	. . .	70	. . .	. . .	. . .	. . .	. . .	. . .	. . .
Peru	862	1,618	465	138	1,993	1,463	. . .	. . .	530	750	. . .
Trinidad & Tobago	. . .	230	301	70	303	. . .	90	. . .	213	46	. . .
Uruguay	550	465	603	1,147	400	250	150	. . .	. . .	. . .	. . .
Venezuela	5,470	1,562	2,263	3,417	1,015	. . .	500	515	. . .	. . .	. . .

Note: Data provided by the Bond, Equity, and Loan database of the IMF sourced from Capital Data. Loan data includes hard currencies only.

Table 15. Emerging Market Bond Issuance
(In millions of U.S. dollars)

	1998	1999	2000	2001	2002	2002 Q1	2002 Q2	2002 Q3	2002 Q4	2003 Q1	2003 Q2
Total	**79,516**	**82,359**	**80,475**	**89,037**	**61,647**	**22,228**	**15,882**	**8,834**	**14,703**	**20,158**	**25,217**
Africa	**1,381**	**2,346**	**1,486**	**2,110**	**2,161**	**250**	**1,650**	**. . .**	**261**	**483**	**1,875**
Mauritius	. . .	160	. . .	. . .	. . .	. . .	. . .	. . .	. . .	. . .	. . .
Morocco	. . .	152	. . .	. . .	. . .	. . .	. . .	. . .	. . .	. . .	465
South Africa	1,381	1,805	1,486	1,648	1,511	250	1,000	. . .	261	126	1,410
Tunisia	. . .	229	. . .	462	650	. . .	650	. . .	. . .	357	. . .
Asia	**12,400**	**23,425**	**24,501**	**35,869**	**22,533**	**7,554**	**5,029**	**3,957**	**5,993**	**4,226**	**8,675**
China	1,794	1,060	1,771	2,342	603	500	90	. . .	13	. . .	225
Hong Kong SAR	725	7,125	7,059	10,459	1,952	1,711	84	157	. . .	. . .	182
India	. . .	100	100	99	153	. . .	. . .	. . .	153	. . .	. . .
Indonesia	. . .	. . .	. . .	125	375	100	. . .	125	150	. . .	417
Korea	5,084	4,906	7,653	7,756	6,706	627	420	2,616	3,042	1,790	4,346
Malaysia	. . .	2,062	1,420	2,150	1,880	750	980	. . .	150	. . .	. . .
Philippines	1,890	4,751	2,467	1,842	4,774	2,300	650	400	1,424	1,025	200
Singapore	1,500	2,147	2,334	8,665	562	409	8	144	2	2	1,400
Sri Lanka	65	. . .	. . .	. . .	. . .	. . .	. . .	. . .	. . .	. . .	. . .
Taiwan Province of China	1,041	475	1,698	2,152	5,481	1,157	2,797	515	1,012	1,409	1,605
Thailand	300	798	. . .	279	48	. . .	. . .	. . .	48	. . .	300
Europe	**24,050**	**13,873**	**14,203**	**11,559**	**14,997**	**5,098**	**4,255**	**698**	**4,947**	**8,151**	**6,386**
Bulgaria	. . .	54	. . .	223	1,248	1,248	. . .	. . .	. . .	. . .	. . .
Croatia	97	601	858	934	848	546	201	. . .	101	768	215
Cyprus	481	289	. . .	480	480	480	. . .	. . .	. . .	. . .	. . .
Czech Republic	815	422	. . .	51	428	. . .	428	. . .	. . .	188	. . .
Estonia	106	85	336	65	293	. . .	95	198	. . .	323	. . .
Hungary	1,897	2,410	541	1,248	71	71	. . .	. . .	. . .	1,081	. . .
Kazakhstan	100	300	350	250	209	109	. . .	100	. . .	. . .	. . .
Latvia	. . .	237	. . .	181	. . .	. . .	. . .	. . .	. . .	. . .	. . .
Lithuania	. . .	532	376	222	356	. . .	356	. . .	. . .	432	. . .
Malta	250	. . .	. . .	. . .	. . .	. . .	. . .	. . .	. . .	. . .	. . .
Poland	1,943	1,653	1,554	2,774	2,680	658	1,000	400	622	1,622	1,130
Romania	. . .	. . .	260	909	1,062	. . .	622	. . .	440	. . .	814
Russia	12,107	. . .	75	1,353	3,391	536	750	. . .	2,105	2,050	475
Slovak Republic	1,336	800	978	220	143	. . .	143	. . .	. . .	. . .	574
Slovenia	556	439	385	490	30	. . .	. . .	. . .	30	. . .	. . .
Turkey	3,261	5,761	8,491	2,159	3,260	1,450	660	. . .	1,150	1,627	2,377
Ukraine	1,100	291	. . .	. . .	499	. . .	. . .	. . .	499	60	800
Middle East	**2,175**	**4,410**	**4,671**	**5,921**	**3,707**	**875**	**725**	**1,728**	**378**	**500**	**1,000**
Bahrain	. . .	209	188	. . .	325	. . .	325	. . .	. . .	500	250
Egypt	. . .	100	. . .	1,500	. . .	. . .	. . .	. . .	. . .	. . .	. . .
Iran, I.R. of	. . .	. . .	. . .	. . .	986	. . .	. . .	608	378	. . .	. . .
Israel	650	1,679	1,330	1,121	344	344	. . .	. . .	. . .	. . .	750
Jordan	. . .	. . .	. . .	. . .	81	81	. . .	. . .	. . .	. . .	. . .
Kuwait	. . .	. . .	. . .	. . .	750	450	300	. . .	. . .	. . .	. . .
Lebanon	1,525	1,421	1,752	3,300	990	. . .	100	890	. . .	. . .	. . .
Qatar	. . .	1,000	1,400	. . .	. . .	. . .	. . .	. . .	. . .	. . .	. . .
United Arab Emirates	. . .	. . .	. . .	. . .	230	. . .	. . .	. . .	230	. . .	. . .
Latin America	**39,511**	**38,307**	**35,615**	**33,579**	**18,250**	**8,451**	**4,223**	**2,451**	**3,125**	**6,799**	**7,282**
Argentina	15,615	14,183	13,025	1,501	. . .	. . .	. . .	. . .	. . .	. . .	. . .
Brazil	9,190	8,586	11,382	12,239	6,375	4,721	1,454	200	. . .	150	3,500
Chile	1,063	1,764	680	1,536	1,729	. . .	864	40	825	1,000	150
Colombia	1,389	1,676	1,547	4,263	1,000	. . .	500	. . .	500	500	250
Costa Rica	200	300	250	250	250	250	. . .	. . .	. . .	450	. . .
Dominican Republic	. . .	. . .	. . .	500	. . .	. . .	. . .	. . .	. . .	600	. . .
El Salvador	. . .	150	50	354	1,252	. . .	500	300	452	349	. . .
Grenada	. . .	. . .	. . .	. . .	100	. . .	100	. . .	. . .	. . .	. . .
Guatemala	. . .	. . .	. . .	325	. . .	. . .	. . .	. . .	. . .	. . .	. . .
Jamaica	250	. . .	421	691	300	. . .	300	. . .	. . .	. . .	. . .
Mexico	8,444	9,854	7,078	9,232	4,914	1,800	355	1,911	848	3,000	3,382
Peru	150	. . .	. . .	. . .	1,930	1,430	. . .	. . .	500	750	. . .
Trinidad & Tobago	. . .	230	250	. . .	. . .	. . .	. . .	. . .	. . .	. . .	. . .
Uruguay	550	350	443	1,106	400	250	150	. . .	. . .	. . .	. . .
Venezuela	2,660	1,215	489	1,583	. . .	. . .	. . .	. . .	. . .	. . .	. . .

Note: Data provided by the Bond, Equity, and Loan database of the IMF sourced from Capital Data.

Table 16. Emerging Market Equity Issuance
(In millions of U.S. dollars)

	1998	1999	2000	2001	2002	2002 Q1	Q2	Q3	Q4	2003 Q1	Q2
Total	**9,436**	**23,187**	**41,773**	**11,246**	**16,359**	**4,076**	**4,345**	**3,816**	**4,122**	**1,153**	**1,940**
Africa	**800**	**659**	**103**	**151**	**341**	**70**	**260**	...	**10**	**621**	**75**
Mali	24	...	...	...	...	...	...	...	...	...	...
Morocco	80	...	56	7	...	...	...	...	...	...	...
South Africa	656	659	47	144	341	70	260	...	10	621	75
Tunisia	40	...	...	...	...	...	...	...	...	...	...
Asia	**4,455**	**18,272**	**31,568**	**9,592**	**12,411**	**2,461**	**3,015**	**3,816**	**3,120**	**517**	**1,657**
China	709	1,477	20,240	2,810	2,546	113	103	316	2,015	509	332
Hong Kong SAR	438	3,370	3,089	297	2,858	82	35	2,725	16	...	86
India	53	874	917	467	265	172	43	50	...	...	...
Indonesia	...	522	28	347	281	...	156	125	...	...	235
Korea	495	6,591	785	3,676	1,554	...	894	431	229	...	254
Macao	...	...	29	...	...	...	...	...	...	...	...
Malaysia	...	...	...	15	891	...	823	3	65	8	4
Papua New Guinea	...	232	...	...	...	...	...	...	...	...	...
Philippines	...	222	195	...	11	...	...	...	11	...	...
Singapore	226	1,726	2,202	626	892	190	6	111	585	...	477
Taiwan Province of China	354	2,500	3,952	1,127	3,058	1,905	954	...	199	...	268
Thailand	2,179	757	132	225	56	...	...	56	...	...	...
Europe	**2,532**	**1,412**	**3,340**	**259**	**1,612**	**457**	**163**	...	**992**	**14**	**74**
Croatia	205	...	...	22	...	...	...	...	...	...	...
Czech Republic	126	...	...	...	...	...	...	...	...	...	...
Estonia	52	190	...	...	...	...	...	...	...	...	...
Hungary	383	529	19	...	...	...	...	...	...	...	...
Latvia	4	...	...	...	23	...	23	...	...	...	...
Lithuania	...	...	150	...	...	...	...	...	...	...	...
Malta	46	...	...	...	...	...	...	...	...	...	...
Poland	957	636	359	...	217	...	...	...	217	...	20
Romania	45	...	...	...	...	...	...	...	...	...	...
Russia	...	56	388	237	1,301	386	140	...	775	14	54
Turkey	713	...	2,424	...	71	71	...	...	...	...	...
Middle East	**1,486**	**2,084**	**1,618**	**87**	...	...	...	...	...	...	...
Egypt	102	89	319	...	...	...	...	...	...	...	...
Israel	497	1,995	1,299	87	...	...	...	...	...	...	...
Lebanon	145	...	...	...	...	...	...	...	...	...	...
Qatar	742	...	...	...	...	...	...	...	...	...	...
Latin America	**164**	**761**	**5,144**	**1,157**	**1,995**	**1,088**	**907**	...	...	...	**135**
Argentina	...	350	393	34	...	...	...	...	...	...	1
Brazil	...	161	3,103	1,123	1,148	1,088	61	...	...	...	134
Chile	72	...	...	...	...	...	...	...	...	...	...
Dominican Republic	74	...	74	...	...	...	...	...	...	...	...
Mexico	...	162	1,574	...	847	...	847	...	...	...	...
Peru	17	88	...	...	...	...	...	...	...	...	...

Note: Data provided by the Bond, Equity, and Loan database of the IMF sourced from Capital Data.

Table 17. Emerging Market Loan Syndication
(In millions of U.S. dollars)

	1998	1999	2000	2001	2002	2002 Q1	2002 Q2	2002 Q3	2002 Q4	2003 Q1	2003 Q2
Total	**60,025**	**58,025**	**94,158**	**61,855**	**57,637**	**10,740**	**12,660**	**19,484**	**14,752**	**14,641**	**15,299**
Africa	**1,711**	**1,703**	**7,794**	**4,731**	**4,668**	**1,010**	**...**	**2,220**	**1,438**	**1,250**	**1,286**
Algeria	...	...	...	50	150	...	...	150	...	75	...
Angola	310	...	...	455	350	...	...	350	...	...	117
Botswana	...	...	...	22	...	...	...	...	...	...	...
Cameroon	...	...	...	54	...	...	...	...	...	...	...
Chad	...	...	...	400	...	...	...	...	...	...	...
Côte d'Ivoire	...	179	...	15	...	...	...	...	...	...	...
Ghana	509	30	320	300	420	...	...	420	...	...	...
Guinea	130	...	...	...	...	...	...	...	...	...	...
Kenya	...	...	8	80	...	...	...	...	...	134	...
Mali	...	...	...	...	150	...	...	...	150	...	...
Morocco	200	171	...	129	...	...	...	...	...	...	...
Mozambique	...	...	...	200	...	...	...	...	...	36	...
Nigeria	...	90	...	100	1,000	...	...	...	1,000	460	169
Senegal	...	...	...	...	40	40	...	...	...	...	...
Seychelles	...	...	50	...	150	...	...	150	...	...	...
South Africa	532	960	7,166	2,855	2,308	970	...	1,100	238	545	1,000
Tanzania	...	...	135	...	...	...	...	50	50	...	...
Tunisia	...	123	94	71	100	...	...	...	...	...	...
Zaire	...	...	21	...	...	...	...	...	...	...	...
Zambia	30	...	...	...	...	...	...	...	...	...	...
Zimbabwe	...	150	...	...	...	...	...	...	...	...	...
Asia	**17,356**	**14,262**	**29,814**	**22,023**	**18,957**	**3,296**	**3,831**	**6,320**	**5,510**	**8,213**	**5,596**
Brunei	...	...	...	...	129	...	129	...	...	...	...
China	4,472	924	1,053	415	1,902	110	940	772	80	730	817
Hong Kong SAR	930	994	10,899	7,552	2,206	407	652	402	744	538	80
India	1,380	1,402	1,208	1,816	1,142	240	246	123	533	382	419
Indonesia	374	943	1,255	493	100	...	100	...	...	2,928	...
Korea	680	2,046	5,793	5,588	6,287	713	917	1,909	2,748	595	1,638
Lao P.D.R.	...	...	...	...	30	...	30	...	...	...	...
Malaysia	2,527	3,115	3,087	2,267	2,338	1,058	368	835	77	1,818	731
Marshall Islands	...	...	...	...	35	...	...	35	...	...	...
Nepal	57	...	...	...	...	...	...	...	...	...	...
Pakistan	323	...	...	182	85	...	...	...	85	...	9
Philippines	2,223	2,209	2,360	1,816	1,012	100	...	840	72	675	48
Singapore	741	466	1,544	1,093	1,630	610	90	800	130	419	689
Sri Lanka	...	23	100	105	...	...	...	...	...	...	...
Taiwan Province of China	1,044	1,044	1,054	515	770	40	93	141	496	...	162
Thailand	2,568	996	1,441	181	899	18	266	170	445	128	958
Vietnam	37	100	20	...	392	...	...	293	100	...	45
Europe	**9,003**	**10,909**	**19,479**	**10,970**	**13,721**	**1,670**	**2,863**	**6,173**	**3,016**	**2,352**	**2,975**
Azerbaijan	...	77	...	16	...	...	...	...	...	...	...
Bulgaria	10	...	9	19	13	13	...	...	...	...	...
Croatia	226	904	641	810	552	15	106	325	106	...	309
Cyprus	75	...	86	152	68	...	68	...	...	...	...
Czech Republic	723	119	127	514	35	...	...	10	25	...	...
Estonia	223	14	77	137	147	...	147	...	...	88	35
Gibraltar	...	65	80	...	...	...	...	...	...	...	...
Hungary	773	532	749	117	986	195	96	424	270	...	887
Kazakhstan	85	117	80	324	564	26	130	204	205	30	20
Kyrgyz Republic	...	...	...	...	95	...	95	...	...	...	...
Latvia	110	52	23	31	52	...	52	...	...	...	...
Lithuania	35	428	157	25	19	19	...	...	...	...	...
Macedonia	15	...	...	...	...	...	...	...	...	...	...
Malta	207	57	...	85	...	...	...	...	...	...	...
Moldova	...	40	...	...	...	...	...	...	...	...	...
Poland	1,262	1,492	3,340	2,063	3,105	219	...	2,810	76	549	456
Romania	293	176	335	439	680	150	80	450	...	202	162
Russia	1,049	111	3,488	1,610	3,992	788	1,218	1,064	922	1,302	829

Table 17 *(concluded)*

	1998	1999	2000	2001	2002	2002 Q1	Q2	Q3	Q4	2003 Q1	Q2
Europe *(continued)*											
Slovak Republic	165	195	488	...	...	...	...	...	...	79	...
Slovenia	91	249	288	337	279	9	56	86	129		239
Tajikistan	75	...	...	...	...	...	...	...	...		...
Turkey	2,974	6,139	9,471	4,246	3,054	221	815	754	1,264	98	27
Turkmenistan	612	...	...	...	...	...	...	...	...		
Ukraine	...	...	...	15	15	15	...	...	...	...	...
Uzbekistan	...	142	40	30	46	...	...	46	...	4	...
Yugoslavia	...	...	...	...	19	...	...	...	19	...	11
Middle East	**5,906**	**8,894**	**8,711**	**5,013**	**7,124**	**2,435**	**2,787**	**1,128**	**774**	**1,331**	**1,600**
Bahrain	650	152	1,202	207	340	...	...	340	...	...	1,050
Egypt	544	1,344	600	1,045	670	...	485	...	185	...	...
Iran, I.R. of	...	692	758	887	1,685	500	1,185	...	...		250
Israel	...	45	280	395	...	...	...	...	...		...
Jordan	...	...	60	...	...	...	...	...	...		...
Kuwait	365	148	250	770	...	...	...	...	...		
Lebanon	100	...	...	...	...	...	...	...	...		
Libya	...	...	50	...	...	...	...	...	...		
Oman	100	357	685	...	2,417	1,300	210	438	469	...	...
Qatar	160	1,000	580	913	1,572	545	607	300	120	771	...
Saudi Arabia	3,837	4,375	2,201	275	300	...	300	...	...	400	...
United Arab Emirates	150	781	2,045	521	140	90	...	50	...	160	300
Latin America	**26,049**	**22,257**	**28,360**	**19,118**	**13,167**	**2,329**	**3,179**	**3,643**	**4,014**	**1,495**	**3,842**
Argentina	7,547	3,312	3,231	1,889	824	56	82	86	599	87	60
Bolivia	...	...	...	20	90	...	...	90	...	...	...
Brazil	5,024	4,205	8,754	6,171	3,508	1,223	1,385	225	675	198	240
Chile	4,091	6,268	5,103	2,399	1,283	170	166	366	580	150	285
Colombia	558	1,880	1,546	632	1,221	485	...	616	120	...	...
Costa Rica	74	...	...	150	...	...	...	...	...	...	...
Dominican Republic	...	...	...	31	333	188	...	...	145	...	24
Ecuador	...	73	...	910	10	...	...	10	...	...	...
El Salvador	60	166	110	135	...	...	...	...	...	...	...
Guadeloupe	...	...	...	...	17	...	...	...	17	...	...
Guatemala	120	222	505	...	44	44	...	...	...	...	...
Jamaica	...	...	...	36	45	...	45	...	...	...	...
Mexico	5,070	4,084	6,661	4,592	4,411	130	911	1,735	1,635	1,014	3,233
Paraguay	...	55	...	70	...	...	...	...	...	...	...
Peru	695	1,530	465	138	63	33	...	...	30	...	...
Trinidad & Tobago	...	...	51	70	303	...	90	...	213	46	...
Uruguay	...	115	160	41	...	...	...	...	...	...	...
Venezuela	2,810	347	1,774	1,834	1,015	...	500	515	...	...	...

Note: Data provided by the Bond, Equity, and Loan database of the IMF sourced from Capital Data. Includes hard currencies only.

Table 18. Equity Valuation Measures: Dividend-Yield Ratios

| | 2003 | | 2002 | | | | | | | | |
	Q1	Q2	Q1	Q2	Q3	Q4	1998	1999	2000	2001	2002
Argentina	1.49	1.57	3.20	3.67	4.11	3.42	3.88	3.29	4.62	5.16	3.42
Brazil	5.25	5.03	5.30	5.63	6.92	5.51	9.34	2.95	3.18	4.93	5.51
Chile	2.64	1.98	2.43	2.81	3.27	2.76	4.31	1.88	2.33	2.31	2.76
China	3.52	2.92	2.03	2.39	2.40	2.41	3.71	3.14	0.95	1.95	2.41
Colombia	5.78	4.95	6.61	6.10	5.62	4.78	6.02	6.78	11.12	5.63	4.78
Czech Republic	2.23	7.63	2.10	2.76	2.48	2.36	1.08	1.36	0.95	2.28	2.36
Egypt	6.89	5.19	6.03	7.03	7.98	7.53	8.24	3.92	5.75	6.48	7.53
Hong Kong SAR	4.15	3.93	3.11	3.34	3.88	3.85	3.87	2.31	2.58	3.25	3.85
Hungary	1.43	1.13	1.15	1.51	1.52	1.40	1.14	1.14	1.46	1.30	1.40
India	2.12	2.12	1.94	1.59	1.76	1.81	2.00	1.25	1.59	2.03	1.81
Indonesia	4.46	4.13	2.78	2.97	4.27	4.17	1.16	0.91	3.05	3.65	4.17
Israel	1.18	0.56	2.53	2.50	2.52	1.47	3.58	1.87	2.26	2.24	1.47
Jordan	3.46	3.11	3.34	3.44	3.76	3.77	3.77	4.24	4.54	3.51	3.77
Korea	2.75	2.25	0.97	1.25	1.46	1.38	1.19	0.81	2.05	1.54	1.38
Malaysia	2.52	2.44	1.66	1.88	2.01	2.04	1.85	1.15	1.70	1.87	2.04
Mexico	2.58	2.22	1.70	2.18	2.47	2.30	2.12	1.27	1.63	1.98	2.30
Morocco	4.71	4.38	4.24	4.50	4.89	4.84	2.01	2.49	3.59	3.97	4.84
Pakistan	11.30	11.07	12.74	15.11	14.07	10.95	13.75	4.00	5.12	16.01	10.95
Peru	2.43	2.34	2.55	2.39	2.58	2.37	4.64	2.86	3.38	3.16	2.37
Philippines	1.86	1.40	1.06	2.33	1.69	1.97	1.24	1.08	1.44	1.43	1.97
Poland	1.92	1.56	1.81	2.26	2.06	1.84	1.21	0.70	0.68	1.87	1.84
Russia	2.19	1.76	0.91	1.85	1.99	1.87	0.72	0.14	0.92	1.11	1.87
Singapore	2.43	2.50	1.55	1.90	2.19	2.27	1.41	0.86	1.40	1.80	2.27
South Africa	4.72	7.16	3.31	3.30	4.08	3.83	3.96	2.09	2.75	3.47	3.83
Sri Lanka	3.74	2.12	4.57	3.72	3.06	3.35	2.49	3.22	5.59	4.79	3.35
Taiwan Province of China	1.64	1.66	1.28	1.46	1.81	1.60	1.15	0.97	1.71	1.42	1.60
Thailand	3.13	2.54	2.26	2.37	2.78	2.48	1.84	0.70	2.13	2.02	2.48
Turkey	1.67	1.58	1.51	1.92	1.54	1.35	3.17	0.76	1.91	1.15	1.35
Venezuela	5.86	5.00	4.11	2.41	2.63	2.38	6.93	5.80	5.05	3.89	2.38
Emerging Markets Free	2.99	3.06	2.09	2.32	2.58	2.43	3.13	1.52	2.09	2.30	2.43
EMF Asia	2.58	2.29	1.45	1.65	1.89	1.81	1.60	1.01	1.71	1.73	1.81
EMF Latin America	3.69	3.39	3.24	3.71	4.07	3.64	5.18	2.28	2.69	3.37	3.64
EMF Europe & Middle East	1.77	1.55	1.67	2.11	2.11	1.71	2.05	1.16	1.84	1.69	1.71
ACWI Free	2.45	2.14	1.70	1.93	2.36	2.25	1.58	1.27	1.46	1.72	2.25

Source: Morgan Stanley Capital International.

Note: The countries above include the 27 constituents of the Emerging Markets Free index as well as Hong Kong SAR and Singapore. Regional breakdowns conform to Morgan Stanley Capital International conventions. All indices reflect investible opportunities for global investors by taking into account restrictions on foreign ownership. The indices attempt to achieve an 85 percent representation of freely floating stocks.

Table 19. Equity Valuation Measures: Price-to-Book Ratios

	2003		2002				1998	1999	2000	2001	2002
	Q1	Q2	Q1	Q2	Q3	Q4					
Argentina	1.22	1.46	1.39	1.39	1.26	1.20	1.31	1.47	1.04	0.86	1.20
Brazil	1.18	1.19	1.18	1.20	0.95	1.24	0.52	1.24	1.18	1.11	1.24
Chile	1.11	1.29	1.36	1.14	1.05	1.15	1.16	1.69	1.49	1.39	1.15
China	1.24	1.41	1.79	1.58	1.33	1.30	0.63	0.69	2.75	1.88	1.30
Colombia	1.16	1.11	0.52	0.80	0.88	1.18	0.71	0.71	0.49	0.53	1.18
Czech Republic	0.86	0.83	0.88	0.74	0.81	0.84	0.73	0.80	1.00	0.81	0.84
Egypt	1.17	1.61	1.44	1.15	1.05	1.05	2.13	3.57	2.32	1.39	1.05
Hong Kong SAR	1.02	1.10	1.36	1.27	1.08	1.10	1.31	2.27	1.67	1.38	1.10
Hungary	1.76	1.83	2.16	1.82	1.83	1.91	3.05	3.35	2.33	2.03	1.91
India	2.07	2.47	2.29	2.29	2.13	2.15	2.00	3.55	2.71	2.13	2.15
Indonesia	1.38	1.93	3.11	3.08	2.54	2.23	1.39	2.41	1.03	2.72	2.23
Israel	1.83	2.53	1.88	1.75	1.72	1.74	1.48	2.53	3.04	2.22	1.74
Jordan	1.25	1.56	1.45	1.53	1.27	1.26	1.05	1.03	1.02	1.38	1.26
Korea	1.04	1.32	1.70	1.47	1.22	1.21	0.99	1.42	0.82	1.33	1.21
Malaysia	1.62	1.71	1.94	1.85	1.52	1.54	1.25	1.98	1.59	1.76	1.54
Mexico	1.70	1.92	2.27	1.99	1.69	1.77	1.72	2.31	1.91	1.99	1.77
Morocco	1.39	1.44	1.68	1.50	1.39	1.40	4.27	3.53	2.56	1.79	1.40
Pakistan	1.90	1.98	1.26	1.18	1.38	2.04	1.07	1.48	1.41	0.88	2.04
Peru	1.71	1.71	1.63	1.55	1.56	1.84	1.41	1.92	1.13	1.29	1.84
Philippines	0.87	1.18	1.31	1.07	1.03	0.85	1.48	1.64	1.27	1.11	0.85
Poland	1.29	1.49	1.43	1.32	1.22	1.37	1.47	2.12	2.10	1.33	1.37
Russia	1.00	1.25	1.54	1.64	1.24	1.22	0.67	2.41	0.90	1.27	1.22
Singapore	1.23	1.32	1.80	1.51	1.28	1.26	1.55	2.56	2.05	1.63	1.26
South Africa	1.47	1.66	2.03	1.95	1.68	1.72	1.52	2.75	2.68	1.81	1.72
Sri Lanka	1.04	1.83	0.83	1.10	1.33	1.22	1.15	1.00	0.60	0.83	1.22
Taiwan Province of China	1.49	1.77	2.19	1.71	1.35	1.53	2.21	3.46	1.87	1.98	1.53
Thailand	1.78	2.17	2.11	2.05	1.72	1.83	1.14	2.04	1.51	1.68	1.83
Turkey	1.43	1.31	3.08	2.25	2.04	1.76	2.55	9.21	2.72	3.80	1.76
Venezuela	0.66	1.00	0.50	0.75	0.78	0.87	0.57	0.63	0.67	0.48	0.87
Emerging Markets Free	1.33	1.54	1.79	1.64	1.38	1.45	1.21	2.12	1.64	1.59	1.45
EMF Asia	1.30	1.56	1.92	1.65	1.37	1.41	1.40	2.09	1.53	1.68	1.41
EMF Latin America	1.35	1.44	1.52	1.45	1.26	1.44	0.87	1.57	1.36	1.35	1.44
EMF Europe & Middle East	1.28	1.51	1.71	1.61	1.41	1.42	1.88	3.41	2.15	1.70	1.42
ACWI Free	2.01	2.31	2.71	2.40	1.96	2.07	3.49	4.23	3.46	2.67	2.07

Source: Morgan Stanley Capital International.
Note: The countries above include the 27 constituents of the Emerging Markets Free index as well as Hong Kong SAR and Singapore. Regional breakdowns conform to Morgan Stanley Capital International conventions. All indices reflect investible opportunities for global investors by taking into account restrictions on foreign ownership. The indices attempt to achieve an 85 percent representation of freely floating stocks.

Table 20. Equity Valuation Measures: Price-Earnings Ratios

| | 2003 | | 2002 | | | | | | | | |
	Q1	Q2	Q1	Q2	Q3	Q4	1998	1999	2000	2001	2002
Argentina	−3.09	17.51	31.12	−8.35	−7.59	−12.86	12.95	24.82	20.69	19.13	−12.86
Brazil	11.45	10.00	9.18	8.92	9.46	11.23	6.60	18.64	12.83	8.49	11.23
Chile	31.79	32.83	17.60	19.30	15.72	17.16	16.89	46.40	31.96	18.02	17.16
China	11.95	11.76	13.33	13.46	11.39	12.14	10.58	14.97	40.60	14.09	12.14
Colombia	8.85	8.79	393.04	7.31	8.10	9.55	7.62	20.30	−103.44	64.91	9.55
Czech Republic	11.23	10.18	10.01	8.92	10.02	10.40	33.42	−42.04	16.49	9.21	10.40
Egypt	10.03	14.94	6.68	7.72	7.37	7.33	7.54	16.54	9.35	6.28	7.33
Hong Kong SAR	13.46	13.47	19.09	17.23	14.57	14.91	17.82	30.81	7.64	20.47	14.91
Hungary	10.11	10.15	18.66	15.27	14.47	10.06	14.54	18.50	14.82	19.34	10.06
India	12.46	13.25	14.17	12.77	11.94	13.56	11.64	22.84	15.61	13.84	13.56
Indonesia	5.64	7.49	10.64	10.93	7.19	7.14	−9.04	−48.73	18.68	8.37	7.14
Israel	65.79	68.83	192.41	−32.58	−74.84	−46.62	16.74	25.51	23.88	228.84	−46.62
Jordan	12.85	13.94	15.85	12.89	12.42	12.39	13.30	13.51	−107.11	15.10	12.39
Korea	8.12	8.88	19.54	21.18	11.71	11.44	527.74	23.24	8.12	15.23	11.44
Malaysia	16.05	16.26	27.10	21.81	13.75	13.21	−46.93	−8.41	20.63	22.62	13.21
Mexico	13.73	17.04	16.58	13.64	12.97	14.07	15.20	14.64	13.78	14.23	14.07
Morocco	9.53	21.61	10.22	10.61	9.77	9.87	22.53	18.65	9.30	10.77	9.87
Pakistan	7.41	7.81	7.47	5.31	6.18	8.07	8.15	17.60	8.39	4.53	8.07
Peru	13.84	12.42	15.91	19.84	17.30	20.42	11.30	18.46	15.44	14.08	20.42
Philippines	17.49	19.35	49.36	22.09	22.48	18.21	17.67	142.83	−35.06	43.72	18.21
Poland	−30.30	36.79	19.91	19.65	13.30	−261.14	11.86	22.33	14.30	18.32	−261.14
Russia	9.42	14.24	6.05	5.92	5.94	7.33	12.68	−126.43	5.69	5.03	7.33
Singapore	18.64	18.00	24.75	24.62	22.06	21.07	25.33	41.18	18.94	16.53	21.07
South Africa	8.71	9.44	12.26	12.02	10.13	10.50	11.35	18.73	14.87	11.30	10.50
Sri Lanka	8.67	14.77	9.82	12.67	15.53	14.35	8.10	7.59	4.24	8.53	14.35
Taiwan Province of China	61.54	37.30	22.89	51.48	43.95	73.13	23.49	38.26	14.06	21.08	73.13
Thailand	12.56	14.47	18.91	18.39	16.03	15.52	−3.76	−8.94	−14.61	16.67	15.52
Turkey	40.76	9.33	41.19	26.59	21.50	101.33	7.59	38.60	11.77	25.51	101.33
Venezuela	8.94	14.40	13.04	15.15	11.90	13.43	6.93	17.68	21.76	18.43	13.43
Emerging Markets Free	12.70	12.81	15.59	16.01	12.87	13.95	17.70	27.17	14.85	13.99	13.95
EMF Asia	12.51	12.72	19.07	21.30	14.26	14.85	83.45	40.98	15.47	16.73	14.85
EMF Latin America	15.87	13.55	12.88	11.88	12.38	13.84	10.58	18.28	14.93	11.67	13.84
EMF Europe & Middle East	17.24	17.84	13.62	12.85	11.82	16.27	16.37	37.25	14.05	13.10	16.27
ACWI Free	22.11	22.93	28.46	30.05	24.53	23.18	29.05	35.70	25.44	26.76	23.18

Source: Morgan Stanley Capital International.

Note: The countries above include the 27 constituents of the Emerging Markets Free index as well as Hong Kong SAR and Singapore. Regional breakdowns conform to Morgan Stanley Capital International conventions. All indices reflect investible opportunities for global investors by taking into account restrictions on foreign ownership. The indices attempt to achieve an 85 percent representation of freely floating stocks.

Table 21. United States Mutual Fund Flows
(In millions of U.S. dollars)

	2003		2002				1998	1999	2000	2001	2002
	Q1	Q2	Q1	Q2	Q3	Q4					
Asia Pacific (Ex-Japan)	6	100	38	14	−119	24	−696	152	−1,208	−496	−43
Corporate High Yield	7,162	9,051	4,322	146	−821	4,436	9,857	−510	−6,162	5,938	8,082
Corporate Investment Grade	10,636	6,993	8,178	8,403	9,875	6,232	17,028	7,136	4,254	21,692	32,688
Emerging Markets Debt	343	285	168	28	49	204	523	18	−500	−448	450
Emerging Markets Equity	−186	539	338	−25	−507	−137	−1,485	24	−350	−1,663	−331
European Equity	13	−236	−69	−236	−267	−472	3,087	−1,665	621	−1,791	−1,045
Global Equity	−1,620	−659	−185	−1,224	−2,318	−1,426	1,289	4,673	12,627	−3,006	−5,152
Growth-Aggressive	−1,895	3,419	7,377	2,118	−3,913	30	5,046	15,248	46,610	17,883	5,612
International & Global Debt	791	1,031	−248	305	−521	−359	−90	−1,582	−3,272	−1,602	−823
International Equity	−655	2,590	1,913	3,235	−2,017	1,108	7,373	2,999	13,322	−4,488	4,240
Japanese Equity	28	509	−43	133	−85	−86	154	731	−831	−270	−82
Latin American Equity Funds	−27	43	203	3	−119	−55	−781	−121	−95	−147	33

Note: Data are provided by AMG Data Services and cover net flows of U.S.-based mutual funds. Fund categories are distinguished by a primary investment objective that signifies an investment of 65 percent or more of a fund's assets. Primary sector data are mutually exclusive, but emerging and regional sectors are all subsets of international equity.

Table 22. Bank Profitability

	Return on Assets (In percent)							Return on Equity (In percent)						
	1998	1999	2000	2001	2002	2003	Month	1998	1999	2000	2001	2002	2003	Month
Latin America														
Argentina	0.5	0.2	0.0	0.1	−4.1*	...	...	4.0	1.5	−0.2	0.8	−33.5*	...	...
Bolivia	0.7	0.7	−0.9	−0.4	0.1	0.0	March	7.8	7.9	−9.4	−4.2	0.6	0.4	March
Brazil	0.6	1.6	1.0	0.2	1.9	...	...	7.4	18.9	11.3	2.4	20.8	...	...
Chile	0.9	0.7	1.0	1.3	1.1	1.4	March	11.5	9.4	12.7	17.7	14.4	15.7	March
Colombia	−2.2	−3.2	−1.7	0.1	1.2	...	...	−19.6	−33.4	−15.8	1.2	10.9	...	...
Ecuador	0.8	0.2	−2.8	−6.6	1.5	1.9	March	5.3	1.3	−21.3	−36.0	15.3	23.1	March
Jamaica	...	...	0.3	0.5	0.6	...	...	...	...	...	...	...	...	...
Mexico	0.6	0.7	0.9	0.8	−1.1	1.8	March	6.9	5.8	10.4	8.6	−10.4	15.8	March
Paraguay[1]	5.0	1.2	1.7	2.4	1.5	1.7	March	...	...	...	...	...	...	...
Peru	0.7	0.3	0.3	0.4	0.8	0.7	March	8.4	4.0	3.1	4.5	8.4	7.4	March
Uruguay[1,2]	0.9	1.3	0.9	−0.3	−4.8	...	...	7.3	7.8	4.6	−18.7	−189.4*	...	...
Venezuela, Rep. Bol.	4.9	3.1	2.8	2.7	4.8	0.7	February	41.4	24.0	23.1	20.6	31.7	4.6	February
Emerging Europe														
Bulgaria	1.7	2.4	2.8	2.6	2.0	3.4	March	21.5	20.9	22.6	19.3	14.9	24.9	March
Croatia	−2.8	0.8	1.2	1.3	1.3	1.7	March	...	5.0	10.5	6.7	20.4	...	June
Czech Republic	−0.2	−0.3	0.7	0.7	1.2	0.7	March	−17.8	−4.3	13.1	14.4	22.1	14.2	March
Estonia[3]	−1.2	1.4	1.1	2.5	2.6*	...	...	−6.4	7.8	8.6	18.8	19.2*	...	...
Hungary	−2.0	0.6	1.3	2.0	...	...	...	−26.7	6.7	15.1	20.2	...	...	...
Israel	0.5	0.5	0.5	0.3	0.2	...	June	9.9	11.3	11.7	5.9	3.2	...	June
Latvia	−1.5	1.0	2.0	1.5	1.5	1.3	March	−12.9	11.0	19.0	19.0	14.7	...	March
Lithuania	0.9	0.2	0.5	−0.1	1.3	1.6	March	11.9	1.3	5.0	−1.2	9.8	14.1	March
Poland[3]	1.8	1.6	1.5	1.4	0.9	...	...	16.1	12.9	15.2	12.9	6.7	...	...
Russia	−3.5	−0.3	0.9	2.4	2.3	...	September	−28.6	−4.0	8.0	19.4	16.0	...	September
Slovak Republic	−0.5	−2.3	1.4	1.0	1.2	...	...	−13.4	−36.5	25.2	22.7	31.1	...	...
Slovenia	1.2	0.8	1.1	0.5	1.1	...	...	11.3	7.8	11.4	4.8	13.3	...	...
Turkey[4]	1.9	−0.4	−0.8	−5.5	0.9	0.3	March	23.1	−7.2	−10.5	−69.4	7.2	2.3	March
Ukraine	...	2.0	−0.1	1.2	1.2	0.8	March	...	8.7	−0.5	7.5	8.0	5.3	March
Western Europe														
Austria	0.4	0.4	0.4	0.5	0.3	...	...	8.7	8.4	9.9	10.7	5.4	...	...
Belgium	0.3	0.4	0.6	0.4	0.4*	...	...	11.3	17.4	20.8	14.0	10.0*	...	...
Denmark	0.8	0.7	0.8	0.8	0.7*	...	...	12.9	11.8	13.5	12.6	11.7	...	...
Finland	1.2	1.0	1.2	1.2	0.7	...	...	25.8	20.1	22.4	23.8	14.1	...	...
France	0.3*	0.4*	0.6*	0.4*	0.3*	...	...	7.8*	10.5*	14.9*	10.0*	8.1*	...	...
Germany	0.3	0.2	0.2	0.2	0.1	...	...	8.5	5.4	5.3	4.2	2.0	...	...
Greece	0.8	2.4	1.4	1.0	0.5	...	...	12.0	29.0	15.0	12.4	6.8	...	...
Ireland	1.1	1.0	0.9	0.7	0.5	...	...	19.5	17.4	14.8	11.5	10.1	...	...
Italy	0.5	0.6	0.8	0.6	0.5	...	...	7.2	8.7	11.2	8.6	7.0	...	...
Luxembourg	0.6	0.4	0.5	0.5	0.4	...	September	15.6	10.1	11.1	11.6	11.3	...	September
Netherlands	0.4	0.6	0.5	0.5	0.3	...		11.0	14.3	13.2	12.1	9.0	...	
Norway[3]	0.7	1.2	1.2	1.1	0.9	...	June	11.4	14.7	15.1	11.4	4.8	3.4	March
Portugal	0.7	0.7	0.6	0.6	0.4	...	...	15.1	14.6	15.1	15.0	11.5	...	June
Spain	0.9	0.9	1.0	0.9	0.8	...	...	14.4*	12.2*	14.0*	12.7*	12.2	...	...
Sweden	0.7	0.7	0.9	0.8	0.6	...	...	14.2	16.0	15.7	13.0	10.7	10.1	March
Switzerland	0.7	0.8	0.9	0.5	0.2*	...	...	17.1	18.8	18.2	11.2	8.6	...	...
United Kingdom[3,5]	0.8	1.0	0.9	0.6	0.7	...	June	14.5	17.7	14.0	9.2	10.9	...	June

Table 22 *(concluded)*

	Return on Assets (In percent)							Return on Equity (In percent)						
	1998	1999	2000	2001	2002	2003	Month	1998	1999	2000	2001	2002	2003	Month
Asia														
China	...	0.1	0.1	0.1	0.1	...	June	...	...	...	...	...	...	...
Hong Kong SAR	0.4	0.4	0.8	0.8	0.8	...	...	7.8	11.1	13.5	13.9	13.3	...	...
India [6]	0.8	0.5	0.7	0.5	0.8	...	March	...	...	12.8	10.4	11.9	...	March
Indonesia	−19.9	−9.1	0.1	0.8	1.3	...	...	...	...	19.6	13.4	22.7	...	...
Korea	−3.2	−1.3	−0.6	0.7	0.7	...	...	−52.5	−23.1	−11.9	12.9	12.1	...	...
Malaysia	...	0.7	1.5	1.0	1.3	...	...	...	9.8	19.5	13.4	16.8	...	...
Pakistan	0.5	−0.2	−0.2	−0.5	0.7	...	...	9.1	−6.3	−0.3	−0.3	13.0	...	...
Philippines	0.8	0.4	0.4	0.4	0.8	...	...	5.9	2.9	2.6	3.2	6.2	...	...
Singapore	0.4	1.3	1.4	1.0	0.8	0.9	March	4.2	10.9	12.4	9.6	7.6	7.7	March
Sri Lanka	1.3	−0.2	0.8	0.8	...	...	...	13.9	−10.1	13.1	15.5	...	...	...
Thailand	−5.6	−5.7	−1.7	−0.1	0.4	...	...	−38.5	−47.0	−15.9	−1.9	7.6	...	September
Middle East														
Egypt [7]	0.9	0.9	0.9	0.8	0.7	0.6	December	...	14.7	16.1	13.7	12.4	11.1	December
Lebanon	...	1.0	0.7	0.5	0.7	...	...	...	15.7	11.1	9.1	10.4	...	...
Morocco	0.9	0.7	0.7	0.9	0.7	...	September	9.5	8.2	8.1	10.2	7.8	...	September
Oman	1.9	1.6	1.3	0.1	1.4	...	...	16.7	13.2	12.0	1.2	14.3	...	...
Saudi Arabia	1.8	1.5	2.0	2.1	2.0	...	...	30.8	27.6	37.9	42.1	43.0	...	...
Africa														
Ghana	3.6	6.4	6.1	5.1	3.4	...	September	30.8	62.8	60.8	42.3	33.8	...	September
Kenya	0.8	0.0	0.5	2.2	2.0	...	...	8.9	0.3	5.0	16.6	...	...	...
Nigeria	4.5	4.1	4.0	5.2	...	...	...	...	46.7	51.6	54.9	...	...	...
South Africa [3]	1.5	1.4	1.5	1.1	1.0	1.1	March	26.8	21.1	21.0	16.5	14.8	18.8	March
Uganda	...	3.7	4.4	4.4	3.3	...	June	...	56.5	53.1	45.8	33.5	...	June
Zambia	...	...	5.4	2.5	5.3	...	March	...	...	41.7	21.1	41.4	...	March
Zimbabwe	...	...	6.0	5.1	4.0	...	...	...	...	43.2	42.7	57.7	...	...
Other														
Australia	1.0	1.2	1.3	1.0	1.2	...	...	15.0	18.0	19.4	15.6	18.2	...	...
Canada	0.5	0.7	0.7	0.6	0.5	0.7	March	12.2	14.2	13.9	13.0	9.5	14.7	March
Japan** [6]	−0.6	−0.5	0.2	0.0	−0.4	...	March	−22.5	−11.8	3.3	−0.1	−12.4	...	March
United States [8]	1.1	1.3	1.2	1.1	1.4	1.4	March	13.3	15.7	14.0	12.9	15.0	15.9	March

Sources: National authorities; Bankscope (*); Moody's (**); OECD; and IMF staff estimates.
[1]Private banks only.
[2]For 2002 ROA excludes suspended banks and mortgage bank.
[3]Before-tax.
[4]Data for December 2001 onward reflect the results of the audits conducted during the first half of 2002.
[5]Data for U.K. large commercial banks (exclusive of mortgage banks and other banks).
[6]As of March of each calendar year.
[7]As of June of each calendar year.
[8]U.S. banks with assets greater than $1 billion.

Table 23. Bank Asset Quality

	Nonperforming Loans to Total Loans[1] (in percent)							Provisons to Nonperforming Loans[1] (in percent)						
	1998	1999	2000	2001	2002	2003	Month	1998	1999	2000	2001	2002	2003	Month
Latin America														
Argentina[2]	5.3	7.1	8.7	13.2	17.3	18.5	February	61.2	60.0	62.9	66.0	...	...	
Bolivia	4.6	6.6	10.3	14.4	17.6	20.4	April	58.0	55.8	61.4	63.7	63.7	63.3	March
Brazil***	10.2	8.7	8.4	5.7	5.3	...	...	110.9	125.1	82.1	126.1	143.5	...	...
Chile	1.5	1.7	1.7	1.6	1.8	1.9	March	131.4	152.9	145.5	146.5	128.1	121.1	March
Colombia	10.7	13.6	11.0	10.0	8.7	...	...	37.9	36.8	54.5	73.9	86.3	...	...
Ecuador	8.1	26.0	31.0	27.8	8.5	10.0	March	99.6	109.0	104.0	102.2	131.4	108.8	March
Jamaica	...	...	9.5	6.1	3.7	...	...	...	...	136.5	149.6	139.6	...	...
Mexico	11.3	8.9	5.8	5.1	4.6	4.6	March	66.1	107.8	115.3	123.8	138.9	134.3	March
Paraguay[3]	8.1	9.3	11.8	12.3	14.7	17.5	March	48.1	45.1	45.5	39.8	50.2	46.8	March
Peru	7.0	8.7	9.8	9.0	7.6	7.7	March	92.1	99.5	104.3	114.2	133.2	131.9	March
Uruguay[3,4]	...	8.7	8.5	9.3	13.9	...	...	62.8	48.4	47.5	45.4	60.2	...	...
Venezuela, Rep. Bol.	5.5	7.8	6.6	7.1	10.1	10.9	February	123.4	101.8	93.6	92.2	97.6	95.2	February
Emerging Europe														
Bulgaria**	16.4	13.9	8.2	7.0	5.5	9.0	March	75.0	71.9	79.3	74.3	74.3	53.4	March
Croatia***	11.4	11.8	10.6	7.2	5.8	6.3	March	84.4	78.7	79.8	75.7	68.1	63.4	March
Czech Republic	20.7	21.9	19.9	13.7	8.8	8.6	March	54.3	52.2	55.0	59.2	74.0	77.8	March
Estonia	1.4	1.7	1.0	1.3	1.6	...	March	...	...	...	...	...	...	...
Hungary	4.9	3.6	4.1	4.6	5.8	...	September	45.2	51.4	56.7	53.9	...	...	...
Israel*[5]	4.6	4.7	3.5	3.2	3.6	...	June	49.5	45.7	55.8	57.1	54.7	...	June
Latvia	6.0	6.0	4.6	2.8	2.0	1.9	March	78.0	79.3	74.1	80.4	95.5	98.5	March
Lithuania**	12.9	12.5	11.3	8.3	6.5	5.3	March	47.5	37.5	34.6	36.5	...	...	...
Poland**	10.9	13.2	14.9	17.8	21.4	...	...	63.0	58.4	61.5	66.8	71.8	...	...
Russia[6]	17.3	13.4	7.7	6.3	6.1	...	September	40.1	63.4	80.1	79.3	86.0	...	September
Slovak Republic[7]	31.6	23.7	15.3	15.4	11.0	...	...	...	42.5	61.5	70.5	70.9	...	September
Slovenia[8]	5.4	5.2	5.2	7.0	7.0	...	...	...	114.9	101.0	100.5	102.9	...	September
Turkey[9]	6.7	9.7	9.2	29.3	17.5	15.3	March	44.2	61.9	59.8	47.1	63.9	67.6	March
Ukraine	...	35.8	29.6	25.1	21.9	...	...	...	...	...	...	...	...	...
Western Europe														
Austria	2.4	2.3	2.4	2.3	...	...		...	...					
Belgium	2.7	2.7	2.7	2.9	2.9	...	June	61.0	58.0	57.0	57.0	58.0	...	June
Denmark	0.8	0.6	0.5	0.5	0.6	...	...							
Finland*	1.2	1.0	0.6	0.6	0.5	...	...	...	...	...	...	...		
France	5.9	5.1	4.3	4.3	4.4	...	September	58.5	60.7	60.8	59.9	58.4	...	September
Germany[10]	5.0	4.6	5.1	4.9	5.0	...	...	73.3	76.9	81.8	85.7	...	...	
Greece	13.6	15.5	12.3	9.2	8.1	...	...	24.1	26.1	36.8	43.3	45.3	...	
Ireland	2.5	1.8	1.9	1.9	1.7	...	...	60.0	82.0	105.0	110.0	...		
Italy[11]	9.1	8.5	7.7	6.7	6.5	...	...	42.8	48.1	48.6	50.0	...		
Luxembourg	0.5	0.5	0.5	0.4	0.4	...	September	...						
Netherlands	2.6	2.7	2.3	2.4	...	...	...	...	93.1	90.8	88.8	67.3	...	...
Norway	1.5	1.4	1.3	1.3	1.4	1.5	March	61.0	58.0	57.0	57.0	58.0	...	...
Portugal[12]	3.3	2.4	2.2	2.1	2.3	2.4	March	...	...	68.2	66.7	62.8	...	June
Spain	2.0	1.5	1.2	1.2	1.1	1.1	March	69.9	71.1	61.0	55.6	61.1	...	...
Sweden***	2.6	1.7	1.7	1.6	1.4	1.3	March	42.3	55.5	60.0	64.9	73.8	...	...
Switzerland	5.2	4.6	3.8	4.1	3.6	...	...	...	...	...				
United Kingdom[13]	3.1	2.9	2.6	2.3	2.3	...	June	56.0	71.2	65.0	69.5	...	...	...

Table 23 *(concluded)*

	Nonperforming Loans to Total Loans[1] (in percent)							Provisons to Nonperforming Loans[1] (in percent)						
	1998	1999	2000	2001	2002	2003	Month	1998	1999	2000	2001	2002	2003	Month
Asia														
China	...	28.5	22.4	30.5	28.2	...	June	...	...	...	...	...	...	...
Hong Kong SAR	5.3	7.2	6.1	5.7	4.5	...	...	...	...	...	...	...	...	...
India****	14.4	14.7	12.8	11.4	10.4	...	March	...	...	...	...	...	...	...
Indonesia	48.6	32.9	18.8	11.9	5.8	...	...	28.6	77.7	59.4	97.7	125.7	...	...
Korea	7.4	8.3	6.6	2.9	1.9	...	...	46.2	66.6	81.8	85.2	109.4	...	...
Malaysia	18.6	16.6	15.4	17.8	15.8	...	...	42.4	50.2	54.5	50.8	52.0	...	...
Pakistan	23.1	25.9	23.5	23.5	23.7	...	...	58.6	48.6	55.0	56.2	58.7	...	...
Philippines[14]	11.0	12.7	14.9	16.9	15.4	...	...	36.4	45.2	43.7	45.3	53.2	...	...
Singapore	...	12.2	9.1	8.0	7.7	7.5	March	50.4	52.9	52.8	55.5	56.8	...	...
Sri Lanka	16.6	16.6	15.0	16.9	...	...	...	...	...	...	40.8	...	...	...
Thailand[14]	42.9	38.6	17.7	10.5	15.8	15.9	April	29.2	37.9	47.2	54.9	61.8	62.0	April
Middle East														
Egypt	...	...	...	...	...	...	...	...	...	...	...	...	...	...
Lebanon	12.5	14.3	19.2	22.8	27.2	29.7	March	57.4	72.5	72.5	69.3	68.2	73.3	March
Morocco	14.6	15.3	17.5	16.8	18.0	...	September	52.6	51.8	45.7	53.0	53.8	...	September
Oman	6.4	6.0	7.5	10.6	11.3	...	...	70.3	75.0	71.9	68.5	79.7	...	...
Saudi Arabia	8.4	11.4	10.4	10.1	8.8	...	...	83.0	88.0	93.0	106.0	112.0	...	...
Africa														
Ghana	26.5	22.6	12.1	19.6	19.2	...	September	63.6	59.5	78.3	66.4	81.8	...	September
Kenya[15]	32.0	35.0	38.2	42.1	39.4	...	March	53.0	64.0	63.0	66.0	62.0	...	March
Nigeria	19.4	25.6	22.6	16.0	17.3	...	March	...	46.7	49.7	73.6	60.9	...	March
South Africa[16]	4.1	4.9	4.3	3.3	3.3	3.3	March	41.3	41.5	43.8	36.4	42.9	42.7	March
Uganda****	20.2	11.9	9.8	6.5	3.6	...	June	54.2	51.9	50.5	...	...	...	...
Zambia	...	...	26.0	21.2	28.8	...	March	...	...	21.1	48.4	27.8	...	March
Zimbabwe	...	...	19.6	11.4	4.2	...	...	...	...	44.4	28.3	52.8	...	...
Other														
Australia	0.7	0.6	0.5	0.7	0.6	0.6	March	37.9	44.2	38.4	37.0	36.5	35.5	March
Canada	1.1	1.2	1.2	1.5	1.6	1.6	March	50.3	45.4	42.8	44.0	41.1	43.5	March
Japan[17]	6.1	5.8	5.7	8.4	7.2	...	March	49.9	40.3	35.5	31.8	32.2	...	September
United States[18]	1.0	1.0	1.2	1.5	1.6	1.5	March	73.7	76.1	98.2	118.2	85.6	...	...

Sources: National authorities; and IMF staff estimates.

Notes: (*) based on net nonperforming loans; (**) 30-day nonperforming loan classification; (***) 60-day classification; and (****) 180-day classification.

[1]Indicators are not strictly comparable across countries due to differences in definitions.
[2]Uncollectible credits only as percentage of credits to the private sector.
[3]Private banks only.
[4]For 2002 excludes suspended banks and mortgage bank.
[5]NPLs are exclusive of loans in the special mention category.
[6]Doubtful and loss loans.
[7]Excluding KOBL.
[8]Provisions as a percent of legal requirements.
[9]Data for December 2001 onward reflect the results of the audits conducted during the first half of 2002.
[10]German commercial law definition of nonperforming loans.
[11]Doubtful and bad debts.
[12]Only overdue principle and interest payments are reflected in banks' NPL balances.
[13]Data for U.K. large commercial banks (exclusive of mortgage banks and other banks).
[14] The increase in the NPL ratio in 2002 is due to a change in the definition of NPLs.
[15]NPLs include suspended interest.
[16]NPLs are net of collateral.
[17]End-fiscal year, major banks, NPLs defined as risk-management loans.
[18]U.S. banks with assets greater than $1 billion.

Table 24. Bank Capital Adequacy

	Regulatory Capital to Risk-Weighted Assets (in percent)							Capital to Assets (in percent)						
	1998	1999	2000	2001	2002	2003	Month	1998	1999	2000	2001	2002	2003	Month
Latin America														
Argentina	20.4	20.8	19.5	17.9	. . .	. . .	. . .	11.3	10.6	10.1	12.5	13.1	12.9	February
Bolivia	11.8	12.2	13.4	14.6	16.1	16.5	March	8.5	9.2	9.8	10.5	11.9	11.3	April
Brazil	15.6	15.5	14.3	15.3	16.5	. . .	. . .	10.5	11.6	12.1	13.6	13.5	15.1	February
Chile	12.5	13.5	13.3	12.7	14.0	15.2	March	7.5	7.7	7.5	7.2	7.2	7.8	March
Colombia	10.3	10.8	12.4	12.4	12.2	. . .	. . .	7.7	7.7	7.7	7.9	7.8	. . .	. . .
Ecuador	. . .	. . .	. . .	. . .	. . .	. . .	. . .	14.5	12.9	12.9	8.8	10.3	8.2	March
Jamaica	. . .	. . .	21.9	19.7	15.5	. . .	. . .	21.5	19.6	16.2	15.5	14.2	14.0	January
Mexico	14.4	16.2	13.8	14.7	15.5	14.4	March	8.3	8.0	9.6	9.4	11.1	11.2	March
Paraguay[1]	24.8	20.9	21.0	16.2	17.9	20.6	March	14.9	12.6	12.4	12.1	10.9	10.6	March
Peru	11.2	12.0	12.9	13.4	12.5	13.3	March	8.7	8.9	9.1	9.8	10.1	10.4	March
Uruguay[1,2]	11.2	10.2	11.7	11.3	20.9	. . .	. . .	15.3	14.7	11.7	8.1	−2.2	−2.4	January
Venezuela, Rep. Bol.	. . .	. . .	. . .	. . .	. . .	. . .	. . .	14.0	13.5	12.4	14.3	16.1	14.5	February
Emerging Europe														
Bulgaria	36.7	41.8	35.6	31.3	25.2	24.3	March	14.0	15.3	15.2	13.6	13.3	14.0	March
Croatia	12.7	20.6	21.4	18.5	17.6	18.7	March	18.3	15.2	11.9	10.4	9.4	. . .	. . .
Czech Republic	12.0	13.6	14.9	15.5	14.4	13.7	March	7.9	7.9	8.2	6.7	6.8	6.5	March
Estonia	17.0	16.1	13.2	14.4	. . .	. . .	. . .	20.8	19.2	15.2	15.2	13.7	. . .	. . .
Hungary	16.5	14.9	13.5	13.9	11.1	. . .	September	9.7	9.7	9.8	9.5	10.0	. . .	September
Israel	9.2	9.4	9.2	9.4	9.9	. . .	June	6.7	6.8	7.3	7.7	9.2	. . .	June
Latvia	17.0	16.0	14.0	14.2	13.1	13.8	March	3.7	2.0	8.5	9.1	8.8	8.8	March
Lithuania	23.8	17.4	16.3	15.7	14.7	14.7	March	13.9	9.9	9.2	9.4	9.9	10.2	March
Poland	11.7	13.2	12.9	15.1	14.5	. . .	. . .	7.0	7.1	7.2	8.0	8.3	. . .	. . .
Russia	11.5	18.1	19.0	20.3	19.2	. . .	September	. . .	14.3	12.9	12.5	12.4	. . .	June
Slovak Republic	6.6	12.7	13.1	19.7	21.1	. . .	. . .	9.8	8.7	5.9	7.9	9.8	9.9	March
Slovenia	16.0	14.0	13.5	11.9	11.9	. . .	September	13.9	13.5	12.8	10.6	10.9	11.2	March
Turkey[3]	. . .	. . .	17.3	15.3	26.4	26.7	March	8.7	5.2	6.1	9.6	9.7	. . .	June
Ukraine	. . .	19.6	15.5	20.7	18.5	. . .	. . .	. . .	. . .	17.5	16.6	15.5	14.6	March
Western Europe														
Austria	14.3	13.9	13.8	14.6	14.0	. . .	. . .	4.9	5.2	5.2	5.1	5.6	5.4	March
Belgium	11.3	11.9	11.9	12.9	12.5	. . .	June	4.0	4.1	4.6	4.4	4.7	4.4	March
Denmark	10.7	11.1	11.3	12.1	12.6	. . .	. . .	6.3	6.1	6.7	6.2	5.2	. . .	. . .
Finland	11.5	11.9	11.6	10.5	10.7	. . .	. . .	5.9	5.6	6.3	10.2	10.1	9.2	March
France	10.7*	10.8*	10.9*	10.6*	. . .	. . .	. . .	6.4	6.8	6.7	6.7	6.7	6.6	March
Germany	10.5	11.3	10.9	11.5	11.3	. . .	. . .	4.0	4.1	4.2	4.3	4.5	4.6	March
Greece	10.2	16.2	13.6	12.5	11.6	. . .	September	. . .	10.1	8.9	9.2	9.4	8.2	May
Ireland	11.0	10.4	9.7	11.2	12.5	. . .	. . .	7.2	7.3	6.5	5.9	5.5	5.6	March
Italy	11.3	10.6	10.3	10.6	11.2	. . .	. . .	6.7	7.0	6.9	7.2	7.2	7.0	March
Luxembourg	12.6	13.4	13.4	13.7	14.6	. . .	September	3.5	3.8	3.9	3.9	3.7	. . .	September
Netherlands	11.4	11.2	11.3	11.5	11.9	. . .	. . .	5.0	4.8	5.1	4.8	4.7	4.5	March
Norway	12.4	12.4	12.1	12.2	12.8	. . .	. . .	6.0	6.6	6.4	6.0	5.5	5.4	May
Portugal	12.4	11.8	10.4	9.3	9.6	. . .	. . .	5.6	6.7	7.3	7.0	7.3	8.6	March
Spain	12.9	12.6	12.5	13.0	12.2	. . .	June	7.1	6.6	7.5	7.2	7.3	. . .	November
Sweden	10.4	11.4	9.9	10.0	10.1	10.1	March	5.0	5.5	5.3	5.6	5.2	. . .	. . .
Switzerland	11.4	11.4	12.8	11.8	12.6	. . .	. . .	4.3	4.5	4.8	4.5	4.2	. . .	March
United Kingdom[4]	12.4	13.6	11.8	12.2	12.5	. . .	June	7.0	7.5	6.5	6.6	6.7	. . .	June

Table 24 (concluded)

	Regulatory Capital to Risk-Weighted Assets (in percent)							Capital to Assets (in percent)						
	1998	1999	2000	2001	2002	2003	Month	1998	1999	2000	2001	2002	2003	Month
Asia														
China	...	...	...	...	...	...	...	...	5.2	5.3	5.1	4.0	...	June
Hong Kong SAR	18.5	18.7	17.8	16.5	15.8	...	...	7.7	8.1	9.0	9.8	10.7	11.5	March
India[5,6]	11.5	11.2	10.7	11.2	11.8	...	March	6.2	5.9	5.3	5.1	5.6	...	March
Indonesia	−13.0	−2.4	−18.2	19.2	19.7	...	...	−12.9	−4.1	5.2	5.4	7.3	...	...
Korea	8.2	10.8	10.5	10.8	10.5	10.2	March	2.8	3.9	3.8	4.1	4.0	3.8	March
Malaysia	11.8	12.5	12.5	13.0	12.8	...	...	8.9	8.9	8.5	8.5	8.7	...	November
Pakistan	10.9	10.9	9.7	8.8	8.4	...	...	4.1	4.3	4.4	4.3	3.3	...	...
Philippines	17.7	17.5	16.2	14.5	15.7	...	September	14.8	16.0	15.3	15.4	15.8	...	October
Singapore	18.3	21.3	19.9	18.5	17.2	17.4	March	7.5	7.8	7.1	9.6	8.3	8.5	March
Sri Lanka	10.7	10.6	8.3	7.8	...	...	...	5.9	4.3	3.7	3.8	...	...	...
Thailand	10.9	12.4	12.0	13.7	13.7	13.3	April	4.8	5.5	4.5	5.5	5.8	5.9	April
Middle East														
Egypt	...	...	...	...	...	...	...	...	...	...	...	...	...	...
Lebanon	18.9	15.0	16.9	18.0	17.0	...	June	6.6	6.6	6.4	6.2	6.4	6.4	March
Morocco	12.6	12.1	12.8	12.6	12.5	...	September	9.8	9.9	9.2	9.3	8.9	8.7	March
Oman	...	16.5	16.5	15.6	16.9	...	...	...	13.0	13.0	12.6	12.5	...	...
Saudi Arabia	21.2	21.2	21.0	20.3	21.3	...	...	10.0	10.2	9.6	9.3	9.3	...	...
Africa														
Ghana	...	...	11.6	...	...	...	...	12.2	11.9	11.8	12.5	12.0	...	...
Kenya	...	...	17.6	17.9	18.9	...	March	10.7	8.9	8.7	8.8	8.0	...	...
Nigeria	12.7	19.0	17.5	16.1	...	...	...	9.3	8.2	7.4	8.6	9.5	...	March
South Africa	11.5	12.6	14.5	11.4	12.6	12.2	March	8.2	8.2	8.7	7.8	8.2	7.2	March
Uganda	11.0	13.6	20.5	23.1	23.7	...	June	...	7.0	9.8	10.0	9.5	...	June
Zambia	...	...	22.8	22.0	21.4	...	March	...	...	12.9	11.7	12.8	...	March
Zimbabwe	...	...	44.0	44.5	30.6	...	...	8.0	9.4	9.4	9.3	9.5	...	...
Other														
Australia	10.3	10.1	9.8	10.5	9.9	10.0	March	7.6	7.3	6.9	7.1	6.3	6.2	March
Canada	10.7	11.7	11.9	12.3	12.4	12.6	March	4.2	4.7	4.7	4.6	4.6	4.7	March
Japan[6,7]	11.6	11.8	11.7	10.8	10.0	...	March	2.7	4.4	4.7	4.4	3.8	3.8	September
United States[8]	11.6	11.6	11.7	12.4	12.5	12.7	March	8.2	8.1	8.2	8.9	9.0	9.0	March

Sources: National authorities; Moody's (*); OECD; and IMF staff estimates.

[1]Private banks.
[2]For 2002 the risk-weighted ratio excludes suspended banks and mortgage bank.
[3]Data for December 2001 onward reflect the results of the audits conducted during the first half of 2002.
[4]Data for U.K. large commercial banks (exclusive of mortgage banks and other banks).
[5]Data for public sector banks only for the risk-weighted ratio
[6]End-fiscal year.
[7]Major banks, nonconsolidated.
[8]U.S. banks with assets greater than $1 billion.

Table 25. Moody's Weighted Average Bank Financial Strength Index[1]
(In percent)

	Financial Strength Index			Percent Change		Financial Strength Index			Percent Change
	Dec. 2001	Dec. 2002	May 2003	from Dec. 2002		Dec. 2001	Dec. 2002	May 2003	from Dec. 2002
Latin America					**Western Europe** *(continued)*				
Argentina	13.3	0.0	0.0	0.0	Norway	63.3	65.0	65.0	0.0
Bolivia	25.0	8.3	2.7	−67.5	Portugal	64.6	64.2	64.2	0.0
Brazil	37.9	25.0	25.0	0.0	Spain	77.1	75.0	75.0	0.0
Chile	50.6	52.5	52.5	0.0	Sweden	72.5	73.3	75.0	2.3
Colombia	23.3	24.2	24.2	0.0	Switzerland	70.8	72.1	72.1	0.0
Ecuador	8.3	8.3	8.3	0.0	United Kingdom	83.8	83.8	83.3	−0.5
Jamaica	...	...	...	...					
Mexico	36.3	39.6	39.6	0.0	**Asia**				
Paraguay	...	...	...	...	China	10.0	10.0	10.0	0.0
Peru	22.9	23.3	23.3	0.0	Hong Kong SAR	66.6	62.3	62.3	0.0
Uruguay	31.3	0.0	0.0	0.0	India	25.8	27.5	27.5	0.0
Venezuela, Rep. Bol.	28.8	15.4	8.3	−46.2	Indonesia	1.7	3.0	3.0	0.0
					Korea	14.2	16.7	16.7	0.0
Emerging Europe					Malaysia	30.4	31.7	32.3	2.0
Bulgaria	...	16.7	16.7	0.0	Pakistan	2.1	5.0	5.0	0.0
Croatia	33.3	33.3	33.3	0.0	Philippines	17.5	20.4	20.4	0.0
Czech Republic	29.2	32.5	32.5	0.0	Singapore	75.0	74.7	74.7	0.0
Estonia	38.3	46.7	46.7	0.0	Sri Lanka	...	...	...	...
Hungary	41.7	45.0	45.0	0.0	Thailand	15.8	15.8	15.8	0.0
Israel	48.3	45.8	45.8	0.0					
Latvia	29.2	32.1	32.1	0.0	**Middle East**				
Lithuania	...	...	...	...	Egypt	22.9	22.9	22.9	0.0
Poland	29.6	28.3	29.5	4.2	Lebanon	33.3	33.3	33.3	0.0
Russia	12.5	10.8	10.8	0.0	Morocco	35.8	35.8	35.8	0.0
Slovak Republic	9.6	15.0	15.0	0.0	Oman	31.7	29.2	29.2	0.0
Slovenia	40.2	40.8	40.8	0.0	Saudi Arabia	43.3	43.3	43.3	0.0
Turkey	30.0	20.4	18.3	−10.3					
Ukraine	8.3	8.3	8.3	0.0	**Africa**				
					Ghana	...	...	...	...
Western Europe					Kenya	...	...	...	...
Austria	62.5	61.7	61.7	0.0	Nigeria	...	...	...	...
Belgium	75.0	75.0	75.0	0.0	South Africa	53.5	49.0	50.0	2.0
Denmark	80.0	80.0	80.0	0.0	Uganda	...	...	...	...
Finland	70.0	73.3	73.3	0.0	Zambia	...	...	...	...
France	71.9	74.2	74.2	0.0	Zimbabwe	...	...	...	...
Germany	61.7	54.2	48.0	−11.4					
Greece	40.0	40.0	40.0	0.0	**Other**				
Ireland	69.2	70.0	70.0	0.0	Australia	71.7	72.5	72.5	0.0
Italy	64.6	63.3	63.3	0.0	Canada	77.1	75.0	75.0	0.0
Luxembourg	68.7	68.3	68.3	0.0	Japan	16.7	12.9	12.9	0.0
Netherlands	87.5	84.2	84.2	0.0	United States	77.1	75.0	75.0	0.0

Source: Moody's.

[1]Constructed according to a numerical scale assigned to Moody's weighted average bank ratings by country. Zero indicates the lowest possible average rating and 100 indicates the highest possible average rating.

World Economic and Financial Surveys

This series (ISSN 0258-7440) contains biannual, annual, and periodic studies covering monetary and financial issues of importance to the global economy. The core elements of the series are the *World Economic Outlook* report, usually published in May and October, and the quarterly *Global Financial Stability Report*. Other studies assess international trade policy, private market and official financing for developing countries, exchange and payments systems, export credit policies, and issues discussed in the *World Economic Outlook*. Please consult the IMF *Publications Catalog* for a complete listing of currently available World Economic and Financial Surveys.

World Economic Outlook: A Survey by the Staff of the International Monetary Fund

The *World Economic Outlook*, published twice a year in English, French, Spanish, and Arabic, presents IMF staff economists' analyses of global economic developments during the near and medium term. Chapters give an overview of the world economy; consider issues affecting industrial countries, developing countries, and economies in transition to the market; and address topics of pressing current interest.

ISSN 0256-6877.

$49.00 (academic rate: $46.00); paper.
2002. (Sep.). ISBN 1-58906-179-9. **Stock #WEO EA 0022002.**
2002. (April). ISBN 1-58906-107-1. **Stock #WEO EA 0012002.**
2001. (Dec.). ISBN 1-58906-087-3. **Stock #WEO EA 0172001.**
2001. (Oct.). ISBN 1-58906-073-3. **Stock #WEO EA 0022001.**
2001. (May). ISBN 1-58906-032-6. **Stock #WEO EA 0012001.**
2000. (Oct.). ISBN 1-55775-975-8. **Stock #WEO EA 0022000.**
2000. (May). ISBN 1-55775-936-7. **Stock #WEO EA 012000.**

Official Financing for Developing Countries
by a staff team in the IMF's Policy Development and Review Department led by Anthony R. Boote and Doris C. Ross

This study provides information on official financing for developing countries, with the focus on low-income countries. It updates the 1995 edition and reviews developments in direct financing by official and multilateral sources.

$25.00 (academic rate: $20.00); paper.
2001. ISBN 1-58906-038-5. **Stock #WEO EA 0132001.**
1998. ISBN 1-55775-702-X. **Stock #WEO-1397.**
1995. ISBN 1-55775-527-2. **Stock #WEO-1395.**

Exchange Rate Arrangements and Currency Convertibility: Developments and Issues
by a staff team led by R. Barry Johnston

A principal force driving the growth in international trade and investment has been the liberalization of financial transactions, including the liberalization of trade and exchange controls. This study reviews the developments and issues in the exchange arrangements and currency convertibility of IMF members.

$20.00 (academic rate: $12.00); paper.
1999. ISBN 1-55775-795-X. **Stock #WEO EA 0191999.**

World Economic Outlook Supporting Studies
by the IMF's Research Department

These studies, supporting analyses and scenarios of the *World Economic Outlook*, provide a detailed examination of theory and evidence on major issues currently affecting the global economy.

$25.00 (academic rate: $20.00); paper.
2000. ISBN 1-55775-893-X. **Stock #WEO EA 0032000.**

Global Financial Stability Report: Market Developments and Issues

The *Global Financial Stability Report*, published twice a year, examines trends and issues that influence world financial markets. It replaces two IMF publications—the annual *International Capital Markets* report and the electronic quarterly *Emerging Market Financing* report. The report is designed to deepen understanding of international capital flows and explores developments that could pose a risk to international financial market stability.

$49.00 (academic rate: $46.00); paper.
September 2003 ISBN 1-58906-236-1. **Stock #GFSR EA0022003.**
March 2003 ISBN 1-58906-210-8. **Stock #GFSR EA0012003.**
December 2002 ISBN-1-58906-192-6. **Stock #GFSR EA0042002.**
September 2002 ISBN 1-58906-157-8. **Stock #GFSR EA0032002.**

International Capital Markets: Developments, Prospects, and Key Policy Issues (back issues)

$42.00 (academic rate: $35.00); paper.
2001. ISBN 1-58906-056-3. **Stock #WEO EA 0062001.**

Toward a Framework for Financial Stability
by a staff team led by David Folkerts-Landau and Carl-Johan Lindgren

This study outlines the broad principles and characteristics of stable and sound financial systems, to facilitate IMF surveillance over banking sector issues of macroeconomic significance and to contribute to the general international effort to reduce the likelihood and diminish the intensity of future financial sector crises.

$25.00 (academic rate: $20.00); paper.
1998. ISBN 1-55775-706-2. **Stock #WEO-016.**

Trade Liberalization in IMF-Supported Programs
by a staff team led by Robert Sharer

This study assesses trade liberalization in programs supported by the IMF by reviewing multiyear arrangements in the 1990s and six detailed case studies. It also discusses the main economic factors affecting trade policy targets.

$25.00 (academic rate: $20.00); paper.
1998. ISBN 1-55775-707-0. **Stock #WEO-1897.**

Private Market Financing for Developing Countries
by a staff team from the IMF's Policy Development and Review Department led by Steven Dunaway

This study surveys recent trends in flows to developing countries through banking and securities markets. It also analyzes the institutional and regulatory framework for developing country finance; institutional investor behavior and pricing of developing country stocks; and progress in commercial bank debt restructuring in low-income countries.

$20.00 (academic rate: $12.00); paper.
1995. ISBN 1-55775-526-4. **Stock #WEO-1595.**

Available by series subscription or single title (including back issues); academic rate available only to full-time university faculty and students. For earlier editions please inquire about prices.

The IMF *Catalog of Publications* is available on-line at the Internet address listed below.

Please send orders and inquiries to:
International Monetary Fund, Publication Services, 700 19th Street, N.W.
Washington, D.C. 20431, U.S.A.
Tel.: (202) 623-7430   Telefax: (202) 623-7201
E-mail: publications@imf.org
Internet: http://www.imf.org